T0211756

Lecture Notes in Computer Science 12860

More information about this subseries at http://www.springer.com/series/7407

Catalin Dima · Mahsa Shirmohammadi (Eds.)

Formal Modeling and Analysis of Timed Systems

19th International Conference, FORMATS 2021
Paris, France, August 24–26, 2021
Proceedings

 Springer

Editors
Catalin Dima
Université Paris-Est Créteil
Créteil, France

Mahsa Shirmohammadi
CNRS, Université de Paris
Paris, France

ISSN 0302-9743   ISSN 1611-3349   (electronic)
Lecture Notes in Computer Science
ISBN 978-3-030-85036-4   ISBN 978-3-030-85037-1   (eBook)
https://doi.org/10.1007/978-3-030-85037-1

LNCS Sublibrary: SL1 – Theoretical Computer Science and General Issues

This Springer imprint is published by the registered company Springer Nature Switzerland AG
The registered company address is: Gewerbestrasse 11, 6330 Cham, Switzerland

Preface

This volume contains the papers presented at the 19th International Conference on Formal Modeling and Analysis of Timed Systems (FORMATS 2021), held virtually, and hosted by the Laboratoire d'Algorithmique, Complexité et Logique (LACL), Université Paris-Est Créteil, France, during August 24–26, 2021. The event was part of QONFEST 2021, co-located with CONCUR, FMICS, and QEST.

FORMATS is an annual conference aimed at promoting the study of fundamental and practical aspects of timed systems, and bringing together researchers from different disciplines that share interests in modeling, design, and analysis of timed computational systems. The conference principally aims to attract researchers interested in real-time issues in hardware design, performance analysis, real-time software, scheduling, semantics, and verification of real-timed, hybrid, and probabilistic systems. In response to the call for papers, a total of 19 submissions were received. Each submission was assigned to at least three Program Committee (PC) members, aided by 15 external subreviewers. The PC decided to accept eight papers for inclusion in the scientific program. The selection was made on the basis of novelty, rigour, presentation style, and relevance to the FORMATS community.

The conference also welcomes research works concerning applications of real-time systems on relevant topics in interdisciplinary areas. This year, the conference had a special session on control synthesis and motion planning for cyber-physical and control systems. The papers accepted for this session covered a variety of topics, from model-based and data-driven approaches to analysis and control design for systems with logical and temporal specifications. The selection of papers and coordination for this session was chaired by Morteza Lahijanian (University of Colorado Boulder, USA).

Apart from the contributed talks, the event included invited presentations by Jana Tumova (KTH Royal Institute of Technology, Sweden) and Daniele Magazzeni (J. P. Morgan AI Research, UK). This volume contains all the contributed papers presented at the conference, and the paper and abstract accompanying the two invited talks.

We wish to thank all authors who contributed to FORMATS for their interest in this conference, the Program Committee members for their scholarly effort, and the Organizing Committee for ensuring a lively event despite the difficulties related with organizing it virtually. Finally, we would like to thank the FORMATS Steering Committee for the continuous support, with special thanks to Martin Fränzle, Steering Committee chair.

We were very happy to serve as PC chairs of FORMATS 2021. We hope that you will enjoy and profit from the papers in this volume and that the works herein will inspire further progress and new research directions on timed systems and adjacent areas.

July 2021

Catalin Dima
Mahsa Shirmohammadi

Organization

Program Committee

Parosh Aziz Abdulla	Uppsala University, Sweden
Damien Busatto	Université Libre de Bruxelles, Belgium
Thomas Chatain	LMF, ENS Paris-Saclay, France
Lorenzo Clemente	University of Warsaw, Poland
Liliana Cucu-Grosjean	Inria Paris, France
Catalin Dima	LACL, Université Paris-Est Créteil
Hugo Gimbert	CNRS, LABRI, University of Bordeaux, France
Arnd Hartmanns	University of Twente, The Netherlands
Hsi-Ming Ho	University of Sussex, UK
Sophia Knight	University of Minnesota, USA
Moez Krichen	ReDCAD Research Unit, Tunisia
Morteza Lahijanian	University of Colorado Boulder, USA
Engel Lefaucheux	Max Planck Institute for Software Systems, Germany
Martina Maggio	Saarland University, Germany
Angelo Montanari	University of Udine, Italy
Igor Potapov	University of Liverpool, UK
Mickael Randour	FNRS and Université de Mons, Belgium
Mikhail Raskin	Technical University of Munich, Germany
Cristian Riveros	Pontificia Universidad Católica de Chile, Chile
Matteo Rossi	Politecnico di Milano, Italy
Kristin Yvonne Rozier	Iowa State University, USA
Krishna S.	IIT Bombay, India
Mahsa Shirmohammadi	CNRS, IRIF, Université de Paris, France
Sadegh Soudjani	Newcastle University, UK
Naijun Zhan	Institute of Software, Chinese Academy of Sciences, China

FORMATS Steering Committee

Rajeev Alur	University of Pennsylvania, USA
Eugene Asarin	Université de Paris, France
Martin Fränzle (Chair)	Universität Oldenburg, Germany
Thomas A. Henzinger	IST, Austria
Joost-Pieter Katoen	Aachen University, Germany
Kim G. Larsen	Aalborg University, Denmark
Oded Maler (Founding Chair, 1957–2018)	CNRS, France
Pavithra Prabhakar	Kansas State University, USA
Mariëlle Stoelinga	University of Twente, The Netherlands
Wang Yi	Uppsala University, Sweden

Additional Reviewers

An, Jie
Budde, Carlos E.
Gigante, Nicola
Jackson, John
Kottinger, Justin
Lavaei, Abolfazl
Le Coënt, Adrien
Madnani, Khushraj
Orlandini, Andrea
Otop, Jan
Roychowdhury, Sparsa
Sogokon, Andrew
Vandenhove, Pierre
Wang, Qiuye
Whiteland, Markus

Sponsors

Temporal Reasoning for Intelligent Financial Services: Examples and Challenges (Abstract)

Daniele Magazzeni

J.P. Morgan AI Research, London, UK
daniele.magazzeni@jpmorgan.com

Abstract. Temporal reasoning can play a key role in the financial do-main. In this talk, I will present several research directions we are pursuing and discuss how temporal reasoning can help in a variety of problems faced by large financial institutions. Active research activities include efficient resource allocations, time series analysis, behavioural reasoning, fraud detection, and market predictions. I will offer concrete examples of projects, presenting the contributions and highlighting the main challenges. I will then focus on a more specific area that has strong implications for temporal reasoning, namely Explainable AI (XAI). XAI represents an increasingly critical feature of operations undertaken within the financial industry, as brought about by the growing sophistication of AI models and the demand for fairness, safety and interpretability. I will present some novel XAI techniques we developed that leverage temporal reasoning, and future directions. I will conclude highlighting the many challenges and opportunities for temporal reasoning in the financial do-main.

Contents

Formal Methods for Robot Motion Planning with Time and Space Constraints (Extended Abstract)

Fernando S. Barbosa, Jesper Karlsson, Pouria Tajvar, and Jana Tumova(⊠)

KTH Royal Institute of Technology, Stockholm, Sweden
{fdsb,jeskarl,tajvar,tumova}@kth.se

Abstract. Motion planning is one of the core problems in a wide range of robotic applications. We discuss the use of temporal logics to include complex objectives, constraints, and preferences in motion planning algorithms and focus on three topics: the first one addresses computational tractability of Linear Temporal Logic (LTL) motion planning in systems with uncertain non-holonomic dynamics, i.e. systems whose ability to move in space is constrained. We introduce feedback motion primitives and heuristics to guide motion planning and demonstrate its use on a rover in 2D and a fixed-wing drone in 3D. Second, we introduce combined motion planning and hybrid feedback control design in order to find and follow trajectories under Metric Interval Temporal Logic (MITL) specifications. Our solution creates a path to be tracked, a sequence of obstacle-free polytopes and time stamps, and a controller that tracks the path while staying in the polytopes. Third, we focus on motion planning with spatio-temporal preferences expressed in a fragment of Signal Temporal Logic (STL). We introduce a cost function for a of a path reflecting the satisfaction/violation of the preferences based on the notion of STL spatial and temporal robustness. We integrate the cost into anytime asymptotically optimal motion planning algorithm RRT* and we show the use of the algorithm in integration with an autonomous exploration planner on a UAV.

Keywords: Motion planning · Temporal logic · RRT* · Feedback control · MTL · STL.

1 Introduction

Autonomous robots have permeated a variety of application areas, from industrial automation to transport, to household services. Robot vacuum cleaners clean our homes and mobile robotic solutions have been deployed in warehouses

This work was partially supported by the Swedish Research Council (VR), and the Wallenberg AI, Autonomous Systems and Software Program (WASP) funded by the Knutand Alice Wallenberg Foundation. The authors are with the Division of Robotics, Perception, and Learning at KTH, and also affiliated with Digital Futures.

C. Dima and M. Shirmohammadi (Eds.): FORMATS 2021, LNCS 12860, pp. 1–14, 2021.
https://doi.org/10.1007/978-3-030-85037-1_1

to carry shelves of goods. Gradually, autonomous mobile robots are moving from enclosed environment to the wild. Visions for future include driverless vehicles seamlessly cruising streets, drones delivering goods to our doors, and robot butlers delivering room service in hotels. In all of these applications, *motion planning* is one of the core problems that needs to be addressed in order to achieve successful autonomous behavior. In robotics, motion planning is often traditionally presented as a problem of finding a continuous path leading from a source to destination without colliding with obstacles in 2D or 3D space [16]. However, we might be interested in more sophisticated goals, as well as more sophisticated time and space constraints. For instance, self-driving vehicles should obey the traffic rules; robot butlers in hotels should not only avoid collisions with humans, but stay within a comfortable distance from them; search-and-rescue robots should not only reach a destination, but periodically survey a set of regions. How can we specify such motion planning goals, constraints and preferences? How can we ensure that they are met?

In recent years, temporal logics have gained popularity as an alternative to specify such constraints and preferences for several reasons: They allow to specify a large variety of complex tasks and constraints in a rigorous way, yet with some resemblance to natural language; and they allow to deploy automated formal synthesis techniques to obtain correct-by-construction plans for a discrete system model. In particular, Linear Temporal Logic (LTL) allows to capture a wide range of desired behavior goals and constraints for autonomous robots, such as surveillance (periodically visit locations A, B, and C), sequencing (event A happens before event B), request-response (if A happens then B needs to happen, too), conditional reachability (A needs to happen unless B happens first), safety (A should never happen), or their combinations. Furthermore, given a discrete model of a robot or even a multi-robot system in its environment, formal synthesis – a complementary approach to formal verification – can be used to automatically generate discrete sequences provably compliant with the temporal logic specification.

Formal synthesis can be combined with motion planning techniques that utilize transformation to a discrete planning problem, either by building an exact discrete representation (combinatorial motion planning) or by sampling (sampling-based motion planning) of the original problem. Numerous recent works have demonstrated the great potential of the formal synthesis-based planning approach in single- and multi-robot planning, extending the seminal works [13,14] towards efficient planning with performance guarantees in known or partially unknown environments, with the use of deterministic, nondeterministic, or probabilistic models, under hard and soft requirements, and consideration of additional optimization criteria [15]. Specifically for sampling-based motion planning under different temporal logic specifications, Rapidly-exploring Random Tree (RRT) technique was used to find a motion plan that fulfills μ-calculus specifications [9], while RRT* [10] was used for minimum-violation motion planning under finite-LTL specifications [6], and later on complemented to deal with syntactically co-safe LTL (sc-LTL) in workspaces with limited perception horizons [27], as well as in multi-agent settings [12]. A reactive sampling-based motion planner that takes into account imperfect state information has been proposed in [20]. Another reactive planner was proposed to deal with long-term and short-term, dynamic specifications [25].

Many research challenges in motion planning for robotic systems stem from the need to find a corresponding discrete model for a continuous one. Finite exact discrete representations (e.g., bisimilar or language equivalent to the original dynamical system) might not exist or might be extremely large. On the other hand, sampling-based approaches yield underapproximation of the original system and thus offer only probabilistic or resolution completeness. Even then, application of sampling-based planning is challenging due to the size of the search space that combines the robot's state space (the discretization) and the task space (the specification automaton). Various approaches thus have been proposed to bias sampling to make a progress towards specification satisfaction, guided by the geometry of the environment, or the specification automaton [4,18]. Especially the geometrical guiding is shown to significantly speed-up the search algorithm, but is restricted to two and in some cases small three dimensional environments. Furthermore, for highly complex dynamics, tracking a computed motion plan is challenging, and the obtained guarantees apply to the discrete plan, but not necessarily to the continuous trajectory.

All of these challenges are even more pronounced when explicit time and spatial constraints are involved in the specification and the specification is to be interpreted over continuous trajectories as opposed to discrete ones. The discrete abstractions need to be designed accordingly to accommodate them. At the same time, support for such specifications is highly desired in robotics domain.

In this extended abstract, we overview our contributions in three areas: Sec. 2 summarizes our approach to treating spatial and temporal constraints imposed by the robot's continuous dynamics and allowing for efficient LTL planning for such systems [23]. In Sec. 3, we tackle time constraints by specifying tasks in Metric Interval Temporal Logic (MITL) and include them in integrated motion planning and control [3]. In Sec. 4, we focus on planning with spatio-temporal preferences expressed in Signal Temporal Logic (STL) [11]. We also present use cases showing the applicability of the algorithms in autonomous exploration [2].

2   Motion Planning for Uncertain Non-holonomic Systems with LTL Specifications

The problem of finding a feasible trajectory for an uncertain dynamical system under LTL specification is usually tackled hierarchically: A motion planner finds a trajectory assuming simplified and deterministic dynamics, and relies on a low-level controller to follow the prescribed trajectory. In this context, sampling-based approaches such as [18] are shown to be faster in comparison with earlier abstraction based approaches. The search space nevertheless grows proportionally to the size of the automaton, making this problem significantly larger than A-to-B motion planning, and furthermore tracking the prescribed trajectory is often not possible with sufficiently small error.

Research integrating sampling based motion planning with feedback control laws aims to allow for systems with complex dynamics in this context. For instance, LQR-trees [24] build stabilized sets along the vertices of a sampling based tree; however given the size of the search space in LTL planning, synthesizing new controllers along every tree vertex becomes intractable. On the other hand, FaSTrack [7] creates safe envelopes around a planned trajectory a-posteriori; however when the dynamical system is non-holonomic, e.g. a car-like robot, it is not possible to find a controller that follows an arbitrary trajectory a-posteriori and as a result the dynamical constraints should already be incorporated during the planning phase.

In [23] we have proposed an approach based on constructing a library of feedback multi-step motion primitives. Through motion primitives, the dynamical constraints of the system are incorporated and the error after applying them is bound. This means that they are suitable for chaining to satisfy long-term missions specified in LTL. We have further developed a sampling-based approach to guide the planning with such motion primitives. We have shown that higher scalability with respect to state-space dimensions can be achieved in comparison with both abstraction-based and abstraction-free LTL planners.

Motion Primitives. To construct motion primitives, we consider the robot to have a generic continuous-time nonlinear model with uncertainty expressed as the following differential equation:

$$\dot{x} = f(x, u) + w, \tag{1}$$

where $x \in X \subset \mathbb{R}^{n_x}$ is the robot state, $u \in U \subset \mathbb{R}^{n_u}$ is the robot input, and $w \in W \subset \mathbb{R}^{n_x}$ is a disturbance with known bounds. The robot described by this system operates in an environment that is partitioned into regions, and its goal is defined as an LTL formula over these regions.

Each motion primitive that we design consists of a constant input term $\hat{u} \in U$ and a multi-step feedback control to ensure a bounded reachable set after the execution of the primitive. The idea of bounded and shrinking reachable set has also been explored in works such as funnel libraries [19] and contraction theory based control [22]. We have however formulated the feedback control synthesis as a linear programming (LP) problem based on local linearizations of the dynamics. This enables efficient synthesis for a large set of nonlinear systems directly from data that can be reused for further expanding the library if the set of motion primitives proves insufficiently fine for the task.

Motion Planning with Motion Primitives. A known challenge regarding planning with a finite set of actions, i.e. motion primitives, is that the search space grows exponentially with the length of trajectory. Solutions to complex LTL specifications are typically trajectories with long prefixes and periodic suffixes, making it particularly difficult to search through primitives' space. However, we know that algorithm such as $A^\star$ can significantly reduce the branching factor of the search when provided with informative heuristics. In theory, an optimal heuristic of the distance of a state to the goal state will result in linear complexity growth with respect to the trajectory length. This is the insight in our design of a near-optimal heuristic to guide the search with motion primitives.

To estimate the robot distance from the goal, i.e. satisfaction of the LTL specification, we first translate it into a Büchi automaton $\mathcal{B}$, and modify it into a language-equivalent automaton $\mathcal{B}^\dagger$, which embeds the information about the robot's possible regions of interest (illustrated in Fig. 1a). We show that by assigning weights to the edges of $\mathcal{B}^\dagger$ corresponding to real distances between regions, the optimal way for the robot to satisfy the specification can be computed through graph search. To compute the weights of edges in $\mathcal{B}^\dagger$, we employ RRT* to construct backward trees from each region of interest as shown in Fig. 1b. We use the constructed trees to estimate the distances between the robot and each region of interest as well as between the regions of interest and these distances become the weights.

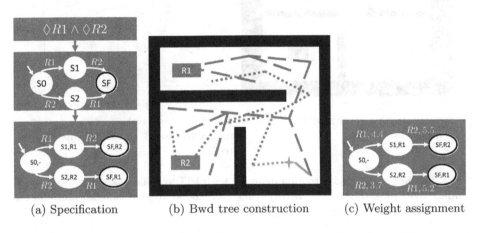

(a) Specification   (b) Bwd tree construction   (c) Weight assignment

Fig. 1. Heuristic construction for evaluating a state: outgoing edges of the current Büchi state are weighted based on robot's current position and other edges use the default weights i.e. based on the distance of a region's root from it's target region.

The computational complexity of computing backward trees is similar to forward trees, however, the advantage is that they are reusable for planning from any state to the root state of the tree. Therefore, after constructing the trees once, we can efficiently compute the distance from the robot to the goal state for any specification and from any initial state in the given environment. Note that if we do not consider the dynamics, this heuristic is already a solution to satisfy the LTL specification.

Results. In Fig. 2a we show a case of guiding motion primitive based planning with our proposed heuristic on a non-holonomic rover model with LTL specification that requires the robot to visit all regions of interest marked in red in an arbitrary order. After the initial tree construction for each tree (12s in total), computing the heuristic takes (80 ms) from any state and the same trees can be reused for any other specification in this space. This is an over $10x$ speedup in comparison to the fastest method prior to our work, i.e. [18] (1.3s). Furthermore, since our method does not rely on geometric biasing in contrast to prior methods such as [4], it is the first method to our best knowledge to handle planning for LTL specifications with non-holonomic dynamics in higher dimensional spaces as demonstrated with the fixed-wing drone model in Fig. 2b. The tree construction in this problem took 8s, each invocation of the heuristic was 20 ms and the full planning with motion-primitives took 40s.

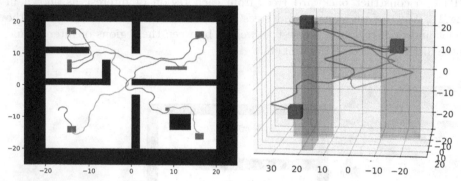

(a) Planning with a rover model to visit 7 regions of interest (in red).

(b) Planning with fixed-wing drone model to visit 3 regions of interest (in red).

Fig. 2. Examples of applying motion planning with LTL specifications in systems with complex dynamics. The colors in trajectory correspond to the changing automaton states. (Color figure online)

3   Integrated Planning and Control with MITL Specifications

In order to allow for time constraints in the mission specification, such as "Visit region A within 10 to 20 time units, then visit B within 30 to 35 time units after reaching A, while avoiding collisions", a timed temporal logic is required, such as Metric Interval Temporal Logic (MITL). When it comes to planning under timed temporal logic tasks, finding a suitable discrete abstraction becomes even more challenging due to the need to maintain the explicit information about time it takes to transition between two states. Related literature often assumes that a discrete system model is already given, e.g., in a form of a Weighted Timed Automaton [1, 28]. [8] proposes a framework capable of planning in dynamically changing environments with dynamic, but only local MTL mission requirements.

To guarantee that a nonlinear dynamical system fulfills a time-bounded MITL task, we propose an approach that closely integrates motion planning and control theory into one framework [3]. The high-level idea of the approach is to first find a candidate timed path that satisfies the specification, followed by the use of a feedback control law that ensures the system follows such a path while also avoiding collision with obstacles in real time.

Integrated MITL Planning and Control Overview. An overview of our approach is presented in Fig. 3. An MITL task specification is first translated into a Timed Automaton (TA) and then into its time-abstract representation, a Zone Automaton (ZA). The ZA is used by an RRT*-based algorithm to find i) an obstacle-free path – a sequence of waypoints – in the workspace, and ii) a sequence of obstacle-free polytopes enclosing the path. Such a path satisfies the untimed version of task; to fulfill the MITL task, time-stamps to reach each waypoint in the path are calculated using clock zones of the ZA as constraints of a Linear Program (LP). We now have a timed path that, if followed by the dynamical system, fulfills the task. To execute the timed path, we propose the use of Time-varying Control Barrier Functions controller derived in [17] and translate the constraints into a fragment of STL. Such a controller ensures that, under certain assumptions on the system dynamics, if the system is within a convex, obstacle-free space, such as a polytope computed by the planner, it is able to navigate from an initial to a goal configuration within a given time window. Sequentially reaching each of the waypoints within the time deadline while staying within the polytopes guarantees that the task is accomplished.

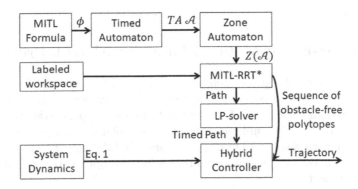

Fig. 3. The approach.

Results. An example of a result using such an approach in an office-like environment is presented in Fig. 4 for the task of reaching region A within 5 to 10 time units, then B within 15 to 20 time units. The dynamical system in question is governed by the following coupled-input equations of motion

$$\dot{x}_1 = u_1 - 0.5u_2, \quad \dot{x}_2 = u_2.$$

Note that the trajectory of the system (blue line in Fig. 4a) never leaves the sequence of obstacle-free polytopes, therefore (indirectly) avoiding collision with surrounding obstacles. Furthermore, since we chose a controller that minimizes the control effort, the system reaches the goal positions exactly at the time deadline (Fig. 4b).

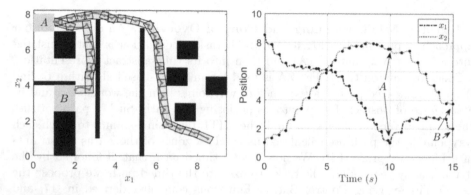

(a) The computed trajectory, in blue, for $\phi_1 = \mathcal{F}_{[5,10]} A \wedge \mathcal{F}_{[15,20]} B$. The robot starts from the bottom right corner, and the controller drives it throughout the way-points marked in red dots.

(b) The evolution of the robot's position in time when subject to ϕ_1. The black dots represent the projection of the timed path onto x_1 and x_2.

Fig. 4. An example of planning in an office-like environment. (Color figure online)

4   Sampling-Based Motion Planning with STL Preferences

So far we have seen the use of temporal logic as a tool to specify tasks that must be fulfilled by the dynamical system, often involving reach, avoid and react specifications. But what if a user wants to specify properties that should be satisfied as much as possible, but that can be violated, to a certain extent, if need be? With such a scenario in mind, we proposed the use of Signal Temporal Logic (STL) as a way of specifying preferences in the robot's trajectory in relation to the environment.

In contrast to LTL, which only offers a qualitative metric in regards to the satisfaction (or not) of a specification, STL allows for a quantitative evaluation, reflecting the level of satisfaction (or violation) of the specification. Such a quantitative evaluation is often called robustness metric, and can be of two forms: space and time. In our works we describe how such metrics can be used in RRT*-based algorithms in order to find trajectories that minimally violate spatial preferences.

Closely related work includes the use of a restricted fragment of Signal Temporal Logic (STL) for control over a short time horizon [17]. For motion planning over longer time horizons, the work by [26] the authors present a sampling-based method for synthesizing control policies that maximize the spatial robustness of STL specifications. In contrast, our work [11] aims to balance between spatial robustness and time robustness.

Motion Planning with User-Adjustable Space-Time Robustness. Our contribution can be summarized as follows: we design an extension to the RRT* that allows for specifying complex missions in scLTL and spatial preferences in a fragment of STL. Our approach measures the cost of a motion plan in terms of a newly developed combined space-time robustness that includes user-adjustable parameters α and A. Intuitively, these represent the hard limit for acceptable space robustness and the relative importance of space robustness and trajectory duration. They can thus be used to tune the prioritization of temporal vs. spatial aspects of the specification. The motion planning algorithm preserves the important properties of RRT*, including asymptotic optimality; furthermore, it guarantees that, if a trajectory that satisfies the scLTL mission exists, it will be found in the asymptotic limit.

Thanks to the user-adjustable parameters, the same framework can provide many different types of trajectories based on the user's preference. In one case, a detour could be preferable over a risky, but more efficient route (e.g., in an autonomous driving scenario). In another, a trajectory that violates the preference might be better, as long as the mission is completed quickly (e.g., in the case of a robotic vacuum cleaner). Our approach provides functionality similarly to what can be found using penalty methods in constrained optimization, without the risk of numerical ill-conditioning.

Results. We present examples that illustrate different compromises between temporal and spatial aspects based on different user-given priorities. The first case study deals with a large and obstacle-filled office depicted in Fig. 5a. It has tables, walls, a corridor and four doors; three regular sized and one smaller, barely the size of the robot. The mission and spatial preference are:

$$\varphi = \mathcal{F}\,G_1 \wedge \mathcal{F}\,G_2$$
$$\Psi = \widehat{\mathcal{G}}_{[0,T_\varphi]}(dist(x(t)) - 0.5),$$

where G_1, G_2 corresponds to the first and second goal regions, respectively (dark gray regions in Fig. 5a). The resulting trajectories can be seen for different values of A in Fig. 5a. Besides different parameter values, the case also provides trajectories using vanilla RRT* and RRT* with obstacles inflated by the robot size, 0.3. Note how the trajectories generated by the vanilla RRT* and the lower values of parameter A pass through the small door at the top of the figure, while for $A = 100$ the planner judges that area too dangerous and takes a longer detours instead. Similarly, we expanded the spatial preference Ψ to include the connectivity constraints depicted in green areas in Fig. 5b. Note that now every trajectory goes through the more dangerous area not to lose connection.

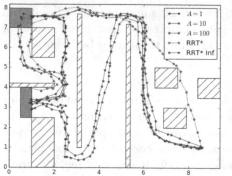 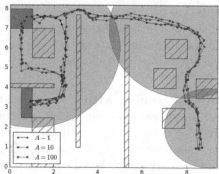

(a) Office environment, with five trajectories; one generated by the vanilla RRT*, one by RRT* with inflated obstacles and three with $\alpha = 0.3$ and varying A.

(b) Scenario with wireless network constraints, with three trajectories with $\alpha = 0.3$ and varying choice of A.

Fig. 5. Case study results using different values of parameter A.

STL-guided Autonomous Exploration. We showcased the use of STL formalism for the robotic exploration problem [2]. Traditionally, algorithms developed for mapping and exploring 3D environments are information-greedy [5,21]. The trajectories generated by such approaches are usually erratic, leading to unorganized exploration and potentially dangerous manoeuvres. Similarly as before, by using a user-defined specification written in a fragment of STL, our proposed approach finds trajectories that minimally violate it while, at the same time, balancing greediness and violation of specification.

A series of simulations and experiments are presented showing the effectiveness of the proposed approach when implemented into AEP [21], an existing receding-horizon, sampling-based motion planning algorithm for exploration of 3D environments with an Unmanned Aerial Vehicle (UAV).

Fig. 6 shows the performance of the proposed approach when used to map a simple rectangular empty room and an office. Note that in the empty room, AEP alone creates a very disorganised trajectory (Fig. 6c), while using our approach the robot swiftly follows the walls (where the actual information is) in a more organized way (Fig. 6e). The improvement in the trade-off between safety and exploration when using our approach can be seen in the real office case. When using UAVs in complex missions, it is common to have a safety bubble around it (an over-approximation of its volume) in order to find relatively safe trajectories, i.e. to maintain a minimum distance to obstacles. However, in exploration tasks, such a safety bubble can hinder the progress of the task if not well tuned, as seen in Fig. 6d. With our proposed approach, the UAV is able to quickly find a safe trajectory that pass through smaller gaps, as in Fig. 6f.

Lastly, Fig. 7 compares the progress of the exploration task along time with both AEP and our proposed approach. We highlight that, besides progressing

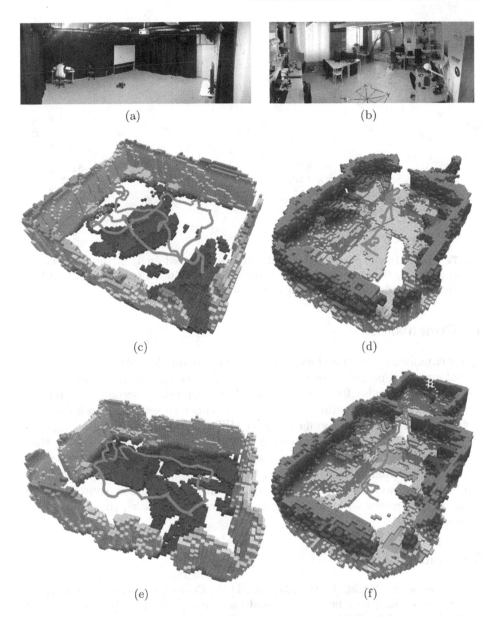

Fig. 6. Experimental results comparing the state-of-the-art exploration algorithm AEP (c), (d) with our proposed approach (e), (f) in two environments, the Real Room (a) and the Real Office (b).

at similar pace for most of the time, our approach is capable of exploring more area than the original AEP, in less time. This is mainly due to the organized exploration feature embedded in our approach.

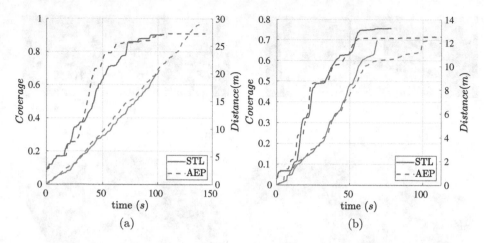

Fig. 7. Exploration progress (blue) and distance travelled (red) of the experiments performed in (a) the Real Room and (b) the Real Office. In both cases, vanilla AEP is depicted with dashed lines, while our approach is with solid lines.

5   Conclusions

In this extended abstract we focused on motion planning for robots that are given spatial and/or time constraints – either through their own dynamics or through specification. We also focused on cases when constraints become preferences. We summarized contributions tackling three concrete set-ups: non-holonomic and uncertain dynamics, specifications in MITL, and preferences in a fragment of STL. One of the main take-aways is that the gap between the models that precisely describe a given system and a discrete model that can be handled by planning algorithms represents a major challenge that cannot be neglected when addressing real-world robotic systems. Our future work will thus continue along those lines, together with expanding on the richness of tasks, constraints, and preferences.

References

1. Andersson, S., Nikou, A., Dimarogonas, D.V.: Control synthesis for multi-agent systems under metric interval temporal logic specifications. IFAC-PapersOnLine **50**(1), 2397–2402 (2017)
2. Barbosa, F.S., Duberg, D., Jensfelt, P., Tumova, J.: Guiding autonomous exploration with signal temporal logic. IEEE Robot. Autom. Lett. **4**(4), 3332–3339 (2019)
3. Barbosa, F.S., Lindemann, L., Dimarogonas, D.V., Tumova, J.: Integrated motion planning and control under metric interval temporal logic specifications. In: 2019 18th European Control Conference (ECC), pp. 2042–2049. IEEE (2019)
4. Bhatia, A., Kavraki, L.E., Vardi, M.Y.: Sampling-based motion planning with temporal goals. In: 2010 IEEE International Conference on Robotics and Automation, pp. 2689–2696. IEEE (2010)

5. Bircher, A., Kamel, M., Alexis, K., Oleynikova, H., Siegwart, R.: Receding horizon "next-best-view" planner for 3D exploration. In: 2016 IEEE International Conference on Robotics and Automation (ICRA), pp. 1462–1468. IEEE (2016)
6. Castro, L.I.R., Chaudhari, P., Tumova, J., Karaman, S., Frazzoli, E., Rus, D.: Incremental sampling-based algorithm for minimum-violation motion planning. In: 52nd IEEE Conference on Decision and Control, pp. 3217–3224. IEEE (2013)
7. Herbert, S.L., Chen, M., Han, S., Bansal, S., Fisac, J.F., Tomlin, C.J.: FaSTrack: a modular framework for fast and guaranteed safe motion planning. In: 2017 IEEE 56th Annual Conference on Decision and Control (CDC), pp. 1517–1522. IEEE (2017)
8. Hoxha, B., Fainekos, G.: Planning in dynamic environments through temporal logic monitoring. In: Workshops at the Thirtieth AAAI Conference on Artificial Intelligence (2016)
9. Karaman, S., Frazzoli, E.: Sampling-based motion planning with deterministic μ-calculus specifications. In: Proceedings of the 48h IEEE Conference on Decision and Control (CDC) held jointly with 2009 28th Chinese Control Conference, pp. 2222–2229. IEEE (2009)
10. Karaman, S., Frazzoli, E.: Sampling-based algorithms for optimal motion planning. Int. J. Robot. Res. **30**(7), 846–894 (2011)
11. Karlsson, J., Barbosa, F.S., Tumova, J.: Sampling-based motion planning with temporal logic missions and spatial preferences. IFAC-PapersOnLine **53**(2), 15537–15543 (2020)
12. Karlsson, J., Vasile, C.I., Tumova, J., Karaman, S., Rus, D.: Multi-vehicle motion planning for social optimal mobility-on-demand. In: 2018 IEEE International Conference on Robotics and Automation (ICRA), pp. 7298–7305. IEEE (2018)
13. Kloetzer, M., Belta, C.: A fully automated framework for control of linear systems from temporal logic specifications. IEEE Trans. Autom. Control **53**(1), 287–297 (2008)
14. Kress-Gazit, H., Fainekos, G.E., Pappas, G.J.: Temporal-logic-based reactive mission and motion planning. IEEE Trans. Robot. **25**(6), 1370–1381 (2009)
15. Kress-Gazit, H., Lahijanian, M., Raman, V.: Synthesis for robots: guarantees and feedback for robot behavior. Annu. Rev. Control Robot. Auton. Syst. **1**, 211–236 (2018)
16. LaValle, S.M.: Planning Algorithms. Cambridge University Press (2006)
17. Lindemann, L., Dimarogonas, D.V.: Control barrier functions for signal temporal logic tasks. IEEE Control Syst. Lett. **3**(1), 96–101 (2019)
18. Luo, X., Kantaros, Y., Zavlanos, M.M.: An abstraction-free method for multirobot temporal logic optimal control synthesis. IEEE Trans. Robot. (2021)
19. Majumdar, A., Tedrake, R.: Funnel libraries for real-time robust feedback motion planning. Int. J. Robot. Res. **36**(8), 947–982 (2017)
20. Montana, F.J., Liu, J., Dodd, T.J.: Sampling-based reactive motion planning with temporal logic constraints and imperfect state information. In: Critical Systems: Formal Methods and Automated Verification, pp. 134–149. Springer (2017). https://doi.org/10.1007/978-3-319-67113-0_9
21. Selin, M., Tiger, M., Duberg, D., Heintz, F., Jensfelt, P.: Efficient autonomous exploration planning of large-scale 3-D environments. IEEE Robot. Autom. Lett. **4**(2), 1699–1706 (2019)
22. Singh, S., Majumdar, A., Slotine, J.J., Pavone, M.: Robust online motion planning via contraction theory and convex optimization. In: 2017 IEEE International Conference on Robotics and Automation (ICRA), pp. 5883–5890. IEEE (2017)

23. Tajvar, P., Barbosa, F.S., Tumova, J.: Safe motion planning for an uncertain non-holonomic system with temporal logic specification. In: 2020 IEEE 16th International Conference on Automation Science and Engineering (CASE), pp. 349–354. IEEE (2020)
24. Tedrake, R., Manchester, I.R., Tobenkin, M., Roberts, J.W.: LQR-trees: feedback motion planning via sums-of-squares verification. Int. J. Robot. Res. **29**(8), 1038–1052 (2010)
25. Vasile, C.I., Li, X., Belta, C.: Reactive sampling-based path planning with temporal logic specifications. Int. J. Robot. Res. **39**(8), 1002–1028 (2020)
26. Vasile, C.I., Raman, V., Karaman, S.: Sampling-based synthesis of maximally-satisfying controllers for temporal logic specifications. In: 2017 IEEE/RSJ International Conference on Intelligent Robots and Systems (IROS), pp. 3840–3847. IEEE (2017)
27. Vasile, C.I., Tumova, J., Karaman, S., Belta, C., Rus, D.: Minimum-violation scltl motion planning for mobility-on-demand. In: 2017 IEEE International Conference on Robotics and Automation (ICRA), pp. 1481–1488. IEEE (2017)
28. Zhou, Y., Maity, D., Baras, J.S.: Timed automata approach for motion planning using metric interval temporal logic. In: 2016 European Control Conference (ECC), pp. 690–695. IEEE (2016)

On the Complexity of Timed Pattern Matching

Eugene Asarin[1]([⊠]) [iD], Thomas Ferrère[2], Dejan Ničković[3] [iD], and Dogan Ulus[4] [iD]

[1] IRIF, Université de Paris, Paris, France
asarin@irif.fr
[2] Imagination Technologies, Kings Langley, UK
thomas.ferrere@imgtec.com
[3] AIT Austrian Institute of Technology, Vienna, Austria
dejan.nickovic@ait.ac.at
[4] Bogazici University, Istanbul, Turkey
dogan.ulus@boun.edu.tr

Abstract. Timed pattern matching consists in finding occurrences of a timed regular expression in a timed word. This problem has been addressed using several techniques, its solutions are implemented in tools (quite efficient in practice), and used, for example in log analysis and runtime verification. In this article, we explore computational complexity of timed pattern matching, and prove P, NP and PSPACE bounds, depending on connectives used in expressions and other details. We conclude with a couple of open questions.

Keywords: Timed regular expressions · Pattern matching · Complexity

1 Introduction

The timed pattern matching (TPM) problem, first formulated in [21], consists in finding in a timed word all (or some) occurrences of a timed regular expression (TRE). Several algorithms have been proposed, using recursion on expression [21] or timed automata [5,23,25], as well as for online [22], quantitative [4], and parametric [24] versions of pattern matching. Experiments conducted using tools such as [19], show that practical complexity of TPM is often low, close to linear in the length of the timed word, which makes possible applications such as [10,13–15].

In this article, we study the complexity of TPM. While this problem has an obvious theoretical interest, several important practical aspects are also addressed herein. First, we are able to identify kinds of timed regular expressions that have tractable worst-case complexity. Second, we are able to characterize the type of signals that cause the worst-case behavior and thus better understand the class of problems for which the low practical complexity of TPM holds.

E. Asarin—Supported by ANR-JST grant CyPhAI.

C. Dima and M. Shirmohammadi (Eds.): FORMATS 2021, LNCS 12860, pp. 15–31, 2021.
https://doi.org/10.1007/978-3-030-85037-1_2

In the untimed case, the problem is thoroughly explored, and became in part textbook material, see e.g. [12, ex. 3.23], or [16] and references therein. It is well known that the problem is polynomial even if complementation or intersection is allowed in the expressions.[1]

However, the TPM problem has a more difficult, arithmetical aspect. Indeed, a timed expression should not only match the sequence of events, but also all the delays between them, that should thus satisfy quite involved constraints. Several results in this direction can be found in [11,17], where fragments of Presburger arithmetic augmented with Kleene stars are considered, and their complexity, from NP to EXPTIME is established.

TPM combines easy combinatorial and hard arithmetical aspects, hence exhibits a large spectrum of complexity. We show that for timed words of polynomially-bounded duration (or equivalently when the word has its delays represented in unary), all pattern matching problems considered in this article remain in P. As soon as the word has delays written in binary (and can thus have an exponential duration), the pattern matching becomes NP-complete even for expressions without Kleene star. On the other side of the spectrum, matching generalized expressions (with complementation) is shown to be PSPACE-complete. Unfortunately, for the most interesting case (expressions with star of unbounded depth and no complementation), we were unable to close the complexity gap, between NP-hardness and PSPACE-easyness.

Another contribution of this article, instrumental for complexity analysis, consists in revisiting the recursive TPM algorithm from [21] using the worst-case complexity perspective. We show that this algorithm can be performed in a region-graph-like structure of quadratic size, and this guarantees that all relevant operations (including complementation and Kleene iteration) can be performed in polynomial time.

The article is organized as follows: in Sect. 2 we present our statement of and approach to TPM; in Sect. 3 we explore the complexity of underlying data structures and operations; in Sect. 4 we establish the main results regarding complexity classes of TPM problems; finally, we conclude in Sect. 5.

2   Background Material

2.1   Terminology and Problem Statement

Here we recall the TPM setting introduced in [20,21].

Timed relations. Throughout the paper, we use a bounded *time domain* $[0; d] \subset \mathbb{R}$ for some rational d. A *time period* (t, t') is defined by a pair of boundary time points in $[0; d]$ such that $t < t'$; its *duration* is $t' - t$. We denote the set of all such time periods $\Omega([0; d])$ or merely Ω. Geometrically speaking, a time period (t, t') can be viewed as a single point on the standard two-dimensional plane. On the

---

[1] To avoid confusion, we recall that high complexity bounds, such as the famous non-elementary bound of [18], deal with quite a different problem of emptiness checking.

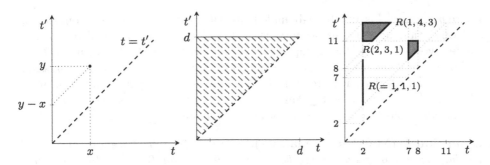

Fig. 1. Left: Geometric representations of a time period (x, y). **Middle:** The set Ω for time domain $[0; d]$. **Right:** Regions on $[0, 13]$ over constants $\{2, 7, 8, 11\}$.

left of Fig. 1, we illustrate attributes of a time period (t, t'), its beginning t, its end t', and its duration $t' - t$. Then we can view the set of all time periods Ω as a (triangular) set of points such that $\Omega = \{(t, t') \mid t, t' \in [0; d], t' - t > 0\}$ on the plane as depicted in the middle of Fig. 1.

We call a *zone* any set of timed periods that can be expressed as

$$Z = \{(t, t') \in \Omega \mid c_6 \prec t \prec c_1 \wedge c_5 \prec t' \prec c_2 \wedge c_4 \prec t' - t \prec c_3\}, \qquad (1)$$

where $c_1, \ldots, c_6 \in [0; d]$ and $\prec \in \{<, \leq\}$. Thus a zone is a polygon on the plane with vertical, horizontal and 45 degree diagonal bounds only.

We call a set of time periods a *timed relation* if it can be expressed as a finite union of zones. Clearly the empty set, the set $\Omega([0; d])$ of all time periods, and all finite sets of time periods are timed relations.

Timed behaviors. Let $P = \{p_1, \ldots, p_m\}$ be a finite set of atomic propositions that correspond to qualitative states or actions of some real-time system observed continuously for a finite amount of time. We represent their evolution over time as a *timed behavior* that is a finite sequence of the form

$$w = (t_0, t_1, a_1), (t_1, t_2, a_2), \ldots, (t_{n-1}, t_n, a_n),$$

with $a_k \in \{0, 1\}^m$, and $t_{k-1} < t_k$ for $k \in 1 \ldots n$. We also require that $t_0 = 0, t_n = d$, i.e. the observation interval is $[0; d]$.

Each time period (t_{k-1}, t_k) is thus associated with a Boolean vector a_k such that $a_k(i) = 1$ if the proposition p_i holds on the time period (t_{k-1}, t_k) and $a_k(i) = 0$ if it does not.

Timed regular expressions. The syntax of *timed regular expressions* (a variant of [2,3]) over a finite set P of propositions is given by the following grammar[2] (or its fragments):

$$\varphi := p \mid \neg p \mid \langle \varphi \rangle_I \mid \varphi_1 \vee \varphi_2 \mid \varphi_1 \wedge \varphi_2 \mid \varphi_1 \circ \varphi_2 \mid \varphi^+ \mid \overline{\varphi},$$

[2] We avoid empty matches, and for this reason use $^+$ rather than * for Kleene iteration.

where $p \in P$ and I is an integer-bounded interval of duration values. Atoms $p, \neg p$, and operation $\langle \varphi \rangle_I$ are mandatory, we will explicitly mention which of other connectives are used (for example, $\wedge, \vee, \circ, {}^+$-TRE mean the fragment of TRE without complement operator). The duration restriction $\langle \varphi \rangle_I$ of an expression φ is the characteristic feature of TRE [2,3]. We use an exponent notation with $\varphi^1 = \varphi$, $\varphi^k = \varphi^{k-1} \circ \varphi$ for $k \geq 2$ and sometimes juxtaposition for concatenation. Kleene *plus* connective φ^+ stands for an infinite sum $\bigcup_{k \geq 1} \varphi^k$ as usual.

Definition 1 (Matchset Semantics). *The satisfaction relation $\models$ of a timed regular expression φ on a timed behavior w defined on $[0; d]$, relative to a time period $(t, t') \in \Omega([0; d])$ is defined as follows:*

$$
\begin{aligned}
(w, t, t') &\models p & &\leftrightarrow (t, t') \in \mathcal{V}(p); \\
(w, t, t') &\models \neg p & &\leftrightarrow (t, t') \in \mathcal{V}(\neg p); \\
(w, t, t') &\models \langle \varphi \rangle_I & &\leftrightarrow (w, t, t') \models \varphi \text{ and } t' - t \in I \\
(w, t, t') &\models \varphi_1 \vee \varphi_2 & &\leftrightarrow (w, t, t') \models \varphi_1 \text{ or } (w, t, t') \models \varphi_2; \\
(w, t, t') &\models \varphi_1 \wedge \varphi_2 & &\leftrightarrow (w, t, t') \models \varphi_1 \text{ and } (w, t, t') \models \varphi_2; \\
(w, t, t') &\models \varphi_1 \circ \varphi_2 & &\leftrightarrow \exists t''. \, (w, t, t'') \models \varphi_1 \text{ and } (w, t'', t') \models \varphi_2; \\
(w, t, t') &\models \varphi^+ & &\leftrightarrow \exists k \geq 1. \, (w, t, t') \models \varphi^k; \\
(w, t, t') &\models \overline{\varphi} & &\leftrightarrow (w, t, t') \not\models \varphi,
\end{aligned}
$$

where $\mathcal{V}(p)$ (resp. $\mathcal{V}(\neg p)$) is the set of all time periods on which p is permanently true (resp. false). We call the set of time periods such that $(w, t, t') \models \varphi$ the matchset of φ. We say that w matches φ, written $w \models \varphi$, whenever $(w, 0, d) \models \varphi$.

2.2 Computing the Matchset

The TPM method introduced in [21] and implemented in [19] computes the matchset by induction over the regular expression, and it is summarized in Algorithm 1. We leave out optimisations not relevant to worst-case complexity.

The main insight of this algorithm is that the matchset of any TRE is a timed relation. A Boolean combination of timed relations is a timed relation, and the restriction to a duration in interval I amounts to intersection with a single zone—a diagonal stripe. The composition of timed relations, resulting from a concatenation, is again a timed relation. For the Kleene plus, we can compute a bounded iteration $\psi^{\leq 2^k}$ instead of ψ^+. We provide in Sect. 2.3 a choice of k guaranteeing the correctness of the computation.

The relevant data structures, algorithms and complexity of all auxiliary operations are discussed in Sect. 3.3. A comprehensive example of TPM is given on Fig. 2.

2.3 Bounds on Kleene Plus

There remains one important thing to analyze in Algorithm 1: in line 18 we compute a bounded iteration $\psi^{\leq 2^k}$. What is a choice of k such that the resulting timed relation covers ψ^+? This question has been answered in [21, Theorem

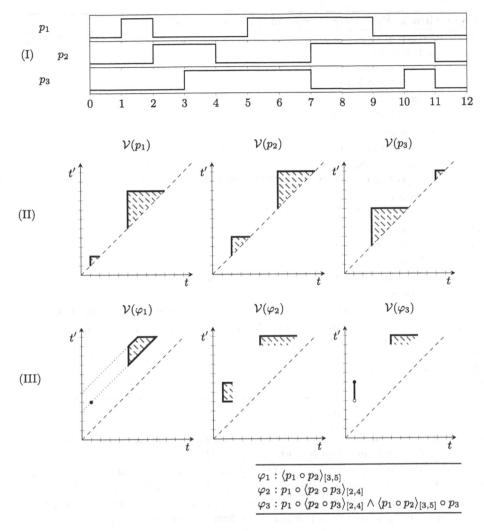

$\varphi_1 : \langle p_1 \circ p_2 \rangle_{[3,5]}$
$\varphi_2 : p_1 \circ \langle p_2 \circ p_3 \rangle_{[2,4]}$
$\varphi_3 : p_1 \circ \langle p_2 \circ p_3 \rangle_{[2,4]} \wedge \langle p_1 \circ p_2 \rangle_{[3,5]} \circ p_3$

Fig. 2. (I) Three example timed behaviors, namely p_1, p_2, p_3, starting from time 0 and ending at time point 12. (II) Matchsets for atomic expressions, p_1, p_2, and p_3. (III) Example matchsets for timed regular expressions φ_1, φ_2, and φ_3 computed by our TPM algorithm over these behaviors.

2], we reproduce it here for completeness.[3] We show that for a timed relation R covering d time units and represented as union of N zones with smallest diagonal constraint c, the squaring procedure KLEENE converges within $k = \log(N + \frac{d}{c})$. A sequence of zones $z_1, \ldots, z_n$ is said to be *redundant* if there exists $1 \le i < j \le n$ with $z_1 \circ \cdots \circ z_j \subseteq z_1 \circ \cdots \circ z_i$. We will show that all sequences of zones of

---

[3] Note that the present bound, unlike the ones in [21], does not rely on expressions having integer interval bounds.

Algorithm 1. Procedure for computing the matchset

```
1:  procedure MATCHSET(TRE φ)                          ▷ returns a TimedRelation
2:      switch φ do
3:          case p
4:              return 𝒱(p)
5:          case ¬p
6:              return 𝒱(¬p)
7:          case ψ₁ ∨ ψ₂
8:              return MATCHSET(ψ₁) ∪ MATCHSET(ψ₂)
9:          case ψ₁ ∧ ψ₂
10:             return MATCHSET(ψ₁) ∩ MATCHSET(ψ₂)
11:         case ψ̄
12:             return Ω \ MATCHSET(ψ)
13:         case ⟨ψ⟩ᵢ
14:             return MATCHSET(ψ) ∩ {(t,t′) | t′ − t ∈ I}
15:         case ψ₁ ∘ ψ₂
16:             return MATCHSET(ψ₁) ∘ MATCHSET(ψ₂)
17:         case ψ⁺
18:             return KLEENE(MATCHSET(ψ), k)   ▷ see below the right choice of k
19: procedure KLEENE(TimedRelation R, Integer k)      ▷ returns a TimedRelation
20:     if k = 0 then
21:         return R
22:     S ← KLEENE(R, k − 1)
23:     return S ∪ (S ∘ S)
```

---

length greater than $N + \frac{d}{c}$ are redundant. It follows that $\text{KLEENE}(R, k+1) \subseteq \text{KLEENE}(R, k)$ and therefore $\text{KLEENE}(R, k) = R^+$.

Let us denote $(\pi_1^-(z), \pi_1^+(z), \pi_2^-(z), \pi_2^+(z), \delta^-(z), \delta^+(z))$ the tight representation of a zone z, given as the lower and upper bounds of its horizontal, vertical and diagonal projections $\pi_1(z), \pi_2(z)$, and $\delta(z)$ respectively. First, we show that in a non-redundant sequence the maximal duration never decreases.

Lemma 1. *For any z, z' such that $z \circ z' \not\subseteq z$ we have $\delta^+(z \circ z') \geq \delta^+(z)$.*

Proof. The propagation of difference constraints gives us $\delta^+(z \circ z') = \min\{\delta^+(z) + \delta^+(z'), \pi_2^+(z') - \pi_1^-(z)\}$. Suppose $\delta^+(z \circ z') < \delta^+(z)$ and show $z \circ z' \subseteq z$. First note that $\pi_1(z \circ z') \subseteq \pi_1(z)$. By hypothesis $\pi_2^+(z') - \pi_1^-(z) < \delta^+(z)$, yet $\delta^+(z) \leq \pi_2^+(z) - \pi_1^-(z)$ so that $\pi_2^+(z') < \pi_2^+(z)$. This implies that $\pi_2(z \circ z') \subseteq \pi_2(z)$. Finally the hypothesis $\delta^+(z \circ z') < \delta^+(z)$ gives us $\delta(z \circ z') \subseteq \delta(z)$.

We call *repeated* a position i in the sequence $z_1, \ldots, z_n$ such that there exists $j > i$ with $z_i = z_j$. Now when appending a zone that may be repeated, the maximal duration increases by the corresponding amount.

Lemma 2. *For any z, z' such that there exists z'' with $z \circ z' \circ z'' \circ z' \not\subseteq z \circ z'$ we have $\delta^+(z \circ z') = \delta^+(z) + \delta^+(z')$.*

Proof. Suppose $\delta^+(z \circ z') < \delta^+(z) + \delta^+(z')$, take z'' a zone and show $z \circ z' \circ z'' \circ z' \subseteq z \circ z'$. Similarly to the proof of Lemma 1 it is sufficient to show that π_2^+ and δ^+ do not increase. On the one hand $\pi_2^+(z \circ z' \circ z'' \circ z') \leq \pi_2^+(z') = \pi_2^+(z \circ z')$, and on the other hand $\delta^+(z \circ z' \circ z'' \circ z') \leq \pi_2^+(z') - \pi_1^-(z) = \delta^+(z \circ z')$.

Assume a timed relation R representable using zones with smallest diagonal constraint c. Remark that any repeated zone z' such that $\pi^+(z') < c$ would make the corresponding sequence redundant. Hence over such a timed relation R, Lemma 2 guarantees $\delta^+(z \circ z') \geq \delta^+(z) + c$.

Proposition 1. *Let R be a timed relation covering d time units and represented as union of N zones with smallest diagonal constraint c. The squaring procedure* KLEENE *converges within $k = \log(N + \frac{d}{c})$.*

Proof. We first show that any non-redundant sequence of zones $z_1, \ldots, z_n$ with m repetitions verifies $\delta^+(z_1 \circ \cdots \circ z_n) \geq mc$.

Let i be a position in the sequence. If z_i is repeated there exists $j > i$ with $z_i = z_j$. Factoring the prefix $(z_1 \circ \cdots \circ z_{i-1}) \circ z_i \circ (z_{i+1} \circ \cdots \circ z_{j-1}) \circ z_j$ we see by Lemma 2 that $\delta^+(z_1 \circ \cdots \circ z_i) = \delta^+(z_1 \circ \cdots \circ z_{i-1}) + \delta^+(z_i)$ and by our remark $\delta^+(z_1 \circ \cdots \circ z_i) \geq \delta^+(z_1 \circ \cdots \circ z_{i-1}) + c$, the maximal duration increases by c. Else z_i is not repeated and by Lemma 1 we ensure $\delta^+(z_1 \circ \cdots \circ z_i) \geq \delta^+(z_1 \circ \cdots \circ z_{i-1})$, the maximal duration does not decrease. By a straightforward induction, with m repetitions the sequence $z_1, \ldots, z_n$ verifies $\delta^+(z_1 \circ \cdots \circ z_n) \geq mc$.

We now show that KLEENE$(R, k+1) \subseteq$ KLEENE(R, k). Let x be a zone in KLEENE$(R, k+1) \setminus$ KLEENE(R, k). There exists a sequence $z_1, \ldots, z_n$ such that $x = z_1 \circ \cdots \circ z_n$ with $n > 2^k \geq N + \frac{d}{c}$. If this sequence is non-redundant it has at least $n - N$ repeated zones, and by the above, a maximal duration $\delta^+(z_1 \circ \cdots \circ z_n) \geq (n - N)c > d$. This is a contradiction, therefore x is redundant. Hence the squaring procedure KLEENE converges within $k = \log(N + \frac{d}{c})$.

3   Complexity of Our Pattern Matching Procedures

3.1   Regions, and Representations of Timed Relations

In this section, we estimate the number of zones needed to represent a timed relation. The main construction, inspired by Alur and Dill's region construction for timed automata [1], is illustrated on the right of Fig. 1. Let us fix a set of constants $\{c^1, \ldots, c^k\}$, sorted in ascending order (we also augment the set with special constants $c^0 = 0$ and $c^{k+1} = d$). We define open regions (smallest zones) $R(i, j, \ell)$ for $i, j, \ell \in 0 \ldots k$ as follows:

$$R(i, j, \ell) = \{(t, t') \mid c^i < t < c^{i+1} \wedge c^j < t' < c^{j+1} \wedge c^\ell < t' - t < c^{\ell+1}\}.$$

In other words, we partition the plane in $k + 1$ vertical, $k + 1$ horizontal, and $k + 1$ diagonal stripes. We also define degenerate 1-dimensional regions

$$R(=i, j, \ell) = \{(t, t') \mid c^i = t \wedge c^j < t' < c^{j+1} \wedge c^\ell < t' - t < c^{\ell+1}\}.$$

Similarly we define two other kinds of 1-dimensional, as well as 0-dimensional regions:

$$R(i, =j, \ell), R(i, j, =\ell), R(=i, =j, \ell), R(i, =j, =\ell), R(=i, j, =\ell).$$

Lemma 3. *The number of distinct regions $R(., ., .)$ is $O(k^2)$ only.*

Lemma 4. *Every zone definable using the constants $c^1 \dots c^k$ is a finite union of regions.*

The following theorem is now immediate.

Theorem 1 (Number of zones vs number of constants). *Let $R = \bigcup_i z_i$ be a timed relation expressed as a union of zones using k constants $c^1, \dots, c^k$ only. Then it is possible to express R as a union of $O(k^2)$ zones (in fact regions), this bound is tight.*

3.2   Complexity of the Matchset

Proposition 2. *For a timed behavior of length n (no constraints are imposed on occurrence times of events), and duration d and a TRE with integer interval bounds, the matchset can be expressed using $O(nd)$ constants. Hence, it can be represented as a union of $O(d^2 n^2)$ regions.*

Proof. Let $X \subset \mathbb{R}$ be the set of all the discontinuities in the timed behavior; then we will prove by structural induction on the regular expression the following property P of the matchset. It can be expressed as a finite union of zones definable using only the constants $c_1, c_2, c_5, c_6 \in X + \mathbb{Z}$ and $c_3, c_4 \in \mathbb{N}$.

As a basis, consider a proposition p that holds on several intervals of the form $[a, a']$ (by definition $a, a' \in X$). To such an interval corresponds a matchset $a \prec t < t' \prec a'$, which can be written as a zone with parameters $c_5 = c_6 = a$, $c_1 = c_2 = a'$, $c_4 = 0$, $c_3 = \infty$, and satisfies the property. The matchset for the expression p consists of such zones for all the maximal validity intervals of p, and also satisfies P. The proof for $\neg p$ is similar.

The inductive case is based on the following main lemma:

Lemma 5. *Let zones z^1 and z^2 satisfy the property P, then the same is true for $z^1 \cap z^2$ and $z^1 \circ z^2$, and even $\overline{z^1}$.*

Proof. Let z^i be represented using parameters $c_1^i, \dots, c_6^i$ satisfying property P. Then $z^1 \cap z^2$ is a zone with parameters

$$c_1' = \min(c_1^1, c_1^2); \qquad c_2' = \min(c_2^1, c_2^2); \qquad c_3' = \min(c_3^1, c_3^2);$$
$$c_4' = \max(c_4^1, c_4^2); \qquad c_5' = \max(c_5^1, c_5^2); \qquad c_6' = \max(c_6^1, c_6^2);$$

the property P is preserved.

For the concatenation, $z^1 \circ z^2$ is a zone with parameters

$$c'_1 = \min(c^1_1, c^2_1 - c^1_4, c^1_2 - c^1_4); \qquad c'_2 = \min(c^2_2, c^1_2 + c^2_3, c^2_1 + c^2_3);$$
$$c'_3 = c^1_3 + c^2_3; \qquad\qquad\qquad c'_4 = c^1_4 + c^2_4;$$
$$c'_5 = \max(c^2_5, c^1_5 + c^2_4, c^2_6 + c^2_4); \qquad c'_6 = \max(c^1_6, c^2_6 - c^1_3, c^1_5 - c^1_3);$$

the property P is preserved again.

The complement of the zone z^1 is the union of 6 zones defined by inequations

$$t \prec c^1_6; \qquad c^1_1 \prec t; \qquad t' \prec c^1_5; \qquad c^1_2 \prec t'; \qquad t' - t \prec c^1_4; \qquad c^1_3 \prec t' - t,$$

each of those satisfies P. The Lemma is proved.

The property P is trivially preserved by the union operation. Due to the Lemma above it is preserved by intersection and concatenation. Expression φ^+ can be rewritten in terms of union and concatenation. A time restricted expression $\langle \varphi \rangle_{[a,b]}$ is equivalent to the intersection $\varphi \wedge \langle \mathbf{true} \rangle_{[a,b]}$, and the second term has a matchset definable by $a \prec t < t' \prec b$, and has the property P (we use the hypothesis that interval bounds a and b are integer). Thus in all cases the property P is preserved by regular operations.

All the constants can be brought to the interval $[0, d]$ without changing the zone. Thus the total number of constants is $O(nd)$, and due to Theorem 1 the matchset is a union of $O(n^2 d^2)$ zones (regions).

3.3   All Operations are Polynomial

Proposition 3 (Complexity of operations on timed relations). *Given timed relations R_1 and R_2 represented as unions of n_1 and n_2 zones, the following estimates hold. When estimating time (bit) complexity, we also suppose that all zones have binary rational bounds represented in b bits.*

$R_1 \cup R_2$ *is definable using at most $n_1 + n_2$ zones and computable in $O(n_1 + n_2)$ operations.*

$R_1 \cap R_2$ *is definable using at most $n_1 n_2$ zones and computable in $O(b n_1 n_2)$ operations.*

$R_1 \circ R_2$ *is definable using at most $n_1 n_2$ zones and computable in $O(b n_1 n_2)$ operations.*

$\overline{R}$ *is definable using $O(n^2)$ zones, computable in $O(b n^3)$ operations.*

$\langle R \rangle_I$ *is definable using at most n zones, and computable in $O(bn)$ operations.*

All the bounds on numbers of zones are tight.

Proof. Upper bounds for the number of zones in first three cases are easy: $\cup$ can be computed by merging lists of zones, while $\cap$ and $\circ$ by combining each zone of R_1 and of R_2. Time complexity follows immediately since elementary operations on zones (intersection, concatenation) can be computed in $O(b)$ time.

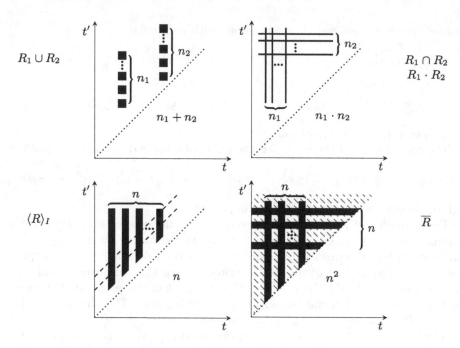

Fig. 3. Bounds on numbers of zones are tight

Time restriction can be seen as intersection with a convex zone $\{(t, t') \mid t' - t \in I\}$, which implies the upper bounds for $\langle R \rangle_I$. The examples on Fig. 3 show that the bounds for $\cup, \cap, \circ, \langle \rangle_I$, and $\overline{R}$ are tight.

Consider now the complement. Theorem 1 yields a quadratic estimate: indeed, $\overline{R}$ is definable using the same $6n$ constants as R, thus $O(n^2)$ zones are sufficient. The time complexity bound follows from the pseudocode in Algorithm 2.

4   Complexity of Timed Pattern Matching

4.1   Pattern Matching on $\mathbb{R}$

The hardness of TPM mostly comes from that of pattern matching on $\mathbb{R}$. Following [7] (see also [6]), we define *real-time expressions*:

- integer bounded intervals I are atomic expressions;
- one can apply connectives $\wedge, \vee, \circ, {}^+, {}^-$ to obtain new expressions.

An example real-time expression is $([21; 23]^+ \circ 37^+) \wedge [100; 110)$. The concatenation corresponds to a Minkowski sum, and other connectives are as expected. Given a real-time expression φ, one can easily define its semantics $[\varphi] \subset (0; \infty)$ by structural induction. For $x \in (0; \infty)$ we write $x \models \varphi$ whenever $x \in [\varphi]$.

Algorithm 2. Computing the complement using regions

```
 1: procedure COMPLEMENT(Z[1, . . . , n])
 2:     M ← ∅
 3:     for all R ∈ Regions do
 4:         ok = true
 5:         if R ⊈ Ω then
 6:             ok = false
 7:         for i = 1 to n do
 8:             if R ⊆ Z[i] then
 9:                 ok = false
10:         if ok then
11:             M ← M ∪ {R}
12:     return M
```

The *matching* problem on $\mathbb{R}$ is formulated as follows: given a rational number x and a real-time regular expression φ, both written in binary, decide whether $x \models \varphi$. Here we only prove hardness results, because easyness is proved in a more general setting in the next section.

Proposition 4. *Matching an* $\vee, \circ$*-expression (or an* $\wedge, \vee, \circ$*-expression) on* $\mathbb{R}$ *is* NP*-complete.*

Proof. By reduction of SubsetSum. Given a set of integers $A = \{a_1, \ldots, a_k\}$ and a target sum W in binary we consider the following expression:

$$\varphi_A = (1 \vee a_1 + 1) \circ (1 \vee a_2 + 1) \circ \cdots \circ (1 \vee a_k + 1).$$

Each subset $S \subset A$ summing up to W corresponds to a match $W + k \models \varphi_A$. Indeed we should just take a term $(a_i + 1)$ in each parenthesis with $a_i \in S$, and 1 in all the others. Symmetrically, every match $W + k \models \varphi_A$ yields a subset of A summing up to W.

Proposition 5. *Matching an* $\vee, \circ, \bar{}$*-expression (or an* $\wedge, \vee, \circ, ^+, \bar{}$*-expression) on* $\mathbb{R}$ *is* PSPACE*-complete.*

*Proof (*PSPACE*-hardness).* We proceed by reduction of SubsetSum−Game problem from [9]: Given natural numbers W and a_i, b_i, c_i, d_i for $i = 1 \ldots n$ decide whether

$$\bigwedge_{x_1 \in \{a_1, b_1\}} \bigvee_{y_1 \in \{c_1, d_1\}} \cdots \bigwedge_{x_n \in \{a_n, b_n\}} \bigvee_{y_n \in \{c_n, d_n\}} \left(\sum_{i=1}^{n} (x_i + y_i) = W \right). \quad (2)$$

Consider the regular expression

$$\varphi_{abcd} = \overline{(a_1 \vee b_1) \circ \overline{(c_1 \vee d_1)} \circ \cdots \circ (a_n \vee b_n) \circ \overline{(c_n \vee d_n)}}.$$

We will now formalize and prove the fact that matching $W \models \varphi_{abcd}$ and winning the game (2) are equivalent.

First we define sets $H_i, i \in 0 \ldots n$ and $G_i, i \in 1 \ldots n$ by the following descending induction:

$$H_n = \{0\};$$
$$G_k = (H_k + c_k) \cup (H_k + \dot{} d_k);$$
$$H_{k-1} = (G_k + a_k) \cap (G_k + b_k).$$

We can use the sets H_i, G_i to describe semantics of the game formula (2) and all its suffixes.

Lemma 6. – *Vector* $x_{1..k}, y_{1..k}$ *satisfies the suffix of* (2) *with first* $2k$ *quantifiers removed, iff*

$$W - \sum x - \sum y \in H_k.$$

– *Vector* $x_{1..k}, y_{1..k-1}$ *satisfies the suffix of* (2) *with first* $2k - 1$ *quantifiers removed, iff*

$$W - \sum x - \sum y \in G_k.$$

– *Hence, the subset game is won iff* $W \in H_0$.

The proof is by straightforward induction.

We will use a couple of simple formulas on how some idioms transform the semantics of an expressions:

Lemma 7 (Transforming semantics). *Given an expression* ψ,

$$[(c \vee d) \circ \psi] = (c + [\psi]) \cup (d + [\psi]);$$
$$\overline{[(a \vee b) \circ \overline{\psi}]} = (a + [\psi]) \cap (b + [\psi]).$$

Proof. The former equality is evident, let us prove the latter:

$$(0, x, (1)) \models \overline{(a \vee b) \circ \overline{\psi}} \Leftrightarrow (0, x, (1)) \not\models (a \vee b) \circ \overline{\psi} \Leftrightarrow$$
$$x - a \notin [\overline{\psi}] \wedge x - b \notin [\overline{\psi}] \Leftrightarrow x - a \in [\psi] \wedge x - b \in [\psi] \Leftrightarrow$$
$$x \in (a + [\psi]) \cap (b + [\psi]),$$

which concludes the proof.

Semantics of φ and its suffixes can also be described in terms of the sets H_i, G_i.

Lemma 8. – *Semantics of the suffix of* φ *starting at* $(a_k \vee b_k)$ *(with the bar over the whole suffix) is* H_{k-1}.
– *Semantics of the suffix of* φ *starting at* $(c_k \vee d_k)$ *(without bar) is* G_k.
– *Hence, semantics of the whole* φ *is* H_0.

Proof. The basis of induction is

$$[(c_n \vee d_n)] = \{C_n; D_n\} = G_n.$$

Alternating the two identities from Lemma 7 we deduce required results for $H_{n-1}, G_{n-1}, H_{n-2}, \ldots, G_1, H_0$.

Finally from Lemmata 6 and 8 it follows that (2) is equivalent to $W \in H_0 = [\varphi]$, which in turn is equivalent to $W \models \varphi_{abcd}$, and we have a required reduction. The hardness is proved.

4.2   Timed Pattern Matching: Main Complexity Results

We consider the following setting: the timed behavior (with rational dates) is presented in binary, the TRE uses integer-bounded intervals, also in binary.

Let us consider the decision problem: given a timed behavior and a TRE, does the whole timed behavior match the expression. It is easy to see that the problem of deciding whether the behavior contains an infix matching the expression belongs to the same complexity class.

First we notice that on polynomial duration the matching problem is easy.

Theorem 2. *Given a duration d **in unary**, a timed behavior w and a TRE φ (using all connectives), the match problem can be solved in polynomial time.*

Proof. We will follow Algorithm 1, representing all the intermediate matchsets as lists of regions. Recursive calls of MATCHSET correspond to subexpressions of φ, their number is polynomial. Due to Proposition 2, there are only $O(d^2 n^2)$ regions that can occur in each of the matchsets. Due to Proposition 1, all the Kleene $^+$ involve a polynomial number of operations. By virtue of Proposition 3, each operation is computable in polynomial time. The whole computation is thus polynomial.

The general case, when the duration (as all other dates) is written in binary, and can thus be exponentially large, TPM is much more complex, even for very simple expressions. We will use the results on $\mathbb{R}$-expressions with the following simple reduction.

Lemma 9. *The problem of matching a real-time expression (using some set of connectives) can be polynomially reduced to TPM (with the same set of connectives).*

Proof. Let φ be a real-time expression. We denote $\varphi(p)$ the TRE obtained from φ by replacing each interval I by $\langle p \rangle_I$. Then $x \models \varphi$ whenever $(0, x, p) \models \varphi(p)$.

Theorem 3. *Given a timed behavior and an $\vee, \circ$-TRE (or an $\wedge, \vee, \circ$-TRE), the matching problem is NP-complete.*

NP-hardness is immediate from Proposition 4 and Lemma 9.

Proof (NP-easyness). The nondeterministic recursive Algorithm 3, instead of computing the whole set of matching zones guesses only one matching region.[4] If at the end the region contains $[0, d]$, we know that the timed behavior matches the expression.

---

[4] This would not work for Kleene $^+$.

Algorithm 3. Nondeterministic procedure for guessing a matching region

```
1:  procedure GUESSMATCH(TRE φ)                          ▷ returns a Region
2:      switch φ do
3:          case p                                  ▷ case of ¬p is similar
4:              guess region R ⊂ 𝒱(p)
5:              return R
6:          case ψ₁ ∨ ψ₂
7:              guess i ∈ {1, 2}
8:              return GUESSMATCH(ψᵢ)
9:          case ψ₁ ∧ ψ₂
10:             R1 = GUESSMATCH(ψ₁)
11:             R2 = GUESSMATCH(ψ₂)
12:             if R1 = R2 then
13:                 return R1
14:         case ⟨ψ⟩_I
15:             R = GUESSMATCH(ψ₁)
16:             if Duration(R) ⊂ I then
17:                 return R
18:         case ψ₁ ∘ ψ₂
19:             guess region R ⊂ GUESSMATCH(ψ₁) ∘ GUESSMATCH(ψ₂)
20:             return R
```

Theorem 4. *Given a timed behavior and an* $\vee, \circ, ^-$*-TRE (or even the most general* $\wedge, \vee, \circ, ^+, ^-$*-TRE), the matching problem is* PSPACE-*complete.*

PSPACE-hardness is immediate from Proposition 5 and Lemma 9.

We remark that our matching algorithm manipulates a potentially exponential set of zones, and thus is EXPTIME. It can be slightly modified (and proceed region-by-region) to remain in PSPACE.

Proof (PSPACE-*easyness*). Let us fix a timed behavior w. First we apply Proposition 2 and fix an enumeration of all $O((nd)^2)$ (thus exponentially many) regions that can potentially occur in the matchset, we also fix a polynomial-size representation of such regions. Let also 2^K be an upper bound on Kleene $^+$ from Proposition 1.

The recursive procedure in Algorithm 4 describes a Boolean function MATCH(φ, R) returning **true** iff the region R belongs to the matchset of the TRE φ.

Recursion can be implemented in the standard way using a stack. The auxiliary procedure in Algorithm 4 is used to compute the Kleene $^+$. Recursion depth does not exceed Ks (with s the size of the TRE), each entry on the stack is of polynomial size, hence the whole algorithm is in PSPACE.

4.3   The Unsettled Case

Given an $\vee, \circ, ^+$-timed or real-time regular expression (eventually also with $\wedge$), it follows from the previous results that matching is in PSPACE and NP-hard. We

---

Algorithm 4. Matching generalized expressions in PSPACE

1: **procedure** MATCH(TRE φ, Region R)
2:   **switch** φ **do**
3:     **case** p ▷ case of $\neg p$ is similar
4:       **return** $R \subseteq \mathcal{V}(p)$
5:     **case** $\psi_1 \vee \psi_2$ ▷ case of $\psi_1 \wedge \psi_2$ is similar
6:       **return** MATCH(φ_1, R) $\vee$ MATCH(φ_2, R)
7:     **case** $\overline{\psi}$
8:       **return** $\neg$MATCH(ψ, R)
9:     **case** $\langle \psi \rangle_I$
10:      **return** MATCH(ψ, R) $\wedge$ Duration(R) $\subseteq I$
11:     **case** $\psi_1 \circ \psi_2$
12:       **for all** Region R_1 **do**
13:         **for all** Region R_2 **do**
14:           **if** $R \subseteq R_1 \circ R_2 \wedge$ MATCH(ψ_1, R_1) $\wedge$ MATCH(ψ_2, R_2) **then**
15:             **return** true
16:       **return** false
17:     **case** ψ^+
18:       **return** KLEE(R, ψ, k)
19: **procedure** KLEE(TRE φ, Region R, Integer k)
20:   **if** Match(φ, R) **then**
21:     **return** true
22:   **if** $k \geq 1$ **then**
23:     **for all** Region R_1 **do**
24:       **for all** Region R_2 **do**
25:         **if** $R \subseteq R_1 \circ R_2 \wedge$ KLEE($\varphi, R_1, k-1$) $\wedge$ KLEE($\varphi, R_2, k-1$) **then**
26:           **return** true
27:   **return** false

---

do not know the exact complexity. Using techniques based on [8] we were able to prove the following fact, similar in spirit to results on Presburger arithmetic with stars in [11].

Proposition 6. *Pattern matching* $\wedge, \vee, \circ, ^+$*-timed or real-time regular expressions with the depth of embedded* $^+$ *operators bounded by some constant, is* NP-*complete.*

5   Conclusions

In this paper, we answered multiple questions regarding the complexity of TPM. Previous works on timed pattern matching had mainly focused on the algorithmic improvements and extensions to new applications. These algorithms have worked well on timed behaviors with a length of more than millions and demonstrate a complexity close to linear in the length of the timed behavior unlike the worst-case complexity as we investigated here. One reason for such low practical complexity is the rarity of the occurrence of interesting patterns we seek to find.

By nature we are interested in patterns occurring rarely over temporal behaviors and this fact helps keep the complexity low in practice. However, the inclusion of the complement operator in the pattern specification would reverse this argument and we would see existing approaches and algorithms struggling, getting close to bounds presented in this paper. Hence, TPM with the complement (and its interplay with Kleene iteration) is indeed a new challenge for both theoretical and practical purposes.

Acknowledgement. We would like to thank Thao Dang, Nicolas Basset, and Akshay Mambakam for motivating and technically relevant discussions.

References

1. Alur, R., Dill, D.L.: A theory of timed automata. Theor. Comput. Sci. **126**(2), 183–235 (1994). https://doi.org/10.1016/0304-3975(94)90010-8
2. Asarin, E., Caspi, P., Maler, O.: A Kleene theorem for timed automata. In: LICS, pp. 160–171 (1997). https://doi.org/10.1109/LICS.1997.614944
3. Asarin, E., Caspi, P., Maler, O.: Timed regular expressions. J. ACM **49**(2), 172–206 (2002). https://doi.org/10.1145/506147.506151
4. Bakhirkin, A., Ferrère, T., Maler, O., Ulus, D.: On the quantitative semantics of regular expressions over real-valued signals. In: Abate, A., Geeraerts, G. (eds.) FORMATS 2017. LNCS, vol. 10419, pp. 189–206. Springer, Cham (2017). https://doi.org/10.1007/978-3-319-65765-3_11
5. Bakhirkin, A., Ferrère, T., Nickovic, D., Maler, O., Asarin, E.: Online timed pattern matching using automata. In: Jansen, D.N., Prabhakar, P. (eds.) FORMATS 2018. LNCS, vol. 11022, pp. 215–232. Springer, Cham (2018). https://doi.org/10.1007/978-3-030-00151-3_13
6. Choffrut, C., Goldwurm, M.: Timed automata with periodic clock constraints. J. Autom. Lang. Comb. **5**(4), 371–403 (2000). https://doi.org/10.25596/jalc-2000-371
7. Dima, C.: Real-time automata. J. Autom. Lang. Comb. **6**(1), 3–23 (2001). https://doi.org/10.25596/jalc-2001-003
8. Eisenbrand, F., Shmonin, G.: Carathéodory bounds for integer cones. Oper. Res. Lett. **34**(5), 564–568 (2006). https://doi.org/10.1016/j.orl.2005.09.008
9. Fearnley, J., Jurdzinski, M.: Reachability in two-clock timed automata is PSPACE-complete. Inf. Comput. **243**, 26–36 (2015). https://doi.org/10.1016/j.ic.2014.12.004
10. Bakhirkin, A., Ferrère, T., Nickovic, D., Maler, O., Asarin, E.: Online timed pattern matching using automata. In: Jansen, D.N., Prabhakar, Pavithra (eds.) FORMATS 2018. LNCS, vol. 11022, pp. 215–232. Springer, Cham (2018). https://doi.org/10.1007/978-3-030-00151-3_13
11. Haase, C., Zetzsche, G.: Presburger arithmetic with stars, rational subsets of graph groups, and nested zero tests. In: LICS, pp. 1–14 (2019). https://doi.org/10.1109/LICS.2019.8785850
12. Hopcroft, J., Ullman, J.: Introduction to Automata Theory, Languages, and Computation. Addison-Wesley (1979)
13. Narayan, A., Cutulenco, G., Joshi, Y., Fischmeister, S.: Mining timed regular specifications from system traces. ACM Trans. Embed. Comput. Syst. **17**(2),(2018). https://doi.org/10.1145/3147660

14. Ničković, D., Lebeltel, O., Maler, O., Ferrère, T., Ulus, D.: AMT 2.0: qualitative and quantitative trace analysis with extended signal temporal logic. In: Beyer, D., Huisman, M. (eds.) TACAS 2018. LNCS, vol. 10806, pp. 303–319. Springer, Cham (2018). https://doi.org/10.1007/978-3-319-89963-3_18
15. Ničković, D., Qin, X., Ferrère, T., Mateis, C., Deshmukh, J.: Shape expressions for specifying and extracting signal features. In: Finkbeiner, B., Mariani, L. (eds.) RV 2019. LNCS, vol. 11757, pp. 292–309. Springer, Cham (2019). https://doi.org/10.1007/978-3-030-32079-9_17
16. Petersen, H.: The membership problem for regular expressions with intersection is complete in LOGCFL. In: Alt, H., Ferreira, A. (eds.) STACS 2002. LNCS, vol. 2285, pp. 513–522. Springer, Heidelberg (2002). https://doi.org/10.1007/3-540-45841-7_42
17. Piskac, R., Kuncak, V.: Linear arithmetic with stars. In: Gupta, A., Malik, S. (eds.) CAV 2008. LNCS, vol. 5123, pp. 268–280. Springer, Heidelberg (2008). https://doi.org/10.1007/978-3-540-70545-1_25
18. Stockmeyer, L.J., Meyer, A.R.: Word problems requiring exponential time (preliminary report). In: STOC, pp. 1–9. ACM (1973). https://doi.org/10.1145/800125.804029
19. Ulus, D.: MONTRE: a tool for monitoring timed regular expressions. In: Majumdar, R., Kunčak, V. (eds.) CAV 2017. LNCS, vol. 10426, pp. 329–335. Springer, Cham (2017). https://doi.org/10.1007/978-3-319-63387-9_16
20. Ulus, D.: Pattern matching with time: theory and applications. Ph.D. thesis, Université Grenoble Alpes (2018). https://hal.archives-ouvertes.fr/tel-01901576
21. Ulus, D., Ferrère, T., Asarin, E., Maler, O.: Timed pattern matching. In: Legay, A., Bozga, M. (eds.) FORMATS 2014. LNCS, vol. 8711, pp. 222–236. Springer, Cham (2014). https://doi.org/10.1007/978-3-319-10512-3_16
22. Ulus, D., Ferrère, T., Asarin, E., Maler, O.: Online timed pattern matching using derivatives. In: Chechik, M., Raskin, J.-F. (eds.) TACAS 2016. LNCS, vol. 9636, pp. 736–751. Springer, Heidelberg (2016). https://doi.org/10.1007/978-3-662-49674-9_47
23. Waga, M., Akazaki, T., Hasuo, I.: A Boyer-Moore type algorithm for timed pattern matching. In: Fränzle, M., Markey, N. (eds.) FORMATS 2016. LNCS, vol. 9884, pp. 121–139. Springer, Cham (2016). https://doi.org/10.1007/978-3-319-44878-7_8
24. Waga, M., André, E.: Online parametric timed pattern matching with automata-based skipping. In: Badger, J.M., Rozier, K.Y. (eds.) NFM 2019. LNCS, vol. 11460, pp. 371–389. Springer, Cham (2019). https://doi.org/10.1007/978-3-030-20652-9_26
25. Waga, M., Hasuo, I., Suenaga, K.: Efficient online timed pattern matching by automata-based skipping. In: Abate, A., Geeraerts, G. (eds.) FORMATS 2017. LNCS, vol. 10419, pp. 224–243. Springer, Cham (2017). https://doi.org/10.1007/978-3-319-65765-3_13

Stubborn Set Reduction for Timed Reachability and Safety Games

Frederik M. Bønneland[(⊠)], Peter G. Jensen, Kim G. Larsen, Marco Muñiz, and Jiří Srba

Department of Computer Science, Aalborg University, Aalborg, Denmark
{frederikb,pgj,kgl,muniz,srba}@cs.aau.dk

Abstract. Timed games are an essential formalism for modeling time-sensitive reactive systems that must respond to uncontrollable events triggered by the (hostile) environment. However, the control synthesis problem for these systems is often resource-demanding due to the state space explosion problem. To counter this problem, we present an extension of partial order reduction, based on stubborn sets, into timed games. We introduce the theoretical foundations on the general formalism of timed game labeled transition systems and then instantiate it to the model of timed-arc Petri net games. We provide an efficient implementation of our method as part of the model checker TAPAAL and discuss an experimental evaluation on several case studies that show increasing (sometimes even exponential) savings in time and memory as the case studies scale to larger instances. To the best of our knowledge, this is the first application of partial order reductions to a game formalism that includes time.

1 Introduction

Even for simple concurrent systems, the reachable state space can become too large and render formal methods such as model checking intractable. This so-called state space explosion problem can be induced by exponentially many, and often redundant (for the validity of the verified property), interleavings of concurrent and independent system actions. Many methods exist for alleviating this problem, such as *symmetry reductions* [12,14] or *parametric verification* [1,2, 17]. We focus on a family of methods called *(static) partial order reductions* [19, 31,34], which exploit the commutativity of independent system actions to prune redundant interleavings. The most prevalent variants of partial order reductions are *persistent sets* [19,20], *ample sets* [31,32], and *stubborn sets* [34,35].

We combine the approaches of stubborn sets for timed systems and reachability games, initially presented respectively in [8] and [10], into a unified method for general timed games represented as a timed game labelled transition system (TGLTS). As main contributions, we present a new correctness proof of the method for preserving the existence of winning *reachability* strategies to accomodate for the timed setting. In addition, we show that our method also preserves

© Springer Nature Switzerland AG 2021
C. Dima and M. Shirmohammadi (Eds.): FORMATS 2021, LNCS 12860, pp. 32–49, 2021.
https://doi.org/10.1007/978-3-030-85037-1_3

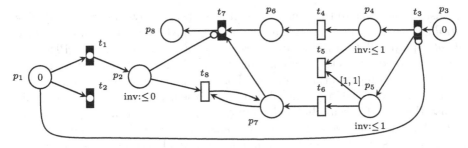

(a) Timed-arc Petri net game

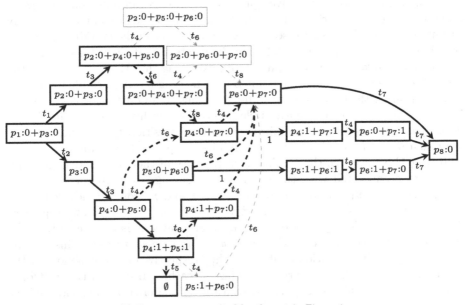

(b) State space generated by the net in Figure 1a

Fig. 1. Example of timed-arc Petri net game and its reachable state space

winning *safety* strategies with minimal changes to the game-theoretic framework. This provides, to the best of our knowledge, the first partial order reduction approach for general timed games. We instantiate our framework to Timed-Arc Petri net Games (TAPG) [25] with inhibitor arcs, and propose syntax-driven, overapproximation algorithms for generating stable stubborn sets. While these algorithms are similar to the algorithms presented for timed systems and games, we leverage further improvements by a detailed analysis of the guard and invaraint We implement our method in the model checker TAPAAL [13,23] and provide an experimental evaluation to showcase the potential of our method.

Let us first intuitively introduce the model of timed-arc Petri net games [25] that extends timed-arc Petri nets [4,21] into a game setting by splitting transitions into the controllable and uncontrollable ones. In our example in Fig. 1a we consider the discrete time semantics (integer time delays) as in [25, 26]. The *controllable* (player 1) transitions are denoted as filled rectangles and the *uncontrollable* (player 2) transitions are shown as transparent rectangles. Places in the net (denoted by circles) can contain tokens which are associated with non-negative integers representing their age. For example, the places p_1 and p_3 each contain a token of age 0 in the initial marking of the net. Delay actions uniformly increase the age of tokens, but delays may be prevented in markings that are *urgent*. A marking is urgent if an urgent transition (denoted with a circle inside the rectangle) is enabled; in our example all controllable transitions are urgent. Furthermore, a marking can be urgent due to place invariants which constrain the allowed age of tokens in a given place, e.g. place p_2 can only contain tokens of age 0 due to the invariant inv: ≤ 0. If a marking is not urgent then a delay action may occur which progresses the age of all tokens in the marking evenly by some numerical value, as long as all place invarints are satisfied. Firing a transition consumes tokens from its input places, assuming that their ages fit into the intervals on the input arcs to the transition; a missing interval stands for $[0, \infty)$. Transition firing then produces fresh 0-age tokens to all output places. The net also contains inhibitor arcs with circle-pointed arrow heads. For example the place p_1 is connected by an inhibitor arc to the transition t_3 and the presence of a token in p_1 in the initial marking inhibits the possibility to fire t_3.

In Fig. 1b we can see the reachable state space of the game net. Each state (marking) is annotated with the tokens and their ages, e.g. $p_4 : 1 + p_7 : 0$ is a marking where p_4 contains a token of age 1 and p_7 contains a token of 0. Solid arrows represent player 1 and delay actions, and dashed arrows represent player 2 actions. The objective of the controller (player 1) is to place a token to the place p_8. Indeed, the controller has a *winning strategy* to reach this goal by initially playing the transition t_1 after which, irrespective of the behaviour of the environment (player 2), the target marking is reached. If instead the controller plays from the initial marking the transition t_2, the environment can enforce to reach the empty marking $\emptyset$ with no tokens, which is clearly not a winning strategy for the controller.

The grayed out arrows and markings can be pruned during the state space exploration as they do not influence the existence of a winning stratety for the controller. For example, in the marking $p_2{:}0 + p_4{:}0 + p_5{:}0$, we can observe that only player 2 transitions are enabled and time cannot progress either, hence we can apply the classical stubborn set reduction and consider only one of the possible interleavings of the transitions t_4, t_6 and t_8.

Related Work. The literature for partial order reductions for both timed systems and games is scarce and generally does not report favourable experimental evaluation, if any at all. For timed systems, early work by Bengtsson et al. [3] and Minea [29] provides partial order reduction methods but no experimental evaluation to show a practical benefit. For Petri nets, various efforts have been made. Examples include one-safe time Petri nets by Yoneda et al. [37]; however, the method is not suitable for larger models [33]. Boucheneb et al. [5–7] present a partial order reduction method for timed Petri nets but only report on experimental results for a small amount of examples on a prototype implementation. Lilius [28] suggests a method that allows for applying partial order reductions for untimed systems; however, no experiments are reported. As an exception, partial order reductions have been used successfully for timed systems that exhibit urgent behaviour [8]. Furthermore, we differentiate from other approaches by preserving both winning reachability and safety strategies as well as extending the approach to games.

Similarly, the extent of applying partial order reductions to games has been limited until recent notable developments. Partial order reductions for bisimulation equivalence were presented in [18,22,36]; however, our approach is more general as we allow for reduction in both controllable and uncontrollable states, and we provide an experimental evaluation. Recently, Neele et al. [30] presented partial order reductions for untimed parity games. This method can model check the full modal μ-calculus, where game semantics are encoded as μ-calculus formulae. This, however, includes conditions that may be redundant and weaken the reduction potential in our less general setting where we preserve the existence of winning two-player reachability and safety strategies [9,10]. Lastly, we preserve winning reachability and safety strategies in the presence of time, which is not yet achieved by other approaches.

2   Preliminaries

Definition 1 (Timed Game Labelled Transition System). *A Timed Game Labelled Transition System (TGLTS) is a tuple $G = (\mathcal{S}, A_1, A_2, \to, Goal)$ where $\mathcal{S}$ is a set of states, $A = A_1 \cup A_2$ is a set of actions divided into a finite set of player 1 actions A_1 and a finite set of player 2 actions A_2 where $A_1 \cap A_2 = \emptyset$, $\to \subseteq \mathcal{S} \times (A \cup \mathbb{R}^{\geq 0}) \times \mathcal{S}$ is a deterministic transition relation s.t. if $(s, \alpha, s') \in \to$ and $(s, \alpha, s'') \in \to$ then $s' = s''$, and $Goal \subseteq \mathcal{S}$ is a set of goal states where for all $s, s' \in \mathcal{S}$ if $(s, d, s') \in \to$ and $d \in \mathbb{R}^{\geq 0}$ then $s \in Goal$ iff $s' \in Goal$.*

Let $G = (\mathcal{S}, A_1, A_2, \to, Goal)$ be a fixed TGLTS for the remainder of the section. Whenever $(s, \alpha, s') \in \to$ we write $s \xrightarrow{\alpha} s'$. The set of *enabled* player actions at a state $s \in \mathcal{S}$ is defined as $en(s) = \{a \in A \mid \exists s' \in \mathcal{S}.\ s \xrightarrow{a} s'\}$. The set of *enabled* player 1 actions in a state $s \in \mathcal{S}$ is given by $en_1(s) = en(s) \setminus A_2$, and similarly for player 2. Alternatively, we also refer to player 1 and 2 as the *controller* and the *environment*, respectively. For a state $s \in \mathcal{S}$ where $en(s) \neq \emptyset$ if $en_2(s) = \emptyset$ then we call s a player 1 state, if $en_1(s) = \emptyset$ then we call s a player 2 state, and otherwise we call it a mixed state. A state s is a *deadlock* state if for all delays $d \in \mathbb{R}^{\geq 0}$ s.t. $s \xrightarrow{d} s'$ we have $en(s') = \emptyset$. The TGLTS G is called non-mixed if all states are either player 1, player 2, or deadlock states.

A state $s \in \mathcal{S}$ is *zero time* if time can not elapse at s. We denote the zero time property of a state s by the predicate $\mathsf{zt}(s)$ and define it as $\mathsf{zt}(s)$ iff for all $s' \in \mathcal{S}$ and all $d \in \mathbb{R}^{\geq 0}$ if $s \xrightarrow{d} s'$ then $d = 0$. We only consider TGLTS that satisfy the following time related axioms for all $s, s', s'' \in \mathcal{S}$ and all $d, d' \in \mathbb{R}^{\geq 0}$:

- If $s \xrightarrow{d} s'$ and $0 \leq d' \leq d$ then there exists $s_{d'} \in \mathcal{S}$ s.t. $s \xrightarrow{d'} s_{d'} \xrightarrow{d-d'} s'$.
- If $s \xrightarrow{d} s'$ and $d = 0$ then $s = s'$.

For a sequence of actions $w = \alpha_1 \alpha_2 \cdots \alpha_n \in (A \cup \mathbb{R}^{\geq 0})^*$ we write $s \xrightarrow{w} s'$ if $s \xrightarrow{\alpha_1} s_1 \xrightarrow{\alpha_2} \cdots \xrightarrow{\alpha_n} s'$ for some $s_1, \ldots, s_{n-1} \in \mathcal{S}$. For an infinite sequence $w \in (A \cup \mathbb{R}^{\geq 0})^\omega$ if for every prefix w' of w there exists $s' \in \mathcal{S}$ s.t. $s \xrightarrow{w'} s'$ then we write $s \xrightarrow{w}$. Actions that are a part of w are said to occur in w.

A (memoryless) strategy is a function which proposes the next move either player 1 or player 2 wants to make, where λ represents the delay action.

Definition 2 (Strategy). *Let $G = (\mathcal{S}, A, \rightarrow, Goal)$ be a TGLTS. A strategy for a player i where $i \in \{1, 2\}$ is a function $\sigma_i : \mathcal{S} \rightarrow (\mathbb{R}^{\geq 0} \times A_i) \cup \{\lambda\}$ where for all $s \in \mathcal{S}$ we have:*

- *If $\sigma_i(s) = \lambda$ then for all $d \in \mathbb{R}^{\geq 0}$ where $s \xrightarrow{d} s'$ we have $\sigma_i(s') = \lambda$, and*
  - *either for all $d \in \mathbb{R}^{\geq 0}$ there exists $s'' \in \mathcal{S}$ s.t. $s \xrightarrow{d} s''$, or*
  - *there exists $d \in \mathbb{R}^{\geq 0}$ s.t. $s \xrightarrow{d} s'$ and for all $d' \in \mathbb{R}^{\geq 0}$ where $s' \xrightarrow{d'} s''$ we have $en_i(s'') = \emptyset$.*
- *If $\sigma_i(s) = (d, a)$ then there exists $s' \in \mathcal{S}$ s.t. $s \xrightarrow{da} s'$.*

Let Σ_G^1 (ranged over by σ_1) and Σ_G^2 (ranged over by σ_2) be the set of all possible strategies for player 1 and player 2 for a TGLTS G, respectively.

A run $\pi = s_0 s_1 \cdots \in \mathcal{S}^* \cup \mathcal{S}^\omega$ is a (possibly infinite) sequence of states where for all $i \geq 0$ there exists $d \in \mathbb{R}^{\geq 0}$ and $a \in A$ s.t. $s_i \xrightarrow{da} s_{i+1}$. The length of a run π (number of actions in the run) is given by $\ell(\pi)$ where $\ell(\pi) = \infty$ if $\pi \in \mathcal{S}^\omega$ and otherwise $\ell(\pi) = n$ where $\pi = s_0 \cdots s_n$. Let $\mathbb{N}^0 = \mathbb{N} \cup \{0\}$. A position in a run $\pi = s_0 s_1 \ldots \in \mathcal{S}^* \cup \mathcal{S}^\omega$ is a natural number $i \in \mathbb{N}^0$ that refers to the state s_i and is written as π_i. A position i can range from 0 to $\ell(\pi)$ s.t. if π is infinite then $i \in \mathbb{N}^0$ and otherwise $0 \leq i \leq \ell(\pi)$.

Let $\Pi_{G, \sigma_1, \sigma_2}^{max}(s)$ be the set of maximal runs subject to σ_1 and σ_2 starting at $s \in \mathcal{S}$ defined as follows: $\pi \in \Pi_{\sigma_1, \sigma_2}^{max}(s)$ iff $\pi_0 = s$ and for all $0 \leq i \leq \ell(\pi)$ (or $0 \leq i$ if π is infinite) we either have:

- $\sigma_1(\pi_i) = (d_1, a_1)$ and $(\sigma_2(\pi_i) = \lambda$ or $\sigma_2(\pi_i) = (d_2, a_2)$ and $d_1 \leq d_2)$ and $\pi_i \xrightarrow{d_1 a_1} \pi_{i+1}$.
- $\sigma_2(\pi_i) = (d_2, a_2)$ and $(\sigma_1(\pi_i) = \lambda$ or $\sigma_1(\pi_i) = (d_1, a_1)$ and $d_2 \leq d_1)$ and $\pi_i \xrightarrow{d_2 a_2} \pi_{i+1}$.
- $\sigma_1(\pi_i) = \sigma_2(\pi_i) = \lambda$ and $\pi_i = \pi_{\ell(\pi)}$.

Let $\Pi_{G, \sigma_1}^{max}(s) = \bigcup_{\sigma_2 \in \Sigma_G^2} \Pi_{G, \sigma_1, \sigma_2}^{max}(s)$ be the set of all maximal runs subject to σ_1 and any possible player 2 strategy, and similarly for player 2. We omit the TGLTS G when possible from the subscript of $\Pi_{G, \sigma_1, \sigma_2}^{max}(s)$ for simplicity.

Definition 3 (Winning Strategy). *Let $G = (\mathcal{S}, A_1, A_2, \rightarrow, Goal)$ be a TGLTS and $s \in \mathcal{S}$ be a state. A strategy $\sigma_1 \in \Sigma_G^1$ is a winning (reachability) strategy for player 1 at s in G iff for all $\sigma_2 \in \Sigma_G^2$ and for all $\pi \in \Pi_{\sigma_1, \sigma_2}^{max}(s)$ there exists a position i s.t. $\pi_i \in Goal$. A state s is winning (for player 1) if there exists a winning strategy for player 1 at s in G.*

Remark: We say that a state s is winning for player 2 iff s is not winning for player 1. Similarly, a strategy for player 2 is a winning strategy at s iff there does not exist a winning strategy for player 1 at s.

3   Stable Stubborn Reduction

We now introduce the central concept of *stable reductions* [10] extended to handle timed games. First, we introduce *interesting sets* and *safe actions*.

Definition 4 (Interesting Set of Actions). *Let* $G = (\mathcal{S}, A, \rightarrow, Goal)$ *be a TGLTS,* $s \in \mathcal{S}$ *a state, and* $X \subseteq \mathcal{S}$ *a set of target states. A set of actions* $A_s(X) \subseteq A$ *is called an* interesting set *of actions for* $s \notin X$ *if whenever* $w = a_1 \cdots a_n \in A^*$, $s \xrightarrow{w} s'$, *and* $s' \in X$ *then there exists* $1 \le i \le n$ *s.t.* $a_i \in A_s(X)$. *If* $s \in X$ *then* $A_s(X) = \emptyset$.

Informally, for any run from s to a target state $s' \in X$ (with $s \notin X$) there must be at least one interesting action. For a given set of target states there may be several possible interesting sets of actions and in the rest of this paper we assume that one such set of interesting actions is fixed.

Let us also restate the notion of player 1 safe actions from [9,10]. Intuitively, we require for a safe player 1 action a in a state s that the addition of a to the beginning of an execution sequence does not hand over control to player 2 earlier than otherwise.

Definition 5 (Safe Action). *Let* $G = (\mathcal{S}, A_1, A_2, \rightarrow, Goal)$ *be a TGLTS and* $s \in \mathcal{S}$ *a player 1 state such that* $en_2(s) = \emptyset$. *An action* $a \in A_1 \cap en_1(s)$ *is safe in* s *if whenever* $w \in (A_1 \setminus \{a\})^*$ *with* $s \xrightarrow{w} s'$ *s.t.* $en_2(s') = \emptyset$ *and* $s \xrightarrow{aw} s''$ *then* $en_2(s'') = \emptyset$. *The set of all safe actions for* s *is written as* $safe(s)$.

A reduced game is defined by a function called a *reduction* that for each state proposes the set of actions to consider at that state.

Definition 6 (Reduction). *Let* $G = (\mathcal{S}, A, \rightarrow, Goal)$ *be a TGLTS. A* reduction *is a function* $St : \mathcal{S} \rightarrow 2^A$.

Definition 7 (Reduced Game). *Let* $G = (\mathcal{S}, A, \rightarrow, Goal)$ *be a TGLTS and* St *be a reduction. The reduced game of* G *by the reduction* St *is given by* $G_{St} = (\mathcal{S}, A, \underset{St}{\longrightarrow}, Goal)$ *where* $s \underset{St}{\xrightarrow{\alpha}} s'$ *iff* $s \xrightarrow{\alpha} s'$ *and* $\alpha \in St(s) \cup \mathbb{R}^{\ge 0}$.

The set of states $St(s)$ is the stubborn set of s with the reduction St. The set of non-stubborn actions for s is defined as $\overline{St(s)} = A \setminus St(s)$. We shall now present the key definition of a stable reduction.

Definition 8 (Stable Reduction Conditions). *A reduction* St *is called stable if* St *satisfies for every* $s \in S$ *Conditions* **I, Z, W, R, T, G1, G2, S, V,** *and* **D.** *For a stable reduction* St *we call* $St(s)$ *a stable stubborn set (of* s).

I If $en_1(s) \neq \emptyset$ and $en_2(s) \neq \emptyset$ then $en(s) \subseteq St(s)$.

Z If $\neg zt(s)$ then $en(s) \subseteq St(s)$.

W For all $w \in \overline{St(s)}^*$ and all $a \in St(s)$ if $s \xrightarrow{wa} s'$ then $s \xrightarrow{aw} s'$.

R $A_s(Goal) \subseteq St(s)$.

T $A_s(\{s \in \mathcal{S} \mid \neg zt(s)\}) \subseteq St(s)$.

G1 If $en_2(s) = \emptyset$ then $A_s(\{s \in \mathcal{S} \mid en_2(s) \neq \emptyset\}) \subseteq St(s)$.

G2 If $en_1(s) = \emptyset$ then $A_s(\{s \in \mathcal{S} \mid en_1(s) \neq \emptyset\}) \subseteq St(s)$.

S $en_1(s) \cap St(s) \subseteq safe(s)$ or $en_1(s) \subseteq St(s)$

V If there exists $w \in A_2^*$ s.t. $s \xrightarrow{w} s'$ and $s' \in Goal$ then $en_2(s) \subseteq St(s)$.

D If $en_2(s) \neq \emptyset$ then there exists $a \in en_2(s) \cap St(s)$ s.t. for all $w \in \overline{St(s)}^*$ where $s \xrightarrow{w} s'$ we have $a \in en_2(s')$.

Conditions **I** and **Z** ensures that all enabled actions are included in the reduction if a state is either non-urgent or mixed. Condition **W** ensures that a stubborn action can commute with any sequence of nonstubborn actions. Condition **R** prevents goal states from being reachable by exploring only nonstubborn actions. In other words, any sequence of actions leading to a goal state must include at least one stubborn action. Conditions **T**, **G1**, and **G2** are similar to Condition **R**. They ensure that reachability of certain states where either time can elapse (**T**, or the opposing player is allowed to make a move (**G1** and **G2**) are preserved. Condition **S** states that either all enabled stubborn player 1 actions are safe, and otherwise all enabled player 1 actions are included in the stubborn set. Condition **V** checks if it is possible to reach a goal state by firing exclusively player 2 actions. If this is possible, then all enabled player 2 actions are included in the stubborn set. Condition **D** ensures at least one player 2 action cannot be disabled by exploring only nonstubborn actions. This condition preserves cycles and runs of exclusively player 2 actions to deadlocks.

We can now present the first of two main theorems showing that stable reductions preserve the winning strategies of both players in the game.

Theorem 1 (Reachability Strategy Preservation for TGLTS). *Let $G = (\mathcal{S}, A_1, A_2, \rightarrow)$ be a TGLTS and St a stable reduction. A state $s \in \mathcal{S}$ is winning for player 1 in G iff s is winning for player 1 in G_{St}.*

Furthermore, we can show that slightly modified stable reductions also preserve *winning safety strategies* for both players, which we define as follows.

Definition 9 (Winning Safety Strategy). *Let $G = (\mathcal{S}, A_1, A_2, \rightarrow, Goal)$ be a TGLTS and $s \in \mathcal{S}$ be a state. A strategy $\sigma_1 \in \Sigma_G^1$ is a winning safety strategy for player 1 at s in G iff for all $\sigma_2 \in \Sigma_G^2$, for all $\pi \in \Pi_{\sigma_1,\sigma_2}^{max}(s)$, and for all positions i we have $\pi_i \notin Goal$. A state s is a winning state (for player 1 and a safety objective) if there exists a winning safety strategy for player 1 at s in G.*

To accommodate safety, we introduce the following set of modified stable reduction conditions.

V′ If there exists $w \in A_1^*$ s.t. $s \xrightarrow{w} s'$ and $s' \in Goal$ then $en_1(s) \subseteq St(s)$.

D' If $en_1(s) \neq \emptyset$ then there exists $a \in en_1(s) \cap St(s)$ s.t. for all $w \in \overline{St(s)}^*$ where $s \xrightarrow{w} s'$ we have $a \in en_1(s')$.

We can then state the second main theorem showing that our modified stable reduction preserves the winning safety strategies of both players.

Theorem 2 (Safety Strategy Preservation for TGLTS). *Let* $G = (\mathcal{S}, A_1, A_2, \rightarrow)$ *be a TGLTS and St a stable reduction with Conditions* **V** *and* **D** *replaced by* **V'** *and* **D'**. *A state* $s \in \mathcal{S}$ *is a winning state with a safety objective in* G *for player 1 iff* s *is a winning state with a safety objective in* G_{St} *for player 1.*

4   Stable Reductions on Timed-Arc Petri Net Games

We now introduce the formalism of *Timed-Arc Petri net Games* (TAPG) [25]. Let $\mathbb{N}^\infty = \mathbb{N} \cup \{\infty\}$. We define the set of *well-formed closed time intervals* as $\int \overset{\text{def}}{=} \{[a, b] \mid a \in \mathbb{N}^0 \wedge b \in \mathbb{N}^\infty \wedge a \leq b\}$ and its subset $\int^{\text{inv}} \overset{\text{def}}{=} \{[0, b] \mid b \in \mathbb{N}^\infty\}$ used in age invariants.

Definition 10. (Timed-Arc Petri Net Game [25]). *A timed-arc Petri net game (TAPG) is a 9-tuple* $N = (P, T_1, T_2, T_{urg}, IA, OA, g, w, Type, I)$ *where*

- *P is a finite set of* places,
- T_1 *and* T_2 *are finite sets of controller and environment transitions, respectively, such that* $T_1 \cap T_2 = \emptyset$, $T = T_1 \cup T_2$ *and* $P \cap T = \emptyset$,
- $T_{urg} \subseteq T$ *is the set of* urgent transitions,
- $IA \subseteq P \times T$ *is a finite set of* input arcs,
- $OA \subseteq T \times P$ *is a finite set of* output arcs,
- $g : IA \rightarrow \int$ *is a time constraint function assigning guards (time intervals) to input arcs s.t.*
    - *if* $(p, t) \in IA$ *and* $t \in T_{urg}$ *then* $g((p, t)) = [0, \infty]$,
- $w : IA \cup OA \rightarrow \mathbb{N}$ *is a function assigning* weights *to input and output arcs,*
- *Type* $: IA \cup OA \rightarrow$ **Types** *is a type function assigning a type to all arcs where* **Types** $= \{Normal, Inhib\} \cup \{Transport_j \mid j \in \mathbb{N}\}$ *such that*
    - *if* $Type(z) = Inhib$ *then* $z \in IA$ *and* $g(z) = [0, \infty]$,
    - *if* $Type((p, t)) = Transport_j$ *for some* $(p, t) \in IA$ *then there is exactly one* $(t, p') \in OA$ *such that* $Type((t, p')) = Transport_j$,
    - *if* $Type((t, p')) = Transport_j$ *for some* $(t, p') \in OA$ *then there is exactly one* $(p, t) \in IA$ *such that* $Type((p, t)) = Transport_j$,
    - *if* $Type((p, t)) = Transport_j = Type((t, p'))$ *then* $w((p, t)) = w((t, p'))$,
- $I : P \rightarrow \int^{inv}$ *is a function assigning* age invariants *to places.*

Note that for transport arcs we assume that they come in pairs (for each type $Transport_j$) and that their weights match. Also for inhibitor arcs and for input arcs to urgent transitions, we require that the guards are $[0, \infty]$.

Before we give the formal semantics of the model, let us fix some notation. Let $N = (P, T_1, T_2, T_{urg}, IA, OA, g, w, Type, I)$ be a TAPG for the rest of the section. We denote by $^\bullet x \overset{\text{def}}{=} \{y \in P \cup T \mid (y,x) \in IA \cup OA \wedge \mathit{Type}((y,x)) \neq \mathit{Inhib}\}$ the *preset* of a transition or a place x. Similarly, the *postset* is defined as $x^\bullet \overset{\text{def}}{=} \{y \in P \cup T \mid (x,y) \in IA \cup OA \wedge \mathit{Type}((x,y)) \neq I\}$. We denote by $^\circ t \overset{\text{def}}{=} \{p \in P \mid (p,t) \in IA \wedge \mathit{Type}((p,t)) = \mathit{Inhib}\}$ the *inhibitor preset* of a transition t. The *inhibitor postset* of a place p is defined as $p^\circ \overset{\text{def}}{=} \{t \in T \mid (p,t) \in IA \wedge \mathit{Type}((p,t)) = \mathit{Inhib}\}$. For a place $p \in P$ we define the *increasing preset* of p as $^+p \overset{\text{def}}{=} \{t \in {}^\bullet p \mid w((t,p)) > w((p,t))\}$, and similarly the *decreasing postset* of p as $p^- \overset{\text{def}}{=} \{t \in p^\bullet \mid w((t,p)) < w((p,t))\}$. For a transition $t \in T$ we define the *decreasing preset* of t as $^-t \overset{\text{def}}{=} \{p \in {}^\bullet t \mid w((t,p)) < w((p,t))\}$, and similarly the *increasing postset* of t as $t^+ \overset{\text{def}}{=} \{p \in t^\bullet \mid w((t,p)) > w((p,t))\}$. For a set $X \subseteq P \cap T$ we extend the notation as $^\bullet X = \bigcup_{x \in X} {}^\bullet x$, and similarly for the other operators. Let $\mathcal{B}(\mathbb{R}^{\geq 0})$ be the set of all finite multisets over $\mathbb{R}^{\geq 0}$. A *marking* M on N is a function $M : P \longrightarrow \mathcal{B}(\mathbb{R}^{\geq 0})$ where for every place $p \in P$ and every token $x \in M(p)$ we have $x \in I(p)$, in other words all tokens have to satisfy the age invariants. The set of all markings in a net N is denoted by $\mathcal{M}(N)$.

We write (p,x) to denote a token at a place p with the age $x \in \mathbb{R}^{\geq 0}$. Then $M = \{(p_1,x_1),(p_2,x_2),\ldots,(p_n,x_n)\}$ is a multiset representing a marking M with n tokens of ages x_i in places p_i. We define the size of a marking as $|M| = \sum_{p \in P} |M(p)|$ where $|M(p)|$ is the number of tokens located in the place p. A marked TAPG (N, M_0) is a TAPG N together with an initial marking M_0 with all tokens of age 0.

Definition 11 (Enabledness). *Let $N = (P, T_1, T_2, T_{urg}, IA, OA, g, w, \mathit{Type}, I)$ be a TAPG. We say that a transition $t \in T$ is enabled in a marking M by the multisets of tokens $In = \{(p, x_p^1), (p, x_p^2), \ldots, (p, x_p^{w((p,t))}) \mid p \in {}^\bullet t\} \subseteq M$ and $Out = \{(p', x_{p'}^1), (p', x_{p'}^2), \ldots, (p', x_{p'}^{w((t,p'))}) \mid p' \in t^\bullet\}$ if*

- *for all input arcs except the inhibitor arcs, the tokens from In satisfy the age guards of the arcs, i.e.*

$$\forall p \in {}^\bullet t.\ x_p^i \in g((p,t)) \ \text{for}\ 1 \leq i \leq w((p,t))$$

- *for any inhibitor arc pointing from a place p to the transition t, the number of tokens in p is smaller than the weight of the arc, i.e.*

$$\forall (p,t) \in IA.\ \mathit{Type}((p,t)) = I \Rightarrow |M(p)| < w((p,t))$$

- *for all input arcs and output arcs which constitute a transport arc, the age of the input token must be equal to the age of the output token and satisfy the invariant of the output place, i.e.*

$$\forall (p,t) \in IA.\forall (t,p') \in OA.\ \mathit{Type}((p,t)) = \mathit{Type}((t,p')) = \mathit{Transport}_j$$
$$\Rightarrow \left(x_p^i = x_{p'}^i \wedge x_{p'}^i \in I(p') \right) \ \text{for}\ 1 \leq i \leq w((p,t))$$

- *for all normal output arcs, the age of the output token is 0, i.e.*

$$\forall (t,p') \in OA.\ \mathit{Type}((t,p')) = \mathit{Normal} \Rightarrow x_{p'}^i = 0 \ \text{for}\ 1 \leq i \leq w((t,p')).$$

A TAPG $N = (P, T_1, T_2, T_{urg}, IA, OA, g, w, Type, I)$ defines a GLTS $G(N) = (\mathcal{S}, A_1, A_2, \rightarrow, Goal)$ where $\mathcal{S} = \mathcal{M}(N)$ is the set of all markings, $A_1 = T_1$ is the set of player 1 actions, $A_2 = \dot{T}_2$ is the set of player 2 actions, $Goal \subseteq \mathcal{M}(N)$ is a subset of markings, and the transition relation is defined as follows:

- If $t \in T$ is enabled in a marking M by the multisets of tokens In and Out then t can *fire* and produce the marking $M' = (M \setminus In) \uplus Out$ where $\uplus$ is the multiset sum operator and $\setminus$ is the multiset difference operator; we write $M \xrightarrow{t} M'$ for this action transition.
- A time *delay* $d \in \mathbb{N}^0$ is allowed in M if
  - $(x + d) \in I(p)$ for all $p \in P$ and all $x \in M(p)$, i.e. by delaying d time units no token violates any of the age invariants, and
  - if $M \xrightarrow{t} M'$ for some $t \in T_{urg}$ then $d = 0$, i.e. enabled urgent transitions disallow time passing.

By delaying d time units in M we reach the marking M' defined as $M'(p) = \{x + d \mid x \in M(p)\}$ for all $p \in P$; we write $M \xrightarrow{d} M'$ for this delay transition.

For defining the set of goal markings $Goal$ we present a Boolean logic over marking expressions. Let e_1 and e_2 be two marking expressions of N and let φ be a formulae with the following syntax:

$$\varphi ::= \ true \mid false \mid t \mid e_1 \bowtie e_2 \mid deadlock \mid \varphi_1 \wedge \varphi_2 \mid \varphi_1 \vee \varphi_2 \mid \neg\varphi$$

where $t \in T$ and $\bowtie \in \{<, \leq, =, \neq, >, \geq\}$. Let E_N be defined by the following syntax: $e ::= \ c \mid p \mid e_1 \oplus e_2$, where $c \in \mathbb{N}^0$, $p \in P$, and $\oplus \in \{+, -, *\}$. We evaluate a marking expression e relative to a marking $M \in \mathcal{M}(N)$ by the function $eval_M(e)$ where $eval_M(c) = c$, $eval_M(p) = |M(p)|$ and $eval_M(e_1 \oplus e_2) = eval_M(e_1) \oplus eval_M(e_2)$.

The semantics for the satisfability relation $M \models \varphi$ for a marking $M \in \mathcal{M}(N)$ and a formula φ is given in the standard way for the Boolean connectives and in particular $M \models t$ iff $t \in en(M)$, $M \models deadlock$ iff $en(M) = \emptyset$, and $M \models e_1 \bowtie e_2$ iff $eval_M(e_1) \bowtie eval_M(e_2)$.

Given a formula φ, we aim to preserve at least one run to the set of goal markings $Goal = \{M \in \mathcal{M}(N) \mid M \models \varphi\}$. To achieve this, we use the definition of interesting transitions $A_M(\varphi)$ relative to a formula φ defined in [10]. Lemma 1 shows that $A_M(\varphi)$ is indeed an interesting set of transitions, and is sufficient to preserve Condition **R**.

Lemma 1. *([10]). Let $N = (P, T_1, T_2, T_{urg}, IA, OA, g, w, Type, I)$ be a TAPG, $M \in \mathcal{M}(N)$ a marking, and φ a formula. If $M \not\models \varphi$ and $M \xrightarrow{w} M'$ where $w \in \overline{A_M(\varphi)}^*$ then $M' \not\models \varphi$.*

We use the overapproximation algorithm $reach(N, M, \varphi)$ presented in [10] to overapproximate Condition **V**. The algorithm returns *true* whenever there is a sequence of player 2 transtions that leads us from a marking $M \in \mathcal{M}(N)$ to a goal marking M' where $M' \models \varphi$ in the TAPG N, and otherwise it returns *false*. The desired property is stated in Lemma 2. For handling Condition **V'** we simply switch all instances of environment transitions T_2 with the controller transitions T_1 in $reach(N, M, \varphi)$ and Lemma 2.

Lemma 2. *([10]). Let $N = (P, T_1, T_2, T_{urg}, IA, OA, g, w, Type, I)$ be a Petri net game, $M \in \mathcal{M}(N)$ a marking on N and φ a formula. If there is $w \in T_2^*$ s.t. $M \xrightarrow{w} M'$ and $M' \models \varphi$ then $reach(N, M, \varphi) = true$.*

Before we can state our main theorem, we need a method for determining safe transitions. This can be done by analysing the increasing presets and postsets of transitions as demonstrated in the following Lemma 3 from [10] that requires a small adaptation to our setting.

Lemma 3. *([10]). Let $N = (P, T_1, T_2, T_{urg}, IA, OA, g, w, Type, I)$ be a TAPG and $t \in T$ a transition. If $t^+ \cap {}^\bullet T_2 = \emptyset$ and ${}^-t \cap {}^\circ T_2 = \emptyset$ then t is safe in any marking of N.*

We can now state our main contribution in Theorem 3. The theorem provides a list of syntactic conditions on TAPG that for a given marking generates a stable stubborn set.

Theorem 3 (Stable Reduction Preserving Closure). *Let $N = (P, T_1, T_2, T_{urg}, IA, OA, g, w, Type, I)$ be a TAPG, φ a formula, and St a reduction of $G(N)$ such that for all $M \in \mathcal{M}(N)$ the following conditions hold.*

1. *If $en_1(M) \neq \emptyset$ and $en_2(M) \neq \emptyset$ then $T \subseteq St(M)$.*
2. *If $\neg\mathsf{zt}(M)$ then $T \subseteq St(M)$.*
3. *If $\mathsf{zt}(M)$ then either*
   (a) *there is $t \in T_{urg} \cap en(M) \cap St(M)$ where ${}^\bullet({}^\circ t) \subseteq St(M)$, or*
   (b) *there is $p \in P$ where $I(p) = [a, b]$ and $b \in M(p)$ such that $t \in St(M)$ for every $t \in p^\bullet$ where $b \in g((p, t))$.*
4. *If $en_1(M) \cap St(M) \nsubseteq safe(M)$ then $T \subseteq St(M)$.*
5. *$A_M(\varphi) \subseteq St(M)$*
6. *If $en_1(M) = \emptyset$ then $T_1 \subseteq St(M)$.*
7. *If $en_2(M) = \emptyset$ then $T_2 \subseteq St(M)$.*
8. *For all $t \in St(M) \setminus en(M)$ either*
   (a) *there is $p \in {}^\bullet t$ such that $|\{x \in M(p) \mid x \in g((p, t))\}| < w((p, t))$ and*
      – $t' \in St(M)$ for all $t' \in {}^+p$ where there is $p' \in {}^-t'$ with $Type((t', p)) = Type((p', t')) = Transport_j$ and where $g((p', t')) \cap g((p, t)) \neq \emptyset$, and
      – if $0 \in g((p, t))$ then also ${}^\bullet p \subseteq St(M)$, or
   (b) *there is $p \in {}^\circ t$ where $|M(p)| \geq w((p, t))$ such that*
      – $t' \in St(M)$ for all $t' \in p^-$ where $M(p) \cap g((p, t')) \neq \emptyset$.
9. *For all $t \in St(M) \cap en(M)$ we have*
   (a) *$t' \in St(M)$ for every $t' \in p^\bullet$ where $p \in {}^\bullet t$ and $g((p, t)) \cap g((p, t')) \neq \emptyset$, and*
   (b) *$(t^\bullet)^\circ \subseteq St(M)$.*
10. *If $en_2(M) \neq \emptyset$ then there exists $t \in en_2(M) \cap St(M)$ s.t. $\{t' \in ({}^\bullet t)^\bullet \mid \exists p \in {}^\bullet t \cup {}^\bullet t' \wedge g((p, t')) \cap g((p, t)) \cap M(p) \neq \emptyset\} \cup {}^+({}^\circ t) \subseteq St(M)$.*
11. *If $en_1(M) = \emptyset$ and $reach(N, M, \varphi) = true$ then $en(M) \subseteq St(M)$.*

*Then St satisfies **I**, **Z**, **W**, **R**, **T**, **G1**, **G2**, **S**, **V**, and **D**.*

Algorithm 1: Computation of $St(M)$ for some stable reduction St.

input : A TAPG $N = (P, T_1, T_2, T_{urg}, IA, OA, g, w, Type, I)$ and $M \in \mathcal{M}(N)$
       and formula φ

output: $X \subseteq T$ where X is a stable stubborn set for M

1 **if** $en(M) = \emptyset$ **then** **return** T; ;
2 **if** $\neg zt(M)$ **then** **return** T; ;
3 **if** $en_1(M) \neq \emptyset \wedge en_2(M) \neq \emptyset$ **then** **return** T; ;
4 $Y := \emptyset$;
5 **if** $en_1(M) = \emptyset$ **then**
6   **if** $reach(N, M, \varphi)$ **then** **return** T; ;
7   Pick any $t \in en_2(M)$; $Y := T_1 \cup t \cup {}^+({}^\circ t) \cup$
      $\{t' \in ({}^\bullet t)^\bullet \mid \exists p \in {}^\bullet t \cup {}^\bullet t' \wedge g((p, t')) \cap g((p, t)) \cap M(p) \neq \emptyset\}$;
8 **else**
9     $Y := T_2$;
10 **if** $T_{urg} \cap en(M) \neq \emptyset$ **then**
11   pick any $t \in T_{urg} \cap en(M)$;
12     $Y := Y \cup \{t\} \cup {}^\bullet({}^\circ t)$;
13 **else**
14   pick any $p \in P$ where $I(p) = [a, b]$ and $b \in M(p)$
15   **forall** $t \in p^\bullet$ **do**
16   **if** $b \in g((p, t))$ **then** $Y := Y \cup \{t\}$; ;
17 $Y := Y \cup A_M(\varphi)$; $X := Saturate(Y)$;
18 **if** $X \cap en_1(M) \not\subseteq safe(M)$ **then** **return** T; ;
19 **return** X;

In Algorithm 1 we now provide a pseudocode for calculating stable stubborn sets for a given marking. The algorithm calls Algorithm 2 that saturates a given set to satisfy Conditions 8 and 9.

Theorem 4. *Algorithm 1 terminates and returns $St(M)$ for some stable reduction St.*

To preserve safety strategies, we can modify Algorithm 1 slightly as well as $reach(N, M, \varphi)$ presented in [10]. The modified algorithm returns *true* whenever there is a sequence of player 1 transtions (instead of player 2 transitions) that leads us from a marking $M \in \mathcal{M}(N)$ to a goal marking M' where $M' \models \varphi$ in the TAPG N. To satisfy Condition **V'** we move the check at Line 6 into the else block at Line 9. For Condition **D'**, we move the assignment at Line 7 also into the else block at Line 9.

5   Implementation and Experiments

We extend the timed-arc Petri net game synthesis engine `verifydtapn` of TAPAAL [25,26] with the implementation of our stubborn set reduction for timed games and evaluate it on the following case studies.

Algorithm 2: *Saturate(Y)*

---

1 $X := \emptyset$;
2 **while** $Y \neq \emptyset$ **do**
3   pick any $t \in Y$;
4   **if** $t \notin en(M)$ **then**
5   **if** $\exists p \in {}^{\bullet}t.\; |\{x \in M(p) \mid x \in g((p,t))\}| < w((p,t))$ **then**
6   pick any such p;
7   **if** $0 \in g((p,t))$ **then**
8                  $Y := Y \cup ({}^{\bullet}p \setminus X)$;
9   **else**
10   **forall** $t' \in \{t'' \in {}^{+}p \setminus X \mid Type((t'',p)) = Transport_j\}$ **do**
11   **forall** $p' \in \{p'' \in {}^{-}t' \mid Type((p'',t')) = Type((t',p))\}$ **do**
12   **if** $g((p',t')) \cap g((p,t)) \neq \emptyset$ **then** $Y := Y \cup \{t'\}$; ;

13   **else**
14   pick any $p \in {}^{\circ}t$ s.t. $|M(p)| \geq w((p,t))$;
15   **forall** $t' \in p^{-} \setminus X$ **do**
16   **if** $M(p) \cap g((p,t')) \neq \emptyset$ **then** $Y := Y \cup \{t'\}$; ;

17   **else**
18   **forall** $p \in {}^{\bullet}t$ **do** $Y := Y \cup (\{t' \in p^{\bullet} | g((p,t)) \cap g((p,t')) \neq \emptyset\} \setminus X)$; ;
19          $Y := Y \cup ((t^{\bullet})^{\circ} \setminus X)$;
20      $Y := Y \setminus \{t\}$; $X := X \cup \{t\}$;
21 **return** $X \cap en(M)$;

- The *Fire Alarm* (FireAlarm-N-game) models a fire alarm system developed by a German company [15,16]. We scale the model by the number of wireless sensors N which report to a central unit. The objective of the game is to ensure the central unit acknowledges the messages of the sensors in the presence of a jammer which can cause message loss.
- The *Blood Transfusion* (BloodTransfusion-N-game) case study models a larger blood transfusion workflow [11], adapted to a timed game. We scale the model by the number of patients N receiving blood transfusions. The goal of the controller is to make sure all patients successfully finish the blood transfusion process on schedule.
- The *Limfjord* (Limfjord-N-K-S) models one direction of the Limfjord lifting bridge that connects the cities of Aalborg and Nørresundby in Northern Jutland, Denmark. We scale the model by the number of lanes N available, the number of cars K crossing the bridge, and the allowed interval of time S for all the cars to cross the bridge. The environment may temporarily either close a lane or raise the bridge to allow for boat traffic. The objective of the controller is to ensure all cars cross the bridge within the time limit.
- The *Railway Scheduling Problem* (LyngbySmall-N) is a model of a smaller variant of the Danish train station Lyngby. The problem and the station layout was initially described in [27]. We scale the model by the number of

Table 1. Experiments with (POR) and without (NORMAL) partial order reduction

Model	Time (seconds)		Markings ×1000		Improvement	
	NORMAL	POR	NORMAL	POR	Time	Markings
FireAlarm-10-game	11.24	3.75	796	498	3.00	1.60
FireAlarm-12-game	52.86	4.55	1727	526	11.62	3.28
FireAlarm-14-game	376.26	7.58	5367	554	49.64	9.69
FireAlarm-16-game	3868.19	8.75	19845	582	442.08	34.10
FireAlarm-100-game	> 3 h	255.80	to	1844	-	-
BloodTransfusion-3-game	3.91	3.45	612	504	1.13	1.21
BloodTransfusion-4-game	96.05	72.70	11864	8118	1.32	1.46
BloodTransfusion-5-game	2323.58	1329.11	196534	111089	1.75	1.77
Limfjord-1-6-12-game	2.48	1.11	212	75	2.23	2.83
Limfjord-1-6-20-game	4.10	1.74	423	156	2.36	2.71
Limfjord-1-10-15-game	5.82	2.16	896	336	2.69	2.67
Limfjord-1-10-20-game	9.18	2.79	1380	468	3.29	2.95
Limfjord-1-14-20-game	18.23	5.51	2550	864	3.31	2.95
Limfjord-1-14-25-game	27.98	8.10	3799	1230	3.45	3.09
Limfjord-2-6-12-game	1119.47	280.71	87718	24099	3.99	3.64
LyngbySmall-2-game	0.49	0.21	41	20	2.33	2.05
LyngbySmall-3-game	2.55	2.38	198	177	1.07	1.12
LyngbySmall-4-game	23.90	85.67	1524	4211	−3.58	−2.76
Covid-9-3-3-900-game	0.42	0.38	112	103	1.11	1.09
Covid-9-4-3-900-game	3.43	3.25	823	697	1.06	1.18
Covid-9-6-3-900-game	164.99	145.46	23609	19296	1.13	1.22

trains (N) entering the station. The controller's goal is to ensure that the trains reach their designated destinations without colliding.

- The *Covid-19 Spreading* (Covid-N-C-I-T-game) models activities of N persons in an indoor area. The goal of the controller is to commute C persons from one room to another via two lobbies and a corridor within T time units while keeping person infections below I. It is not possible to maintain social distancing at the corridor where Covid-19 exposures can occur.

All experiments are run on AMD EPYC 7642 processors with hyperthreading disabled, limited to 30 GB of memory, and a time out of 3 h. The source code of our implementation is available at [24]. For all the experiments, we use a depth-first search order.

Table 1 shows the experimental evaluation both without (NORMAL) and with (POR) partial order reduction. We report the time in seconds and the number of unique explored markings (in thousands). We also show the relative gain and loss of using partial order reduction for both time and unique markings. The results show a significant potential of our approach. In the FireAlarm-N-game models, there is an exponential speed-up with partial order reductions. We can handle up to 16 sensors without partial order reduction before the 3 h time out is reached. With partial order reduction, we can verify all our instances of the model up to 100 sensors, and we observe an increasing reduction growing from being 3 times faster in the 10-sensor instance to more than 422 faster in the 16-sensors instance. In the BloodTransfusion-N-game case study, we see that as the number of patients increases, partial order reduction begins to show increasing savings in both time and number of unique markings explored. We observe that both the number of markings explored and the time used for exploration almost halves in the largest instance. A similar tendency can be observed in the Limfjord-K-N models where the benefit of using POR increases with the problem-size. For the LyngbySmall-N models, while we initially see a speed-up with 2 and 3 trains, partial order reduction with 4 trains becomes, as the only case in our experiments, disadvantageous. Notably, in contrast to the untimed version of the model seen in [10] where a reduction was achieved, virtually no reduction is possible in the timed game variants, leaving only the overhead of calculating stubborn sets. Furthermore, partial order reduction explored more unique markings, which indicates that the reduction changed the search order causing us to explore a larger portion of the state-space. The variants with 2 and 3 trains is the opposite where the search order causes us to explore less of the state-space. We note here that winning strategies exist for the 2 and 3 trains models and not for the 4 trains model. Finally, in the Covid models only moderate reduction in the state-space can be achieved (though improving with the scaling of the model) and the synthesis time improves accordingly, showing that our stubborn set implementation has only a small overhead.

The experiments show that of our approach is generally beneficial and has the potential to achieve exponential speed-up, while having only moderate overhead. The changes in search order may cause large increases in the number of markings explored, as this is usual for on-the-fly verification algorithms.

6 Conclusion

We combined partial order reductions for timed systems and reachability games into a unified framework for timed games on the general formalism timed game labelled transitions systems. This required a new proof of the central theorems to accommodate for the timed setting. Furthermore, we showed that our partial order reduction approach for timed games also preserves winning safety strategies in addition to winning reachability strategies. We instantiated our approach to the formalism of timed-arc Petri net games and suggested specialized overapproximation algorithms. We implemented our approach in the timed-arc Petri net game engine of the TAPAAL model checker suite and evaluated this implementation on a set of scalable case studies. Several of the case studies demonstrate a significant reduction (e.g. the fire alarm case study up to several orders of magnitude in terms of time); the relative time and space reduction is often improving with the increasing scaling of the problems. In the future work, we consider to relax the Conditions **I** and **Z** in order to allow for reductions in mixed and non-urgent states.

References

1. Abdulla, P.A., Cerans, K., Jonsson, B., Tsay, Y.K.: General decidability theorems for infinite-state systems. In: Symposium on Logic in Computer Science, LICS 1996, pp. 313–321. IEEE (1996). https://doi.org/10.1109/LICS.1996.561359
2. Alur, R., Henzinger, T.A., Vardi, M.Y.: Parametric real-time reasoning. In: Symposium on Theory of Computing, STOC 1993, pp. 592–601. ACM (1993). https://doi.org/10.1145/167088.167242
3. Bengtsson, J., Jonsson, B., Lilius, J., Yi, W.: Partial order reductions for timed systems. In: Sangiorgi, D., de Simone, R. (eds.) CONCUR 1998. LNCS, vol. 1466, pp. 485–500. Springer, Heidelberg (1998). https://doi.org/10.1007/BFb0055643
4. Bolognesi, T., Lucidi, F., Trigila, S.: From timed petri nets to timed LOTOS. In: Proceedings of the IFIP WG 6.1 Tenth International Symposium on Protocol Specification, Testing and Verification X, pp. 395–408. North-Holland Publishing Co. (1990). https://doi.org/10.5555/645833.670383
5. Boucheneb, H., Barkaoui, K.: Reducing interleaving semantics redundancy in reachability analysis of time petri nets. ACM Trans. Embed. Comput. Syst. 12(1), 1–24 (2013). https://doi.org/10.1145/2406336.2406343
6. Boucheneb, H., Barkaoui, K.: Stubborn sets for time petri nets. ACM Trans. Embed. Comput. Syst. 14(1), 1–25 (2015). https://doi.org/10.1145/2680541
7. Boucheneb, H., Barkaoui, K.: Delay-dependent partial order reduction technique for real time systems. Real-Time Syst. 54(2), 278–306 (2017). https://doi.org/10.1007/s11241-017-9297-0
8. Bønneland, F.M., Jensen, P.G., Larsen, K.G., Muñiz, M., Srba, J.: Start pruning when time gets urgent: partial order reduction for timed systems. In: Chockler, H., Weissenbacher, G. (eds.) CAV 2018, Part I. LNCS, vol. 10981, pp. 527–546. Springer, Cham (2018). https://doi.org/10.1007/978-3-319-96145-3_28
9. Bønneland, F.M., Jensen, P.G., Larsen, K.G., Muñiz, M., Srba, J.: Partial order reduction for reachability games. In: CONCUR, Leibniz International Proceedings in Informatics, vol. 140, pp. 23:1–23:15. Schloss Dagstuhl-Leibniz-Zentrum fuer Informatik (2019). https://doi.org/10.4230/LIPIcs.CONCUR.2019.23
10. Bønneland, F.M., Jensen, P.G., Larsen, K.G., Muñiz, M., Srba, J.: Stubborn Set Reduction for Two-Player Reachability Games. arXiv preprint arXiv:1912.09875 (2019)
11. Christov, S.C., Avrunin, G.S., Clarke, L.A., Osterweil, L.J., Henneman, E.A.: A benchmark for evaluating software engineering techniques for improving medical processes. In: ICSE Workshop on Software Engineering in Health Care, SEHC 2010, pp. 50–56. ACM (2010). https://doi.org/10.1145/1809085.1809092
12. Clarke, E.M., Enders, T., Filkorn, T., Jha, S.: Exploiting symmetry in temporal logic model checking. Formal Methods Syst. Des. 9(1), 77–104 (1996). https://doi.org/10.1007/BF00625969
13. David, A., Jacobsen, L., Jacobsen, M., Jørgensen, K.Y., Møller, M.H., Srba, J.: TAPAAL 2.0: integrated development environment for timed-arc petri nets. In: Flanagan, C., König, B. (eds.) TACAS 2012. LNCS, vol. 7214, pp. 492–497. Springer, Heidelberg (2012). https://doi.org/10.1007/978-3-642-28756-5_36
14. Emerson, E.A., Jha, S., Peled, D.: Combining partial order and symmetry reductions. In: Brinksma, E. (ed.) TACAS 1997. LNCS, vol. 1217, pp. 19–34. Springer, Heidelberg (1997). https://doi.org/10.1007/BFb0035378

15. Feo-Arenis, S., Westphal, B., Dietsch, D., Muñiz, M., Andisha, A.S.: The wireless fire alarm system: ensuring conformance to industrial standards through formal verification. In: Jones, C., Pihlajasaari, P., Sun, J. (eds.) FM 2014. LNCS, vol. 8442, pp. 658–672. Springer, Cham (2014). https://doi.org/10.1007/978-3-319-06410-9_44

16. Feo-Arenis, S., Westphal, B., Dietsch, D., Muñiz, M., Andisha, A.S., Andreas, P.: The humble programmer. Ready Test. Ensuring Conformance Ind. Stan. Through Formal Verifi. **28**(3), 499–527 (2016). https://doi.org/10.1007/s00165-016-0365-3

17. German, S.M., Sistla, A.P.: Reasoning about systems with many processes. J. ACM **39**(3), 675–735 (1992). https://doi.org/10.1145/146637.146681

18. Gerth, R., Kuiper, R., Peled, D., Penczek, W.: A partial order approach to branching time logic model checking. Inf. Comput. **150**(2), 132–152 (1999). https://doi.org/10.1006/inco.1998.2778

19. Godefroid, P.: Partial-Order Methods for the Verification of Concurrent Systems: An Approach to the State-Explosion Problem, vol. 1032. Springer, Heidelberg (1996). https://doi.org/10.1007/3-540-60761-7

20. Godefroid, P., Wolper, P.: Using partial orders for the efficient verification of deadlock freedom and safety properties. Formal Methods Syst. Des. **2**(2), 149–164 (1993). https://doi.org/10.1007/BF01383879

21. Hanisch, H.-M.: Analysis of place/transition nets with timed arcs and its application to batch process control. In: Ajmone Marsan, M. (ed.) ICATPN 1993. LNCS, vol. 691, pp. 282–299. Springer, Heidelberg (1993). https://doi.org/10.1007/3-540-56863-8_52

22. Huhn, M., Niebert, P., Wehrheim, H.: Partial order reductions for bisimulation checking. In: Arvind, V., Ramanujam, S. (eds.) FSTTCS 1998. LNCS, vol. 1530, pp. 271–282. Springer, Heidelberg (1998). https://doi.org/10.1007/978-3-540-49382-2_26

23. Jensen, J.F., Nielsen, T., Oestergaard, L.K., Srba, J.: TAPAAL and reachability analysis of P/T nets. In: Koutny, M., Desel, J., Kleijn, J. (eds.) Transactions on Petri Nets and Other Models of Concurrency XI. LNCS, vol. 9930, pp. 307–318. Springer, Heidelberg (2016). https://doi.org/10.1007/978-3-662-53401-4_16

24. Jensen, P.G.: `verifydtapn` source code (2021). https://github.com/TAPAAL/verifydtapn/tree/dual_game_pw

25. Jensen, P.G., Larsen, K.G., Srba, J.: Real-time strategy synthesis for timed-arc petri net games via discretization. In: Bošnački, D., Wijs, A. (eds.) SPIN 2016. LNCS, vol. 9641, pp. 129–146. Springer, Cham (2016). https://doi.org/10.1007/978-3-319-32582-8_9

26. Jensen, P.G., Larsen, K.G., Srba, J.: Discrete and continuous strategies for timed-arc Petri net games. Int. J. Softw. Tools Technol. Transf. **20**(5), 529–546 (2017). https://doi.org/10.1007/s10009-017-0473-2

27. Kasting, P., Hansen, M.R., Vester, S.: Synthesis of railway-signaling plans using reachability games. In: Symposium on Theory of Computing, IFL 2016, pp. 1–13. ACM (2016). https://doi.org/10.1145/3064899.3064908

28. Lilius, J.: Efficient state space search for time petri nets. Electron. Notes Theor. Comput. Sci. **18**(1), 113–133 (1998). https://doi.org/10.1016/S1571-0661(05)80254-3

29. Minea, M.: Partial order reduction for model checking of timed automata. In: Baeten, J.C.M., Mauw, S. (eds.) CONCUR 1999. LNCS, vol. 1664, pp. 431–446. Springer, Heidelberg (1999). https://doi.org/10.1007/3-540-48320-9_30

30. Neele, T., Willemse, T.A.C., Wesselink, W.: Partial-order reduction for parity games with an application on parameterised boolean equation systems. TACAS 2020, Part II. LNCS, vol. 12079, pp. 307–324. Springer, Cham (2020). https://doi.org/10.1007/978-3-030-45237-7_19

31. Peled, D.: All from one, one for all: on model checking using representatives. In: Courcoubetis, C. (ed.) CAV 1993. LNCS, vol. 697, pp. 409–423. Springer, Heidelberg (1993). https://doi.org/10.1007/3-540-56922-7_34

32. Peled, D.: Combining Partial Order Reductions With On-The-Fly Model-Checking. Formal Methods Syst. Des. 8(1), 39–64 (1996). https://doi.org/10.1007/BF00121262

33. Sloan, R.H., Buy, U.: Stubborn sets for real-time petri nets. Formal Methods Syst. Des. 11(1), 23–40 (1997). https://doi.org/10.1023/A:1008629725384

34. Valmari, A.: Stubborn sets for reduced state space generation. In: Rozenberg, G. (ed.) ICATPN 1989. LNCS, vol. 483, pp. 491–515. Springer, Heidelberg (1991). https://doi.org/10.1007/3-540-53863-1_36

35. Valmari, A.: A stubborn attack on state explosion. Formal Methods Syst. Des. 1(4), 297–322 (1992). https://doi.org/10.1007/BF00709154

36. Valmari, A.: Stubborn set methods for process algebras. In: Proceedings of the DIMACS Workshop on Partial Order Methods in Verification, POMIV 1996, pp. 213–231. ACM (1997). https://doi.org/10.5555/266557.266608

37. Yoneda, T., Schlingloff, B.-H.: Efficient verification of parallel real-time systems. Formal Methods Syst. Des. 11(2), 187–215 (1997). https://doi.org/10.1023/A:1008682131325

Automatic Dynamic Parallelotope Bundles for Reachability Analysis of Nonlinear Systems

Edward Kim[1]($\boxtimes$), Stanley Bak[2]($\boxtimes$), and Parasara Sridhar Duggirala[1]($\boxtimes$)

[1] University of North Carolina at Chapel Hill, Chapel Hill, USA
{ehkim, psd}@cs.unc.edu
[2] Stony Brook University, New York, USA

Abstract. Reachable set computation is an important technique for the verification of safety properties of dynamical systems. In this paper, we investigate reachable set computation for discrete nonlinear systems based on parallelotope bundles. The algorithm relies on computing an upper bound on the supremum of a nonlinear function over a rectangular domain, which has been traditionally done using Bernstein polynomials. We strive to remove the manual step of parallelotope template selection to make the method fully automatic. Furthermore, we show that changing templates dynamically during computations cans improve accuracy. To this end, we investigate two techniques for generating the template directions. The first technique approximates the dynamics as a linear transformation and generates templates using this linear transformation. The second technique uses Principal Component Analysis (PCA) of sample trajectories for generating templates. We have implemented our approach in a Python-based tool called Kaa and improve its performance by two main enhancements. The tool is modular and use two types of global optimization solvers, the first using Bernstein polynomials and the second using NASA's Kodiak nonlinear optimization library. Second, we leverage the natural parallelism of the reachability algorithm and parallelize the Kaa implementation. We demonstrate the improved accuracy of our approach on several standard nonlinear benchmark systems.

1 Introduction

One of the most widely-used techniques for performing safety analysis of nonlinear dynamical systems is reachable set computation. The reachable set is defined to be the set of states visited by at least one of the trajectories of the system starting from an initial set. Computing the reachable set for nonlinear systems is challenging primarily due to two reasons: First, the tools for performing nonlinear analysis are not very scalable. Second, computing the reachable set using set representations involves wrapping error. That is, the overapproximation acquired at a given step would increase the conservativeness of the overapproximation for all future steps.

One of the techniques for computing the overapproximation of reachable sets for discrete time nonlinear systems is to use parallelotope bundles. Here,

C. Dima and M. Shirmohammadi (Eds.): FORMATS 2021, LNCS 12860, pp. 50–66, 2021.
https://doi.org/10.1007/978-3-030-85037-1_4

the reachable set is represented as a parallelotope bundle, an intersection of several parallelotopes. One of the advantages of this technique is its utilization of a special form of nonlinear optimization problem to overapproximate the reachable set. The usage of a specific form of nonlinear optimization mitigates the drawback involved with the scalability of nonlinear analysis.

However, wrapping error still remains to be a problem for reachability using parallelotope bundles. The template directions for specifying these parallelotopes are provided as an input by the user. Often, these template directions are selected to be either the cardinal axis directions or some directions from octahedral domains. However, it is not clear that the axis directions and octagonal directions are optimal for computing reachable sets. Also, even an expert user of reachable set computation tools may not be able to provide a suitable set of template directions for computing reasonably accurate over-approximations of the reachable set. Picking unsuitable template directions would only cause the wrapping error to increase, thus increasing the conservativeness of the safety analysis.

In this paper, we investigate techniques for generating template directions automatically and dynamically. That is, instead of providing the template directions to compute the parallelotope, the user just specifies the number of templates and the algorithm automatically generates the template directions. We study two techniques for generating the template directions. First, we compute a local linear approximation of the nonlinear dynamics and use the linear approximation to compute the templates. Second, we generate a specific set of sample trajectories from the set and use principal component analysis (PCA) over these trajectories. We observe that the accuracy of the reachable set can be drastically improved by using templates generated using these two techniques. For standard nonlinear benchmark systems, we show that generating templates in a dynamic fashion improves the accuracy of the reachable set by two orders of magnitude. We demonstrate that even when the size of the initial set increases, our template generation technique returns more accurate reachable sets than both manually-specified and random template directions.

2   Related Work

Reachable set computation of nonlinear systems using template polyhedra and Bernstein polynomials has been first proposed in [9]. In [9], Bernstein polynomial representation is used to compute an upper bound of a special type of nonlinear optimization problem [17]. Several improvements to this algorithm were suggested in [10,27] and [7] extends it for performing parameter synthesis. The representation of parallelotope bundles for reachability was proposed in [13] and the effectiveness of using bundles for reachability was demonstrated in [12,14]. However, all of these papers used static template directions for computing the reachable set.

Using template directions for reachable set has been proposed in [26] and later improved in [8]. Leveraging the principal component analysis of sample trajectories for computing reachable set has been proposed in [5,28,30]. More recently, connections between optimal template directions for reachability of linear dynamical systems and bilinear programming have been highlighted in [19]. For static template directions, octahedral domain directions [6] remain a popular choice.

3 Preliminaries

The state of a system, denoted as x, lies in a domain $D \subseteq \mathbb{R}^n$. A discrete-time nonlinear system is denoted as

$$x^+ = f(x) \tag{1}$$

where $f : \mathbb{R}^n \to \mathbb{R}^n$ is a nonlinear function. The trajectory of a system that evolves according to Eq. 1, denoted as $\xi(x_0)$ is a sequence $x_0, x_1, \ldots$ where $x_{i+1} = f(x_i)$. The kth element in this sequence x_k is denoted as $\xi(x_0, k)$. Given an initial set $\Theta \subseteq \mathbb{R}^n$, the *reachable set* at step k, denoted as Θ_k is defined as

$$\Theta_k = \{\xi(x, k) \mid x \in \Theta\} \tag{2}$$

A parallelotope P, denoted as a tuple $\langle a, G \rangle$ where $a \in \mathbb{R}^n$ is called the *anchor* and G is a set of vectors $\{g_1, g_2, \ldots, g_n\}$, $\forall_{1 \leq i \leq n} g_i \in \mathbb{R}^n$ called *generators*, represents the set

$$P = \{x \mid \exists \alpha_1, \ldots, \alpha_n, \text{ such that } 0 \leq \alpha_i \leq 1, x = a + \sum_{i=1}^{n} \alpha_i g_i\}. \tag{3}$$

We call this representation as the *generator representation* of the parallelotope. We refer to a generator of a specific parallelotope P using dot notation, for example $P.g_1$. For readers familiar with zonotopes [2,18], a parallelotope is a special form of zonotope where the number of generators n equals the dimensionality of the set. One can also represent the parallelotope as a conjunction of half-space constraints. In half-space representation, a parallelotope is represented as a tuple $\langle \mathcal{T}, c_l, c_u \rangle$ where $\mathcal{T} \in \mathbb{R}^{n \times n}$ are called *template directions* and $c_l, c_u \in \mathbb{R}^n$ such that $\forall_{1 \leq i \leq n} c_l[i] \leq c_u[i]$ are called *bounds*. The half-space representation defines the set of states

$$P = \{x \mid c_l \leq \mathcal{T}x \leq c_u\}.$$

Intuitively, the ith constraint in the parallelotope corresponds to an upper and lower bound on the function $\mathcal{T}_i x$. That is, $c_l[i] \leq \mathcal{T}_i x \leq c_u[i]$. The half-plane representation of a parallelotope can be converted into the generator representation by computing $n+1$ vertices $v_1, v_2, \ldots, v_{n+1}$ of the parallelotope in the following way. The vertex v_1 is obtained by solving the linear equation $\Lambda x = c_l$. The $j+1$ vertex is obtained by solving the linear equation $\Lambda x = \mu_j$ where $\mu_j[i] = c_l[i]$ when $i \neq j$ and $\mu_j[j] = c_u[j]$. The anchor a of the parallelotope is the vertex v_1 and the generator $g_i = v_{i+1} - v_1$.

Example 1. Consider the xy-plane and the parallelotope P given in half-plane representation as $0 \leq x - y \leq 1$, $0 \leq y \leq 1$. This is a parallelotope with vertices at $(0,0)$, $(1,0)$, $(2,1)$, and $(1,1)$. In the half-space representation, the template directions of the parallelotope P are given by the directions $[1, -1]$ and $[0, 1]$. The half-space representation in matrix form is given as follows:

$$\begin{bmatrix} 0 \\ 0 \end{bmatrix} \leq \begin{bmatrix} 1 & -1 \\ 0 & 1 \end{bmatrix} \begin{bmatrix} x \\ y \end{bmatrix} \leq \begin{bmatrix} 1 \\ 1 \end{bmatrix}. \tag{4}$$

To compute the generator representation of P, we need to compute the *anchor* and the *generators*. The anchor is obtained by solving the linear equations $x - y = 0, y = 0$. Therefore, the anchor a is the vertex at origin $(0,0)$ To compute the two generators of the parallelotope, we compute two vertices of the parallelotope. Vertex v_1 is obtained by solving the linear equations $x - y = 1, y = 0$. Therefore, vertex v_1 is the vertex $(1,0)$. Similarly, vertex v_2 is obtained by solving the linear equations $x - y = 0, y = 1$. Therefore, v_2 is the vertex $(1,1)$. The generator g_1 is the vector $v_1 - a$, that is $(1,0) - (0,0) = (1,0)$ The generator g_2 is the vector $v_2 - a$, that is $(1,1) - (0,0) = (1,1)$. Therefore, all the points in the parallelotope can be written as $(x,y) = (0,0) + \alpha_1(1,0) + \alpha_2(1,1), 0 \leq \alpha_1, \alpha_2 \leq 1$.

A parallelotope bundle Q is a set of parallelotopes $\{P_1, \ldots, P_m\}$. The set of states represented by a parallelotope bundle is given as the intersection

$$Q = \bigcap_{i=1}^{m} P_i. \tag{5}$$

Often, the various parallelotopes in a bundle share common template directions. In such cases, the conjunction of all the parallelotope constraints in a bundle Q is written as $c_l^Q \leq T^Q x \leq c_u^Q$. Notice that the number of upper and lower bound half-space constraints in this bundle are stricly more than n in these cases, i.e., $T^Q \in R^{m \times n}$ where $m > n$. Each parallelotope in such a bundle is represented as a subset of constraints in $c_l^Q \leq T^Q x \leq c_u^Q$. These types of bundles are often considered in the literature [9, 10, 14].

Alternatively, we consider parallelotope bundles where the consisting parallelotopes do not share template directions. We consider such bundles because we generate the n template directions automatically at each step.

The basic building block in this work is a conservative overapproximation to a constrained nonlinear optimization problem with a box domain. Consider a nonlinear function $h : \mathbb{R}^n \to \mathbb{R}$ and the optimization problem denoted as optBox(h) as

$$\max\ h(x) \tag{6}$$

$$s.t.\ x \in [0,1]^n.$$

For computing the reachable set of a nonlinear system, we need an upper bound for the optimization problem. Several techniques using interval arithmetic and Bernstein polynomials have been developed in the recent past [1, 17, 22, 29].

4   Reachability Algorithm

In this work, we develop parallelotope reachability algorithms that are **automatic** with **dynamic** parallelotopes. The state of the art, in contrast, is **manual**, where the user specifies a set of parallelotope directions at the beginning. The parallelotopes are also **static** and do not change during the course of the computation. In this section, we detail the modifications to the algorithm and present their correctness arguments.

4.1   Manual Static Algorithm

We first present the original algorithm [10] where the user manually specifies the number of parallelotopes and a set of static directions for each parallelotope.

Recall the system is n-dimensional with dynamics function $f : \mathbb{R}^n \to \mathbb{R}^n$. The parallelotope bundle Q is specified as a collection of m template directions $T^Q \in \mathbb{R}^{m \times n} (m > n)$ and the set of constraints that define each of the member parallelotopes.

Another input to the algorithm is the initial set, given as a parallelotope P_0. When the initial set is a box, P_0 consists has axis-aligned template directions. The output of the algorithm is, for each step k, the set $\overline{\Theta}_k$, which is an overapproximation of the reachable set at step k, $\Theta_k \subseteq \overline{\Theta}_k$.

The high-level pseudo-code is written in Algorithm 1. The algorithm simply calls `TransformBundle` for each step, producing a new parallelotope bundle computed from the previous step's bundle. To compute the image of Q, the algorithm computes the upper and lower bounds of $f(x)$ with respect to each template direction. Since computing the maximum value of $f(x)$ along each template direction on Q is computationally difficult, the algorithm instead computes the maximum value over each of the constituent parallelotopes and uses the minimum of all these maximum values. The `TransformBundle` operation works as follows. Consider a parallelotope P in the bundle Q. From the definition, it follows that $Q \subseteq P$. Given a template direction T_i, the maximum value of $T_i f(x)$ for all $x \in Q$ is less than or equal to the maximum value of $T_i f(x)$ for all $x \in P$. Similar argument holds for the minimum value of $T_i f(x)$ for all $x \in Q$. To compute the upper and lower bounds of each template direction $T_i f(x)$, for all $x \in P$, we perform the following optimization.

$$\max \; T_i^P \cdot f(x) \tag{7}$$
$$s.t. \quad x \in P.$$

Given that P is a parallelotope, all the states in P can be expressed as a vector summation of anchor and scaled generators. Let $\langle a, G \rangle$ be the generator representation of P. The optimization problem given in Eq. 7 would then transform as follows.

$$\max \; T_i \cdot f(a + \Sigma_{i=1}^n \alpha_i g_i) \tag{8}$$
$$s.t. \quad \overline{\alpha} \in [0, 1]^n.$$

Equation 8 is a form of $\mathsf{optBox}(\mathcal{T}_i \cdot \mathsf{f})$ over $[0,1]^n$. One can compute an upperbound to the constrained nonlinear optimization by invoking one of the Bernstein polynomial or interval-arithmetic-based methods. Similarly, we compute the lowerbound of $\mathcal{T}_i f(x)$ for all $x \in P$ by computing the upperbound of $-1 \times \mathcal{T}_i f(x)$.

We iterate this process (i.e., computing the upper and lower bound of $\mathcal{T}_i f(x)$) for each parallelotope in the bundle Q. Therefore, the tightest upper bound on $\mathcal{T}_i f(x)$ over Q is the least of the upper bounds computed from each of the parallelotopes. A similar argument holds for lower bounds of $\mathcal{T}_i f(x)$ over Q. Therefore, the image of the bundle Q will be the bundle Q' where the upper and lower bounds for templates directions are obtained by solving several constrained nonlinear optimization problems.

Lemma 1. *The parallelotope bundle Q' computed using* `TransformBundle` *(Algorithm 1) is a sound overapproximation of the image of bundle Q w.r.t the dynamics $x^+ = f(x)$.*

4.2 Automatic Dynamic Algorithm

The proposed automatic dynamic algorithm does not require the user to provide the set of template directions $\mathcal{T}$; instead it generates these templates directions automatically at each step. We use two techniques to generate such template directions, first: computing local linear approximations of the dynamics and second, performing principal component analysis (PCA) over sample trajectories. To do this, we first sample a set of points in the parallelotope bundle called *support points* and propagate them to the next step using the dynamics f. Support points are a subset of the vertices of the parallelotope that either maximize or minimize the template directions.

Intuitively, linear approximations can provide good approximations when the dynamics function is a time-discretization of a continuous system. In this case, for small time steps a nonlinear function can be approximated fairly accurately by a linear transformation. We use the support points as a data-driven approach to find the best-fit linear function to use. If the dynamics of a system is linear, i.e., $x^+ = Ax$, the image of the parallelotope $c_l \leq Tx \leq c_u$, is the set $c_l \leq \mathcal{T} \cdot A^{-1}x \leq c_u$. Therefore, given the template directions of the initial set as $\mathcal{T}_0$, we compute the local linear approximation of the nonlinear dynamics and change the template directions by multiplying them with the inverse of the approximate linear dynamics. The second technique for generating template directions performs principal component analysis over the images of the support points. Using PCA is a reasonable choice as it produces orthonormal directions that can construct a rotated box for bounding the points.

Observe that in general, the dynamics is nonlinear and therefore, the reachable set could be non-convex. On the other hand, a parallelotope bundle is always a convex set. To mitigate this discrepancy, we can improve accuracy of this representation by considering more template directions. For this purpose, we use a notion of *template lifespan*, where we use the linear approximation and/or PCA template directions not only from the current step, but also from the previous

---

Input: Dynamics f, Initial Parallelotope P_0, Step Bound S, Template Dirs $\mathcal{T}$,
      indexes for parallelotopes I
Output: Reachable Set Overapproximation $\overline{\Theta}_k$ for each step k
1 $Q_0 = \{P_0\}$
2 **for** $k \in [1, 2, \ldots, S]$ **do**
3     $Q_k = \texttt{TransformBundle}\ (f, Q_{k-1}, \mathcal{T})$
4     $\overline{\Theta}_k = Q_k$
5 **end**
6 **return** $\overline{\Theta}_1 \ldots \overline{\Theta}_S$
7
8 **Proc** $\texttt{TransformBundle}(f, Q, \mathcal{T})$:
9     $Q' \leftarrow \{\}; c_u \leftarrow +\infty; c_l \leftarrow -\infty$
10   **for** *each parallelotope P in Q* **do**
11       $\langle a, G \rangle \leftarrow \mathsf{generatorRepresentation}(P)$
12   **for** *each template direction $\mathcal{T}_i$ in the template directions $\mathcal{T}$* **do**
13          $c'_u[i] \leftarrow \min\{\mathsf{optBox}(\mathcal{T}_i \cdot f), c'_u[i]\}$ (Equation 8)
14          $c'_l[i] \leftarrow \max\{-1 \times \mathsf{optBox}(-1 \times \mathcal{T}_i \cdot f), c'_l[i]\}$
15   **end**
16   **end**
17   Construct parallelotopes $P'_1, \ldots, P'_k$ from $\mathcal{T}, c'_l, c'_u$ and indexes from I
18    $Q' \leftarrow \{P'_1, \ldots, P'_k\}$
19   **return** Q'

Algorithm 1: Reachable set computation using manual and static templates.

L steps. We will demonstrate the effectiveness and tune each of the options (PCA/linear approximation as well as lifespan option) in our evaluation.

The new approach is given in Algorithm 2. In this algorithm, instead of fixing the set of templates, we compute one set of templates (that is, a collection of n template directions), using linear approximation of the dynamics and PCA. The algorithm makes use of helper function $\texttt{hstack}$, which converts column vectors into a matrix (as shown in Eq. 4 provided in Example 1). The notation $M_{*,i}$ is used to refer to the ith column of matrix M. The $\texttt{Maximize}$ function takes in a parallelotope bundle Q and direction vector v (one of the template directions), and returns the point $p \in Q$ that maximizes the dot product $v \cdot p$ (for computing support points). This can be computed efficiently using linear programming. The $\texttt{ApproxLinearTrans}$ function computes the best approximation of a linear transformation given a list of points before and after the one-step transformation f. More specifically, given a matrix X of points before applying the transformation f, a matrix of points after the transformation X', we perform a least-squares fit for the linear transition matrix A such that $X' \approx AX$. This can be computed by $A = X'X^{\dagger}$, where $X^{\dagger}$ is the Moore-Penrose pseudoinverse of X. The $\texttt{PCA}$ function returns a set of orthogonal directions using principal component analysis of a set of points. Finally, $\texttt{TransformBundle}$ is the same as in Algorithm 1.

Input: Dynamics f, Initial Parallelotope P_0, Step Bound S
Output: Reachable Set Overapproximation $\overline{\Theta}_k$ at each step k

1 $Q_0 = \{P_0\}$
2 $\mathcal{T} = \text{hstack}(P_0.\mathcal{T}_1, \ldots, P_0.\mathcal{T}_n)$ // Init Template Directions
3 **for** $k \in [1, 2, \ldots, S]$ **do**
4      $P_{supp} = \text{GetSupportPoints}\ (Q_{k-1})$ (support points of Q_{k-1})
5      $P_{prop} = \text{PropagatePointsOneStep}\ (P_{supp}, f)$ (image of support points)
6      $A = \text{ApproxLinearTrans}\ (P_{supp}, P_{prop})$
7      $\mathcal{T} = \mathcal{T} \cdot A^{-1}$
8      $\mathcal{T}_k^{\text{lin}} = \{\{\mathcal{T}_{*,1}, \ldots, \mathcal{T}_{*,n}\}\}$
9      $\mathcal{T}_k^{\text{pca}} = \{\text{PCA}(P_{prop})\}$
10     $\mathcal{T}_k = \mathcal{T}_k^{\text{lin}} \cup \mathcal{T}_k^{\text{pca}}$
11
12   /* For lifespan L, instead call TransformBundle with
       $\mathcal{T}_k \cup \mathcal{T}_{k-1} \cup \ldots \cup \mathcal{T}_{k-L}$ */
13     $Q_k = \text{TransformBundle}\ (f, Q_{k-1}, \mathcal{T}_k)$
14     $\overline{\Theta}_k \leftarrow Q_k$
15 **end**
16 **return** $\overline{\Theta}_1 \ldots \overline{\Theta}_S$
17
18 **Proc GetSupportPoints**(Q):
19     $P_{supp} = \emptyset$
20   **for** $P \in Q$ **do**
21   **for** $i \in [1, 2, \ldots, n]$ **do**
22             $P_{supp} = P_{supp} \cup \text{Maximize}(Q, P.\mathcal{T}_i) \cup \text{Maximize}(Q, -P.\mathcal{T}_i)$
23   **end**
24   **end**
25   **return** P_{supp}

Algorithm 2: Automatic, Dynamic Reachability Algorithm

Algorithm 2 computes the dynamic templates for each time step k. Line 6 computes the linear approximation of the nonlinear dynamics and this linear approximation is used to compute the new template directions according to this linear transformation in Line 8. The PCA directions of the images of support points is computed in line 9. For the time step k, the linear and PCA templates are given as $\mathcal{T}_k^{lin}$ and $\mathcal{T}_k^{pca}$, respectively. To improve the accuracy of the reachable set, we compute the overapproximation of the reachable set with respect to not just the template directions at the current step, but with respect to other template directions for time steps that are within the lifespan L.

5   Evaluation

We evaluate the efficacy of our dynamic parallelotope bundle strategies with our tool, *Kaa* [21]. Kaa is written in Python and relies on the *numpy* library for matrix computations, *sympy* library for all symbolic substitution, and *scipy*, *matplotlib* for plotting the reachable sets and computing the volume for lower-dimensional systems. The optimization procedure for finding the direction offets is performed through the *Kodiak* library. Finally, parallelization of the offset calculation procedures is implemented through the *multiprocessing* module. To estimate volume of reachable sets, we employ two techniques for estimating volume of individual parallelotope bundles. For systems of dimension fewer than or equal to three, we utilize scipy's convex hull routine. For higher-dimensional systems, we employ the volume of the tightest enveloping box around the parallelotope bundle. The total volume estimate of the overapproximation will be the sum of all the bundles' volume estimates.

Model Dynamics. For benchmarking, we select six non-linear models with polynomial dynamics. Benchmarks against more general dynamics can be found in the appendix of the expanded verison. Many of these models are also implemented in *Sapo* [12], a previous tool exploring reachability with **static** parallelotope bundles. In these cases, we directly compare the performance of our dynamic strategies with the Sapos static parallelotopes. To provide meaningful comparisions, we set the number of dynamic parallelotopes to be equal to the number of static ones excluding the initial box. Here, **diagonal directions** are defined to be vectors created by adding and subtracting distinct pairs of unit axis-aligned vectors from each other. By **diagonal parallelotopes**, we refer to parallelotopes defined only by axis-aligned and diagonal directions. Similarly, **diagonal parallelotope bundles** are parallelotope bundles solely consisting of diagonal parallelotopes. Sapo primarily utilizes **static diagonal parallelotope bundles** to perform its reachability computation. Note that the initial box, which is defined only through the axis-aligned directions, is contained in every bundle. For our experiments, we are concerned with the effects of additional static or dynamic parallelotopes added alongside the initial box. We refer to these parallelotopes as **non-axis-aligned parallelotopes**.

Example 2. In two dimensions, $\mathbb{R}^2$, we have the two unit axis-aligned directions, $[1,0]^T, [0,1]^T$. The diagonal directions will then be

$$[1,1]^T, \ [1,-1]^T$$

Consequently, the diagonal parallelotopes will precisely be defined by unique pairs of these directions, giving us a total $\binom{4}{2} = 6$ diagonal parallelotopes.

Table 1 summarizes five standard benchmarks used for experimentation. The last seven-dimensional COVID supermodel is explained in the subsequent subsection below.

Table 1. Benchmark models and relevant information

Model	Dimension	Parameters	# steps	Δ	Initial box
Vanderpol	2	-	70 steps	0.08	$x \in [0, 0.1], y \in [1.99, 2]$
Jet engine	2	-	100 steps	0.2	$x \in [0.8, 1.2], y \in [0, 8, 1.2]$
Neuron [16]	2	-	200 steps	0.2	$x \in [0.9, 1.1], y \in [2.4, 2.6]$
SIR	3	$\beta = 0.05$ $\gamma = 0.34$	150 steps	0.1	$s \in [0.79, 0.8], i \in [0.19, 0.2], r = 0$
Coupled Vanderpol	4	-	40 steps	0.08	$x1 \in [1.25, 2.25], y1 \in [1.25, 2.25]$ $x2 \in [1.25, 2.25], y2 \in [1.25, 2.25]$
COVID	7	$\beta = 0.05$ $\gamma = 0.0$ $\eta = 0.02$	200 steps	0.08	Stated below

COVID Supermodel: We benchmark our dynamic strategies with the recently introduced COVID supermodel [3, 25]. This model is a modified SIR model accounting for the possibility of *asymptomatic* patients. These patients can infect susceptible members with a fixed probability. The dynamics account for this new group and its interactions with the traditional SIR groups.

$$S'_A = S_A - (\beta S_A(A + I)) \cdot \Delta$$
$$S'_I = S_I - (\beta S_I(A + I)) \cdot \Delta$$
$$A' = A + (\beta S_I(A + I) - \gamma I) \cdot \Delta$$
$$I' = I + (\beta S_I(A + I) - \gamma I) \cdot \Delta \qquad (9)$$
$$R'_A = R_A + (\gamma A) \cdot \Delta$$
$$R'_I = R_I + (\gamma I) \cdot \Delta$$
$$D' = D + (\eta I) \cdot \Delta$$

where the variables denote the fraction of a population of individuals designated as *Susceptible to Asymptomatic* (S_A), *Susceptible to Symptomatic* (S_I), *Asymptomatic (A)*, *Symptomatic (I)*, *Removed from Asymptomatic* (R_A), *Removed from Symptomatic* (R_I), and *Deceased (D)*. We choose the parameters $(\beta = 0.25, \gamma = 0.02, \eta = 0.02)$ where β is the probablity of infection, γ is the removal rate, and η is the mortality rate. The parameters are set based on figures shown in [3]. The discretization step is chosen to be $\Delta = 0.1$ and the initial box is set to be following dimensions: $S_A \in [0.69, 0.7], S_I \in [0.09, 0.1], A \in [0.14, 0.15], I \in [0.04, 0.05], R_A = 0, R_I = 0, D = 0$.

Accuracy of Dynamic Strategies. The results of testing our dynamic strategies against static ones are summarized in Table 2. For models previously defined in Sapo, we set the static parallelotopes to be exactly those found in Sapo. If a model is not implemented in Sapo, we simply use the static parallelotopes defined in a model of equal dimension. To address the unavailability of a four-dimensional model implemented in Sapo, we sampled random subsets of five static non-axis-aligned parallelotopes and chose the flowpipe with smallest volume. A cursory

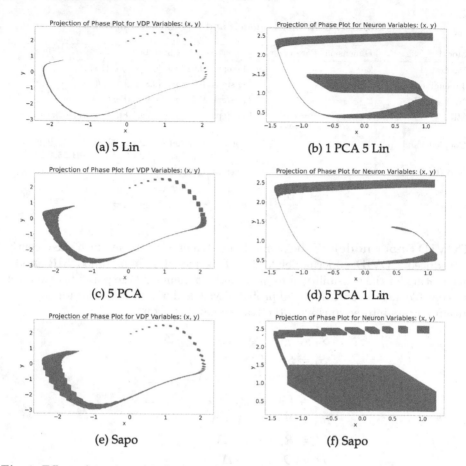

Fig. 1. Effect of varying ratio between the number of PCA and Linear Approximation parallelotopes. The Vanderpol (left) and the FitzHugh-Nagumo Neuron (right) phase plots are shown to illustrate differing effects of varying the PCA/LinApp ratio. The initial set for the Vanderpol model is set to $x \in [0, 0.05]$, $y \in [1.95, 2]$

analysis shows that the number of possible templates with diagonal directions grows with $O(n^n)$ with the number of dimensions and hence an exhaustive search on optimal template directions is infeasible.

From our experiments, we conclude there is no universal optimal ratio between the number of dynamic parallelotopes defined by PCA and Linear Approxiation directions which perform well on all benchmarks. In Fig. 1, we demonstrate two cases where varying the ratio imparts differing effects. Observe that using parallelotopes defined by linear approximation directions is more effective than those defined by PCA directions in the Vanderpol model whereas the Neuron model shows the opposite trend.

Performance Under Increasing Initial Sets. A key advantage of our dynamic strategies is the improved ability to control the wrapping error naturally arising

Table 2. Tables presenting upper bounds on the total reachable set volume by strategy. The static directions are retrieved and/or inspired from Sapo models of equal dimension for benchmarking. The best performing strategy is highlighted in bold.

Strategy	Total volume
5 LinApp	0.227911
1 PCA, 4 LinApp	0.225917
2 PCA, 3 LinApp	0.195573
3 PCA, 2 LinApp	**0.188873**
4 PCA, 1 LinApp	1.227753
5 PCA	1.509897
5 Static Diagonal(Sapo)	2.863307

(a) Vanderpol

Strategy	Total volume
5 LinApp	58199.62
1 PCA, 4 LinApp	31486.16
2 PCA, 3 LinApp	**5204.09**
3 PCA, 2 LinApp	6681.76
4 PCA, 1 LinApp	50505.10
5 PCA	84191.15
5 Static Diagonal (Sapo)	66182.18

(b) Jet Engine

Strategy	Total volume
5 LinApp	154.078
1 PCA, 4 LinApp	136.089
2 PCA, 3 LinApp	73.420
3 PCA , 2 LinApp	**73.126**
4 PCA, 1 LinApp	76.33
5 PCA	83.896
5 Static Diagonal (Sapo)	202.406

(c) FitzHugh-Nagumo

Strategy	Total volume
2 LinApp	**0.001423**
1 PCA, 1 LinApp	0.106546
2 PCA	0.117347
2 Static Diagonal (Sapo)	0.020894

(d) SIR

Strategy	Total volume
5 LinApp	5.5171
1 PCA, 4 LinApp	**5.2536**
2 PCA, 3 LinApp	5.6670
3 PCA, 2 LinApp	5.5824
4 PCA, 1 LinApp	312.2108
5 PCA	388.0513
5 Static Diagonal (Best)	3023.4463

(e) Coupled Vanderpol

Strategy	Total volume
3 LinApp	$2.95582227 * 10^{-10}$
1 PCA, 2 LinApp	$2.33007583 * 10^{-10}$
2 PCA, 1 LinApp	$4.02751770 * 10^{-9}$
3 PCA	$4.02749571 * 10^{-9}$
3 Static Diagonal (Sapo)	$4.02749571 * 10^{-9}$

(f) COVID

from larger initial sets. Figure 2 presents charts showcasing the effect of increasing initial sets on the total flowpipe volume. We vary the initial box dimensions to gradually increase the box's volume. We then plot the total flowpipe volume after running the benchmark. The same initial boxes are also used in computations using Sapo's static parallelotopes. The number of parallelotopes defined by PCA and Linear Approximation directions were chosen based on best performance as seen in Table 2. We remark that our dynamic strategies perform better than static ones in controlling the total flowpipe volume as the initial set becomes larger. On the other hand, the performance of static parallelotopes tends to degrade rapidly as we increase the volume of the initial box.

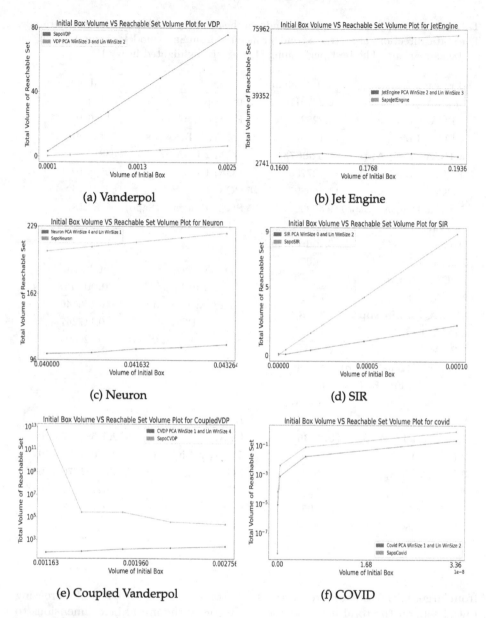

(a) Vanderpol

(b) Jet Engine

(c) Neuron

(d) SIR

(e) Coupled Vanderpol

(f) COVID

Fig. 2. Comparison between the performance of diagonal static parallelotope bundles and that of the best performing dynamic parallelotope bundles as the volume of the initial set grows.

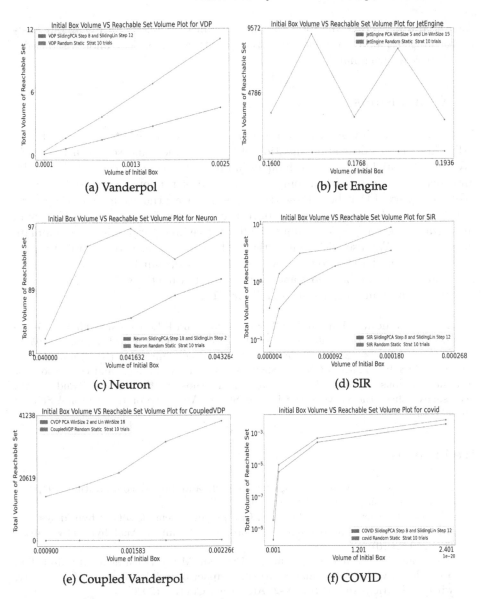

Fig. 3. Comparision between random static strategies and the best performing dynamic strategies as the volume of the initial set grows. The total reachable set volumes for random static strategies are averaged over ten trials for each system.

Performance Against Random Static Templates. We additionally benchmark our dynamic strategies against static random parallelotope bundles. We sample such parallelotopes in n dimensions by first sampling a set of n directions uniformly on the surface of the unit $(n-1)$-sphere, then defining our parallelotope using these sampled directions. We sample twenty of these parallelotopes for each trial and average the total flowpipe volumes. As shown in Fig. 3, our best-performing dynamic strategies consistently outperform static random strategies for all tested benchmarks.

6   Conclusions

In this paper, we investigated two techniques for generating templates dynamically: first using linear approximation of the dynamics, and second using PCA. We demonstrated that these techniques improve the accuracy of reachable set by an order of magnitude when compared to static or random template directions. We also observed that both these techniques improve the accuracy of the reachable sets for different benchamrks. In future, we intend to investigate Koopman linearization techniques for computing alternative linear approximation template directions [4]. We also wish to investigate the use of a massively parallel implementation using HPC hardware such as GPUs for optimizing over an extremely large number of parallelotopes and their template directions. This is inspired by the approach behind the recent tool *PIRK* [11].

Acknowledgements. Parasara Sridhar Duggirala and Edward Kim acknowledge the support of the Air Force Office of Scientific Research under award number FA9550-19-1-0288 and FA9550-21-1-0121 and National Science Foundation (NSF) under grant numbers CNS 1935724 and CNS 2038960. Any opinions, findings, and conclusions or recommendations expressed in this material are those of the author(s) and do not necessarily reflect the views of the United States Air Force or the National Science Foundation.

References

1. Kodiak, a C++ library for rigorous branch and bound computation. https://github.com/nasa/Kodiak. Accessed July 2020
2. Althoff, M., Stursberg, O., Buss, M.: Computing reachable sets of hybrid systems using a combination of zonotopes and polytopes. Nonlinear Anal. hybrid Syst. **4**(2), 233–249 (2010)
3. Ansumali, S., Kaushal, S., Kumar, A., Prakash, M.K., Vidyasagar, M.: Modelling a pandemic with asymptomatic patients, impact of lockdown and herd immunity, with applications to SARS-CoV-2. Ann. Rev. Control (2020)
4. Bak, S., Bogomolov, S., Duggirala, P.S., Gerlach, A.R., Potomkin, K.: Reachability of black-box nonlinear systems after Koopman operator linearization (2021)
5. Chen, X., Ábrahám, E.: Choice of directions for the approximation of reachable sets for hybrid systems. In: Moreno-Díaz, R., Pichler, F., Quesada-Arencibia, A. (eds.) EUROCAST 2011, Part I. LNCS, vol. 6927, pp. 535–542. Springer, Heidelberg (2012). https://doi.org/10.1007/978-3-642-27549-4_69
6. Clarisó, R., Cortadella, J.: The octahedron abstract domain. In: Giacobazzi, R. (ed.) SAS 2004. LNCS, vol. 3148, pp. 312–327. Springer, Heidelberg (2004). https://doi.org/10.1007/978-3-540-27864-1_23

7. Dang, T., Dreossi, T., Piazza, C.: Parameter synthesis using parallelotopic enclosure and applications to epidemic models. In: Maler, O., Halász, Á., Dang, T., Piazza, C. (eds.) HSB 2014. LNCS, vol. 7699, pp. 67–82. Springer, Cham (2015). https://doi.org/10.1007/978-3-319-27656-4_4

8. Dang, T., Gawlitza, T.M.: Template-based unbounded time verification of affine hybrid automata. In: Yang, H. (ed.) APLAS 2011. LNCS, vol. 7078, pp. 34–49. Springer, Heidelberg (2011). https://doi.org/10.1007/978-3-642-25318-8_6

9. Dang, T., Salinas, D.: Image computation for polynomial dynamical systems using the Bernstein expansion. In: Bouajjani, A., Maler, O. (eds.) CAV 2009. LNCS, vol. 5643, pp. 219–232. Springer, Heidelberg (2009). https://doi.org/10.1007/978-3-642-02658-4_19

10. Dang, T., Testylier, R.: Reachability analysis for polynomial dynamical systems using the Bernstein expansion. Reliab. Comput. **17**(2), 128–152 (2012)

11. Devonport, A., Khaled, M., Arcak, M., Zamani, M.: PIRK: scalable interval reachability analysis for high-dimensional nonlinear systems. In: Lahiri, S.K., Wang, C. (eds.) CAV 2020. LNCS, vol. 12224, pp. 556–568. Springer, Cham (2020). https://doi.org/10.1007/978-3-030-53288-8_27

12. Dreossi, T.: Sapo: reachability computation and parameter synthesis of polynomial dynamical systems. In Proceedings of the 20th International Conference on Hybrid Systems: Computation and Control, pp. 29–34 (2017)

13. Dreossi, T., Dang, T., Piazza, C.: Parallelotope bundles for polynomial reachability. In: Proceedings of the 19th International Conference on Hybrid Systems: Computation and Control, pages 297–306 (2016)

14. Dreossi, T., Dang, T., Piazza, C.: Reachability computation for polynomial dynamical systems. Formal Methods Syst. Des. **50**(1), 1–38 (2017)

15. Duggirala, P.S., Viswanathan, M.: Parsimonious, simulation based verification of linear systems. In: Chaudhuri, S., Farzan, A. (eds.) CAV 2016, Part I. LNCS, vol. 9779, pp. 477–494. Springer, Cham (2016). https://doi.org/10.1007/978-3-319-41528-4_26

16. FitzHugh, R.: Impulses and physiological states in theoretical models of nerve membrane. Biophys. J. **1**(6), 445–466 (1961)

17. Garloff, J.: The Bernstein expansion and its applications. J. Am. Rom. Acad. **25**, 27 (2003)

18. Girard, A.: Reachability of uncertain linear systems using zonotopes. In: Morari, M., Thiele, L. (eds.) HSCC 2005. LNCS, vol. 3414, pp. 291–305. Springer, Heidelberg (2005). https://doi.org/10.1007/978-3-540-31954-2_19

19. Gronski, J., Sassi, M.-A.B., Becker, S., Sankaranarayanan, S.: Template polyhedra and bilinear optimization. Formal Methods Syst. Des. **54**(1), 27–63 (2019). https://doi.org/10.1007/s10703-018-0323-1

20. Huang, C., Fan, J., Li, W., Chen, X., Zhu, Q.: ReachNN: reachability analysis of neural-network controlled systems. ACM Trans. Embed. Comput. Syst. (TECS) **18**(5s), 1–22 (2019)

21. Kim, E., Duggirala, P.S.: Kaa: a python implementation of reachable set computation using Bernstein polynomials. EPiC Ser. Comput. **74**, 184–196 (2020)

22. Muñoz, C., Narkawicz, A.: Formalization of Bernstein polynomials and applications to global optimization. J. Autom. Reason. **51**(2), 151–196 (2013)

23. Nataraj, P.S., Arounassalame, M.: A new subdivision algorithm for the Bernstein polynomial approach to global optimization. Int. J. Autom. Comput. **4**(4), 342–352 (2007). https://doi.org/10.1007/s11633-007-0342-7

24. Nataray, P., Kotecha, K.: An algorithm for global optimization using the Taylor-Bernstein form as inclusion function. J. Glob. Optim. **24**(4), 417–436 (2002). https://doi.org/10.1023/A:1021296315884
25. National Supermodel Committee. Indian Supermodel for COVID-19 Pandemic
26. Sankaranarayanan, S., Dang, T., Ivančić, F.: Symbolic model checking of hybrid systems using template polyhedra. In: Ramakrishnan, C.R., Rehof, J. (eds.) TACAS 2008. LNCS, vol. 4963, pp. 188–202. Springer, Heidelberg (2008). https://doi.org/10.1007/978-3-540-78800-3_14
27. Ben Sassi, M.A., Testylier, R., Dang, T., Girard, A.: Reachability analysis of polynomial systems using linear programming relaxations. In: Chakraborty, S., Mukund, M. (eds.) ATVA 2012. LNCS, pp. 137–151. Springer, Heidelberg (2012). https://doi.org/10.1007/978-3-642-33386-6_12
28. Seladji, Y.: Finding relevant templates via the principal component analysis. In: Bouajjani, A., Monniaux, D. (eds.) VMCAI 2017. LNCS, vol. 10145, pp. 483–499. Springer, Cham (2017). https://doi.org/10.1007/978-3-319-52234-0_26
29. Smith, A.P.: Fast construction of constant bound functions for sparse polynomials. J. Glob. Optim. **43**(2–3), 445–458 (2009). https://doi.org/10.1007/s10898-007-9195-4
30. Stursberg, O., Krogh, B.H.: Efficient representation and computation of reachable sets for hybrid systems. In: Maler, O., Pnueli, A. (eds.) HSCC 2003. LNCS, vol. 2623, pp. 482–497. Springer, Heidelberg (2003). https://doi.org/10.1007/3-540-36580-X_35

Closing the Gap Between Discrete Abstractions and Continuous Control: Completeness via Robustness and Controllability

Jun Liu[✉][iD]

University of Waterloo, Waterloo, ON N2L 3G1, Canada
j.liu@uwaterloo.ca

Abstract. A central theoretical question surrounding abstraction-based control of continuous nonlinear systems is whether one can decide through algorithmic procedures the existence of a controller to render the system to satisfy a given specification (e.g., safety, reachability, or more generally a temporal logic formula). Known algorithms are mostly sound but not complete in the sense that they return a correct controller upon termination, but do not offer guarantees of finding a controller if one exists. Completeness of abstraction-based nonlinear control in the general setting, therefore, remains an open question. This paper investigates this theoretical question and presents two sets of main results. First, we prove that sampled-data control of nonlinear systems with temporal logic specifications is robustly decidable in the sense that, given a continuous-time nonlinear control system and a temporal logic formula, one can algorithmically decide whether there exists a robust sampled-data control strategy to realize this specification when the right-hand side of the system is slightly perturbed by a small disturbance. Second, we show that under the assumption of local nonlinear controllability of the nominal system around an arbitrary trajectory that realizes a given specification, we can always construct a (robust) sampled-data control strategy via a sufficiently fine discrete abstraction. In a sense, this shows that temporal logic control for controllable nonlinear systems is decidable.

Keywords: Nonlinear systems · Temporal logic · Control synthesis · Completeness · Robustness · Controllability

1 Introduction

The control of dynamical systems to satisfy formal specifications (e.g., temporal logics) has received considerable attention in the past decade [4,30]. This is partially motivated by the increasing demand of autonomous decision making by

Supported by the Natural Sciences and Engineering Research Council of Canada, the Canada Research Chairs Program, and the Ontario Early Researcher Award Program. The paper has an extended version with Appendix available at [19].

© Springer Nature Switzerland AG 2021
C. Dima and M. Shirmohammadi (Eds.): FORMATS 2021, LNCS 12860, pp. 67–83, 2021.
https://doi.org/10.1007/978-3-030-85037-1_5

physical systems (e.g., mobile robots) in uncertain environments to achieve more complex tasks [6,10,12]. Many system relations have been proposed as abstractions of nonlinear systems [22,24,27,28,32]. Such abstractions are desirable for several reasons. First, they are sound in the sense that they can be used to design provably correct controllers with respect to a given formal specification. Second, they are often finite (e.g., finite transition systems) and the original control design problem over an infinite state space can be effectively solved as a search problem over a finite structure. Third, the construction of these abstractions can be automated with the aid of a computer.

One of the main drawbacks of abstraction-based approaches is their computational cost, which is often incurred when a finer and finer abstraction is used in the hope of finding a controller when a coarser abstraction fails to yield one. However, without theoretical guarantees on completeness, i.e., if a control strategy exists, then it can be found by an abstraction-based approach, such computational efforts can be futile. This motivates the research in this paper.

Related Work. We review several results in the literature that are most relevant to the result presented in this paper. In [31], it is shown that bisimilar (equivalent) symbolic models exist for controllable discrete-time linear systems and, as a result, temporal logic control for discrete-time controllable linear systems is decidable. For nonlinear systems, the authors of [27] showed that approximately bisimilar models can be constructed for incrementally stable systems [1]. The assumption of incremental stability essentially allows one to construct a deterministic transition system that can approximate a sampled-data representation of the original nonlinear system to any degree of precision. For nonlinear systems without the incremental stability assumption, the authors of [32] showed that symbolic models that approximately alternatingly simulate the sampled-data representation of a general nonlinear control system can be constructed. Because a sampled-data representation is used in [27,32], inter-sample behaviours are not considered in such approximations. The authors of [25] (see also [20,24]) considered partition-based transition systems as over-approximations of nonlinear systems for synthesizing controllers for temporal logic specifications. Because no time-discretization is used, correctness guarantee is proved for the continuous-time trajectories. In [21,22], the authors proposed a notion of robust abstractions of continuous-time nonlinear systems using grid-based approximations. A salient feature of such abstractions is that they under-approximate the control space so that all controls used by the abstractions can be implemented by the original system. At the same time, they over-approximate the reachable sets of the original system under a control so that correctness can be guaranteed (behaviours of the original system are included by the behaviours of the abstract system). In addition, the work in [21,22] also tackled the problem of synthesizing robust controllers by introducing robustness margins in the abstractions and reasoned inter-sampling behaviours so that correctness is proved in continuous-time semantics of linear temporal logic. In [28], the authors proposed feedback refinement relations that can be used for control design for systems modelled by difference inclusions. This system relation has the same feature of under-approximating the control space, while over-approximating the reachable sets of the original system.

Nonetheless, all the above mentioned abstraction techniques are sound but not complete, with the exception of [27,31], where additional assumptions on system dynamics are needed (controllable linear and incrementally stable, respectively). In [18], a notion of completeness for abstractions of discrete-time nonlinear systems is proved using a robustness argument (termed as robust completeness). It is shown that with sufficient computational sources, one can construct a finite transition system that robustly abstracts a discrete-time nonlinear system and, at the same time, is robustly abstracted by a slightly perturbed version of the same system. We also note that in [13–17] robust completeness is achieved for invariance and reachability type specifications and beyond using interval analysis for direct control synthesis on the continuous state space without first constructing abstractions. All these results focus on discrete-time control systems. The decidability via robustness for *continuous-time* control systems remains an *open* question.

Main Contributions. In this paper, motivated by the above open question, we establish two sets of theoretical results on abstraction-based control of continuous-time nonlinear systems. First, we prove that robustly complete abstractions of continuous-time control systems exist under a mild assumption (i.e., local Lipschitz continuity) on system dynamics and use this to show decidability of robust realization of temporal logic formulas for continuous-time nonlinear systems by using a sampled-data control strategy. Furthermore, we show that under a suitable assumption on local controllability of the nominal system around a satisfying trajectory, it is guaranteed that a sufficiently fine discrete abstraction will return a (robust) controller. This, in a sense, shows that temporal logic control for controllable nonlinear systems is decidable.

2   Problem Formulation

2.1   Continuous-Time Control System

Consider a *continuous-time nonlinear control system* of the form:

$$x' = f(x, u), \tag{1}$$

where $x \in X \subseteq \mathbb{R}^n$ is the system state and $u \in U \subseteq \mathbb{R}^m$ is the control input. We assume that $f : \mathbb{R}^n \times \mathbb{R}^m \to \mathbb{R}^n$ satisfies the basic regularity assumptions (e.g., local Lipschitz continuity) such that, given any sufficiently regular control input signal and any initial condition, there exists a unique local solution to (1).

A *trajectory* of (1) is a pair $(\mathbf{x}, \mathbf{u})$, where $\mathbf{x} : \mathbb{R}^+ \to X$ is a state trajectory, $\mathbf{u} : \mathbb{R}^+ \to U$ is an input trajectory, and $(\mathbf{x}, \mathbf{u})$ satisfies (1) in the sense that $\mathbf{x}'(t) = f(\mathbf{x}(t), \mathbf{u}(t))$ for all $t \geq 0$.

A *(sampled-data) control strategy* with sampling period $\tau > 0$ for (1) is a partial function of the form:

$$\sigma(x_0, \cdots, x_i) = u_i \in U, \ \forall i = 0, 1, 2, \cdots, \tag{2}$$

where $x_0, \cdots, x_i$ is a finite sequence of sampled states taken at sampling times $t_0 = 0, \cdots, t_i$ and u_i is a constant control input. The sampling times t_0, t_1, t_2, $\cdots$ satisfy $t_{i+1} - t_i = \tau$ for all $i \geq 0$, where $\tau > 0$ is the sampling period that represents the duration for which the constant u_i is applied to the system.

A σ-*controlled trajectory* is a trajectory $(\mathbf{x}, \mathbf{u})$ resulting from executing the control strategy σ, where $\mathbf{u}$ is defined by $\mathbf{u}(t) = u_i$ for $t \in [t_i, t_{i+1})$, where $t_i = i\tau$ and u_i is determined by (2).

Given a positive integer N, a control strategy σ is said to have *dwell time* N, if each control input u_i is used for a multiple of N times, that is, if $i = mN$ for some integer m, then

$$u_i = u_{i+1} = \cdots = u_{i+N-1}. \tag{3}$$

This can be easily encoded by a control strategy with a simple counter. This seemingly peculiar definition plays a role later on in proving completeness for any fixed, but not necessarily small, sampling period.

2.2 δ-perturbed Control System

Given a scalar $\delta \geq 0$, a δ-*perturbation* of the continuous-time nonlinear control system (1) is the differential inclusion

$$x' \in f(x, u) + \delta\mathbb{B}, \tag{4}$$

where $f(x, u) + \delta\mathbb{B}$ denotes the unit closed ball (in infinity norm) centered at $f(x, u)$. A *trajectory* of (4) is a pair $(\mathbf{x}, \mathbf{u})$, where $\mathbf{x} : \mathbb{R}^+ \to X$ is a state trajectory, $\mathbf{u} : \mathbb{R}^+ \to U$ is an input trajectory, and $(\mathbf{x}, \mathbf{u})$ satisfies (4) in the sense that $\mathbf{x}'(t) \in f(\mathbf{x}(t), \mathbf{u}(t)) + \delta\mathbb{B}$ for all $t \geq 0$.

We call system (1) the nominal system and denote it by $\mathcal{S}$. The δ-perturbation of $\mathcal{S}$ defined by (4) is denoted by $\mathcal{S}_\delta$. Apparently, $\mathcal{S}_0$ is exactly $\mathcal{S}$.

2.3 Linear Temporal Logic and Labelling Function

We consider linear-time properties described by linear temporal logic (LTL) [26]. In particular, we consider LTL without the next operator (LTL$_{\backslash \bigcirc}$) and we refer the readers to [3] (or the Appendix of [19]) for its syntax and semantics. We also assume that the formulas are written in a positive form, where negations of atomic propositions are replaced with new atomic propositions (for details, see the Appendix of the extended version [19]).

In the following, we need to reason about satisfaction of LTL formulas by continuous-time trajectories and by discrete-time sequences, and in particular, the implication between the two. For this purpose, we need to introduce the notion of an ε-strengthening of a labelling function [18]. For $\varepsilon > 0$, a labelling function $\mathcal{L}_\varepsilon : \mathbb{R}^n \to 2^\Pi$ is said to be the ε-*strengthening* of another labelling function $\mathcal{L} : \mathbb{R}^n \to 2^\Pi$, if $\pi \in \mathcal{L}_\varepsilon(x)$ *if and only if* $\pi \in \mathcal{L}(y)$ for all $y \in x + \varepsilon\mathbb{B}$. The Appendix includes an illustration of strengthening labelling functions.

The following proposition (proved in the Appendix) relates different strengthening of labelling functions, which is used later in the proof of the main theorems.

Proposition 1. *Given $\varepsilon_2 \geq \varepsilon_1 \geq 0$, let $\mathcal{L}_{\varepsilon_1}$ be the ε_1-strengthening of a labelling function $\mathcal{L}: \mathbb{R}^n \to 2^\Pi$, $(\mathcal{L}_{\varepsilon_1})_{\varepsilon_2}$ be the ε_2-strengthening of $\mathcal{L}_{\varepsilon_1}$, and $\mathcal{L}_{\varepsilon_1 + \varepsilon_2}$ be the $(\varepsilon_1 + \varepsilon_2)$-strengthening of $\mathcal{L}$. Then $\mathcal{L}_{\varepsilon_1 + \varepsilon_2}(x) \subseteq (\mathcal{L}_{\varepsilon_1})_{\varepsilon_2}(x)$ for all $x \in \mathbb{R}^n$.*

2.4   Robust Decidability of Sampled-Data Control

Given a temporal logic formula φ together with a labelling function $\mathcal{L}$, we would like to design a sampled-data control strategy such that the resulting continuous-time state trajectories of $\mathcal{S}_\delta$ satisfy $(\varphi, \mathcal{L})$. If such a control strategy exists, we say $(\varphi, \mathcal{L})$ is *realizable* for $\mathcal{S}_\delta$ (by a sampled-data control strategy).

We formulate the robust decidability problem for system (1) as follows.

Problem 1 (Robust decidability). Given a temporal logic formula φ, a labelling function $\mathcal{L}$, a sampling period $T > 0$, numbers $\delta_2 > \delta_1 \geq 0$ and $\varepsilon > 0$, decide which one of the following is true:

- There exists (and one can algorithmically construct) a sampled-data control strategy with sampling period T for $\mathcal{S}_{\delta_1}$ to realize the specification $(\varphi, \mathcal{L})$;
- There does not exist a sampled-data control strategy with sampling period T for $\mathcal{S}_{\delta_2}$ to realize the specification $(\varphi, \mathcal{L}_\varepsilon)$.

We shall answer this question under the following assumption.

Assumption 1. *The sets X and U are compact and f is locally Lipschitz in both x and u. Let L be the Lipschitz constant (in infinity norm) of f w.r.t. both x and u on $X \times U$.*

3   Transition Systems and Finite Abstractions

In this section, we define finite abstractions of $\mathcal{S}_\delta$ that can be used to synthesize sampled-data control strategies for $\mathcal{S}_\delta$. Due to space limit, the proofs of the preliminary results (Propositions 2–4) are relegated to the Appendix in [19].

3.1   Transition Systems

Definition 1. A *transition system* is a tuple $\mathcal{T} = (Q, A, R)$, where

- Q is the set of states and A is the set of actions;
- $R \subseteq Q \times A \times Q$ is the transition relation.

For each action $a \in A$ and $q \in Q$, we define the a-successor of q by

$$\text{Post}_\mathcal{T}(q, a) = \{q' : q' \in Q \text{ s.t. } (q, a, q') \in R\}.$$

To simplify the presentation, we assume in this paper that, for the transition systems under consideration, every action is admissible for every state in the sense that $\text{Post}_\mathcal{T}(q, a) \neq \emptyset$ for all $q \in Q$ and all $a \in A$.

An *execution* of T is an infinite alternating sequence of states and actions $\rho = q_0, a_0, q_1, a_1, q_2, a_2, \cdots$, where q_0 is some initial state and $(q_i, a_i, q_{i+1}) \in R$ for all $i \geq 0$. The *path* resulting from the execution ρ above is the sequence $\text{Path}(\rho) = q_0, q_1, q_2 \cdots$. A *control strategy* κ for a transition system T is a partial function $\kappa : (q_0, q_1, \cdots, q_i) \mapsto a_i$ that maps the state history to the next action. An κ-*controlled execution* of a transition system T is an execution of T, where for each $i \geq 0$, the action a_i is chosen according to the control strategy κ; κ-controlled paths are defined in a similar fashion. A dwell-time control strategy is defined in the same way as that for $\mathcal{S}_\delta$ in (3).

3.2   Transition Systems for Sampled-Data Control Systems

With a fixed sampling period $\tau > 0$, we define the transition system representation of $\mathcal{S}_\delta$ as follows.

Definition 2. *The system $\mathcal{S}_\delta$ with a sampling period $\tau > 0$ can be interpreted as a transition system $T_{\delta,\tau} = (Q, A, R)$, by defining*

- *$Q = X$ and $A = U$;*
- *$(x_0, u, x_1) \in R$ if and only if there exists a trajectory $\mathbf{x} : [0, \tau] \to X$ such that $x(0) = x_0$, $x_1 = x(\tau)$, and $\mathbf{x}'(s) \in f(\mathbf{x}(s), u) + \delta \mathbb{B}$ for all $s \in [0, \tau]$.*

If $\delta = 0$, we simply write $T_{\delta,\tau}$ as T_τ.

We say that an execution ρ of $T_{\delta,\tau}$ satisfies an $\text{LTL}_{\backslash \bigcirc}$ formula φ with a labelling function $\mathcal{L}$, written as $\rho \vDash (\varphi, \mathcal{L})$, if and only if $\text{Path}(\rho) \vDash (\varphi, \mathcal{L})$. For a control strategy κ for $T_{\delta,\tau}$, if all κ-controlled executions of $T_{\delta,\tau}$ satisfy φ with respect to L, we write $(T_{\delta,\tau}, \kappa) \vDash (\varphi, \mathcal{L})$. If such a control strategy κ exists, we say that $(\varphi, \mathcal{L})$ is *realizable* for $T_{\delta,\tau}$.

The following proposition relates realizability of a temporal logic formula φ on a continuous-time control system with sampled-data control strategies of different sampling periods.

Proposition 2. *Let φ be a temporal logic formula over Π and $\mathcal{L} : X \to 2^\Pi$ be a labelling function. Suppose that $T = N\tau$, where N is a positive integer.*

1. *If $(\varphi, \mathcal{L})$ is realizable for $\mathcal{S}_\delta$ with a sampled-data control strategy with sampling period T, then $(\varphi, \mathcal{L})$ is realizable for $\mathcal{S}_\delta$ with a sampled-data control strategy with sampling period τ and dwell time N.*
2. *Conversely, if $(\varphi, \mathcal{L})$ is realizable for $\mathcal{S}_\delta$ with a sampled-data control strategy with sampling period τ and dwell time N, then $(\varphi, \mathcal{L})$ is realizable for $\mathcal{S}_\delta$ with a sampled-data control strategy with sampling period T.*

By the assumption that X and U are compact sets, we can define $M = \max_{x \in X, \, u \in U} |f(x, u)|$, where $|\cdot|$ is the infinity norm (throughout the paper). The following proposition relates realizability of a temporal logic formula φ on a sampled-data transition system $(T_{\delta,\tau})$ and a continuous-time system $(\mathcal{S}_\delta)$. The main technical part is to show how discrete-time and continuous-time semantics of temporal logic formulas imply each other.

Proposition 3 (Inter-sample correctness). *Let φ be a temporal logic formula over Π. Let $\mathcal{L} : X \rightarrow 2^{\Pi}$ be a labelling function and $\mathcal{L}_\varepsilon$ be an ε-strengthening of $\mathcal{L}$. Suppose that $\varepsilon \geq (M + \delta)\tau/2$.*

1. *If $(\varphi, \mathcal{L}_\varepsilon)$ is realizable for $\mathcal{T}_{\delta,\tau}$ with a dwell-time N control strategy, then $(\varphi, \mathcal{L})$ is realizable for $\mathcal{S}_\delta$ with a sampled-data control strategy with sampling period τ and dwell-time N.*
2. *Conversely, if $(\varphi, \mathcal{L}_\varepsilon)$ is realizable for $\mathcal{S}_\delta$ with a sampled-data control strategy with sampling period τ and dwell-time N, then $(\varphi, \mathcal{L})$ is realizable for $\mathcal{T}_{\delta,\tau}$ with a dwell-time N control strategy.*

3.3 Abstraction

We define control abstraction of transition system that preserves realizability of temporal logic specifications.

Definition 3. Given two transition systems $\mathcal{T}_i = (Q_i, A_i, R_i)$, $i = 1, 2$, a relation $\alpha \subseteq Q_1 \times Q_2$ is said to be an *abstraction* from $\mathcal{T}_1$ to $\mathcal{T}_2$, if the following conditions are satisfied:

(i) for all $q_1 \in Q_1$, there exists $q_2 \in Q_2$ such that $(q_1, q_2) \in \alpha$ (i.e., $\alpha(q_1) \neq \emptyset$);
(ii) for $a_2 \in A_2$, there exists $a_1 \in A_1$ such that, for all $q_2 \in Q_2$ and $q_1 \in \alpha^{-1}(q_2)$,

$$\alpha(\mathrm{Post}_{\mathcal{T}_1}(q_1, a_1)) \subseteq \mathrm{Post}_{\mathcal{T}_2}(q_2, a_2). \tag{5}$$

If such a relation α exists, we say that $\mathcal{T}_2$ *abstracts* $\mathcal{T}_1$ and write $\mathcal{T}_1 \preceq_\alpha \mathcal{T}_2$ or simply $\mathcal{T}_1 \preceq \mathcal{T}_2$. When both Q_1 and Q_2 are subsets of $\mathbb{R}^n$, we say that α is of granularity $\eta > 0$, if for every $q_2 \in Q_2$, $\alpha^{-1}(q_2) \subseteq q_2 + \eta\mathbb{B}$.

The following proposition shows that the abstraction relation defined above is sound in the sense of preserving realization of temporal logic specifications.

Proposition 4 (Soundness). *Consider transition systems $\mathcal{T}_1 = (Q_1, A_1, R_1)$ and $\mathcal{T}_2 = (Q_2, A_2, R_2)$ such that $\mathcal{T}_1 \preceq_\alpha \mathcal{T}_2$. Suppose that Q_1 and Q_2 are subsets of $X \subseteq \mathbb{R}^n$. Let $\mathcal{L} : X \rightarrow 2^{\Pi}$ be a labelling function. Let N be a positive integer.*

- *Suppose that α is proposition preserving with respect to L, defined as $L(q_2) \subseteq L(q_1)$ for all $(q_1, q_2) \in \alpha$. Then $(\varphi, \mathcal{L})$ is realizable for $\mathcal{T}_2$ implies that $(\varphi, \mathcal{L})$ is realizable for $\mathcal{T}_1$.*
- *Suppose that α is of granularity $\eta > 0$ and let $\mathcal{L}_\eta$ denote an η-strengthening of $\mathcal{L}$. Then $(\varphi, \mathcal{L}_\eta)$ is realizable for $\mathcal{T}_2$ implies that $(\varphi, \mathcal{L})$ is realizable for $\mathcal{T}_1$.*

Moreover, a dwell-time N strategy for $\mathcal{T}_2$ can be implemented by a dwell-time N strategy for $\mathcal{T}_1$.

4 Robustly Complete Abstraction and Robust Decidability

In this section, we present the main results on robustly complete abstractions and robust decidability of continuous-time control via discrete abstractions.

4.1 Robustly Complete Abstraction

The key technical result for proving robustly decidability of sampled-data control for nonlinear system is the following result on the possibility of constructing an arbitrarily accurate abstraction of the nonlinear system in the sense that for any $\delta_2 > \delta_1 \geq 0$, one can find a finite transition system $\mathcal{T}$ such that $\mathcal{T}$ abstracts $\mathcal{S}_{\delta_1}$ while $\mathcal{S}_{\delta_2}$ abstracts $\mathcal{T}$. Hence, realizability of a specification by $\mathcal{S}_{\delta_2}$ would imply realizability of the same specification by $\mathcal{S}_{\delta_1}$.

Theorem 1 (Robust completeness). *Given any $\delta_2 > \delta_1 \geq 0$, we can choose $\tau > 0$ and compute a finite transition system $\mathcal{T}$ such that $\mathcal{T}_{\delta_1,\tau} \preceq \mathcal{T} \preceq \mathcal{T}_{\delta_2,\tau}$.*

Proof. We construct $\mathcal{T} = (Q, A, R)$ as follows. Let $\eta > 0$ and $\mu > 0$ be parameters to be chosen. Let Q consist of the centers of the grid cells in $[\mathbb{R}^n]_\eta$ that have a non-empty intersection with X. Let A consist of the centers of the grid cells in $[\mathbb{R}^m]_\mu$ that have a non-empty intersection with U. Because U and X are compact sets, Q and A are both finite. We define a relation $\alpha \subseteq X \times Q$ by $(x, q) \in \alpha$ if and only if $|x - q| \leq \frac{\eta}{2}$. Clearly, α^{-1} is a relation on $Q \times X$. Define $R \subseteq (Q, A, Q)$ by $(q, a, q_1) \in R$ if and only if

$$|q_1 - (q + \tau f(q,a))| \leq \frac{\eta}{2} + \frac{\eta}{2}e^{L\tau} + (\frac{\delta_1}{L} + \frac{\mu}{2})(e^{L\tau} - 1) + \frac{M(e^{L\tau} - L\tau - 1)}{L}. \tag{6}$$

We show that, if η, μ, and τ are chosen sufficiently small, we have $\mathcal{T}_{\delta_1,\tau} \preceq_\alpha \mathcal{T} \preceq_{\alpha^{-1}} \mathcal{T}_{\delta_2,\tau}$. Condition (i) in Definition 3 is clearly satisfied by both α and α^{-1}.

We verify that condition (ii) holds for $\mathcal{T}_{\delta_1,\tau} \preceq_\alpha \mathcal{T}$, that is, for $q \in Q$ and $a \in A$, there exists $u \in U$ such that

$$\alpha(\text{Post}_{\mathcal{T}_{\delta_1,\tau}}(x, u)) \subseteq \text{Post}_\mathcal{T}(q, a); \tag{7}$$

for all $x \in \alpha^{-1}(q)$. Pick $u \in U$ with $|u - a| \leq \frac{\mu}{2}$. Given $x_1 \in \text{Post}_{\mathcal{T}_{\delta_1,\tau}}(x, u)$, there exists a trajectory $\mathbf{x} : [0, \tau] \to X$ such that $\mathbf{x}(0) = x$, $\mathbf{x}(\tau) = x_1$, and $\mathbf{x}'(s) \in f(\mathbf{x}(s), u) + \delta_1 \mathbb{B}$ for all $s \in [0, \tau]$. Define $\mathbf{x}_\tau(t) = q + tf(q, a)$ for $t \in [0, \tau]$. We have

$$|\mathbf{x}'(t) - \mathbf{x}_\tau'(t)| \leq |f(\mathbf{x}(t), u) - f(q, a)| + \delta_1$$
$$\leq |f(\mathbf{x}(t), u) - f(\mathbf{x}_\tau(t), u)| + |f(\mathbf{x}_\tau(t), u) - f(q, u)| + |f(q, u) - f(q, a)| + \delta_1$$
$$\leq L|\mathbf{x}(t) - \mathbf{x}_\tau(t)| + L|\mathbf{x}_\tau(t) - q| + L|u - a| + \delta_1$$
$$\leq L|\mathbf{x}(t) - \mathbf{x}_\tau(t)| + LMt + \frac{L\mu}{2} + \delta_1, \quad t \in [0, \tau]. \tag{8}$$

By Gronwall's inequality (see, e.g., [2]), we have

$$|x_1 - (q + \tau f(q, u))| = |\mathbf{x}(\tau) - \mathbf{x}_\tau(\tau)|$$
$$\leq |x - q| e^{L\tau} + \int_0^\tau (LMs + \frac{L\mu}{2} + \delta_1)e^{L(\tau - s)}ds$$
$$\leq \frac{\eta}{2}e^{L\tau} + (\frac{\delta_1}{L} + \frac{\mu}{2})(e^{L\tau} - 1) + \frac{M(e^{L\tau} - L\tau - 1)}{L}.$$

By (6), this shows $\alpha(x_1) \subseteq \text{Post}_{\mathcal{T}}(q, a)$. Hence (7) holds.

We next verify that condition (ii) holds for $\mathcal{T} \preceq_{\alpha^{-1}} \mathcal{T}_{\delta_2, \tau}$, that is, for $x \in X$ and $u \in U$, there exists $a \in A$ such that

$$\alpha^{-1}(\text{Post}_{\mathcal{T}}(q, a)) \subseteq \text{Post}_{\mathcal{T}_{\delta_2, \tau}}(x, u); \tag{9}$$

for all $q \in \alpha(x)$. Pick a be the center of the grid cell in $[\mathbb{R}^m]_\mu$ that contains u. Given $y_1 \in \alpha^{-1}(\text{Post}_{\mathcal{T}}(q, a))$, there exists $q_1 \in \text{Post}_{\mathcal{T}}(q, a)$ such that $|y_1 - q_1| \leq \frac{\eta}{2}$. By the definition of $\text{Post}_{\mathcal{T}}(q, a)$, we have

$$|q_1 - (q + \tau f(q, a))| \leq \frac{\eta}{2} + \frac{\eta}{2} e^{L\tau} + (\frac{\delta_1}{L} + \frac{\mu}{2})(e^{L\tau} - 1) + \frac{M(e^{L\tau} - L\tau - 1)}{L}.$$

Consider the trajectory $\mathbf{x} : [0, \tau] \to X$ such that $\mathbf{x}(0) = x$, $\mathbf{x}(\tau) = x_1$, and $\mathbf{x}'(s) \in f(\mathbf{x}(s), u)$. By a similar argument as in (8), we can show

$$|x_1 - (q + \tau f(q, a))| \leq \frac{\eta}{2} e^{L\tau} + \frac{\mu}{2}(e^{L\tau} - 1) + \frac{M(e^{L\tau} - L\tau - 1)}{L}.$$

Hence, by the triangle inequality,

$$|y_1 - x_1| \leq \eta + \eta e^{L\tau} + (\frac{\delta_1}{L} + \mu)(e^{L\tau} - 1) + \frac{2M(e^{L\tau} - L\tau - 1)}{L} \tag{10}$$

Define

$$\mathbf{z}(\theta) = \mathbf{x}(\theta) + \frac{\theta}{\tau}(y_1 - x_1), \quad \theta \in [0, \tau].$$

Then $\mathbf{z}(0) = \mathbf{x}(0) = x$ and $\mathbf{z}(\tau) = y_1$, and

$$\mathbf{z}'(\theta) \in f(\mathbf{x}(\theta), u) + \frac{1}{\tau}(y_1 - x_1). \tag{11}$$

Note that

$$|\mathbf{z}(\theta) - \mathbf{x}(\theta)| = |\frac{\theta}{\tau}[y_1 - x_1]| \leq |y_1 - x_1|, \quad \theta \in [0, \tau]. \tag{12}$$

Since $0 \leq \delta_1 < \delta_2$, we can choose τ, μ, η sufficiently small such that

$$[\eta + \eta e^{L\tau} + (\frac{\delta_1}{L} + \mu)(e^{L\tau} - 1) + \frac{2M(e^{L\tau} - L\tau - 1)}{L}][L + \frac{1}{\tau}] < \delta_2. \tag{13}$$

To see this is possible, choose, e.g., $\eta = \tau^2$ and $\mu = \tau$, and note that the limit of the left-hand side as $\tau \to 0$ is given by $\lim_{\tau \to 0} \delta_1 \frac{e^{L\tau} - 1}{L\tau} = \delta_1$. It follows from (10)–(13) and Lipschitz continuity of f that $\mathbf{z}'(\theta) \in f(\mathbf{z}(\theta), u) + \delta_2 B$. Hence $y_1 \in \text{Post}_{\mathcal{T}_{\delta_2, \tau}}(x, u)$ and (9) holds. $\square$

Remark 1. In the proof, we choose the simplest possible validated bounds on a one-step reachable set, i.e., a forward Euler scheme with an error bound. This suffices to prove the required convergence to show approximate completeness. With the template provided by the proof of Theorem 1, one can in fact use any accurate over-approximation of the one-step reachable set for $\mathcal{S}_{\delta_1}$ to replace (6) for defining the transitions in $\mathcal{T}$ and then show that this over-approximation is contained in the actual one-step reachable set of $\mathcal{S}_{\delta_2}$.

Remark 2. Theorem 1 (as well as the problem formulation in the paper) only considers sampled-data control strategies. Later in Sect. 4.3, we also discuss how to approximate arbitrary measurable control signals under the L^1 norm, which plays a role later in proving a notion of completeness via controllability.

4.2   Robust Decidability

The following theorem is an immediate consequence of Theorem 1 and states that sampled-data control for nonlinear system is robustly decidable.

Theorem 2 (Robust decidability). *Given a temporal logic specification φ, a sampling period $T > 0$, any $\delta_2 > \delta_1 \geq 0$, and any $\varepsilon > 0$. Let $\mathcal{L} : X \to 2^\Pi$ be a labelling function and $\mathcal{L}_\varepsilon$ be an ε-strengthening of $\mathcal{L}$. Then there exists a decision procedure that determines which one of the following holds:*

- *there exists (and one can algorithmically construct) a sampled-data control strategy with sampling period T such that $(\varphi, \mathcal{L})$ is realizable for $\mathcal{S}_{\delta_1}$; or*
- *$(\varphi, \mathcal{L}_\varepsilon)$ is not realizable for $\mathcal{S}_{\delta_2}$ with a sampled-data control strategy with sampling period T.*

Proof. Suppose that $(\varphi, \mathcal{L}_\varepsilon)$ is realizable for $\mathcal{S}_{\delta_2}$ with a sampled-data control strategy with sampling period T. Let N be a positive integer and $\tau = \frac{T}{N}$. Let $\varepsilon_1 = \frac{(M+\delta_1)\tau}{2}$ and $\varepsilon_2 = \frac{(M+\delta_2)\tau}{2}$. Choose τ sufficiently small such that

$$\frac{(2M + \delta_1 + \delta_2)\tau}{2} = \varepsilon_1 + \varepsilon_2 \leq \varepsilon. \tag{14}$$

Let $\mathcal{L}_{\varepsilon_1}$ be the ε_1-strengthening of $\mathcal{L}$ and $(\mathcal{L}_{\varepsilon_1})_{\varepsilon_2}$ denote the ε_2-strengthening of $\mathcal{L}_{\varepsilon_1}$. Let $\mathcal{L}_{\varepsilon_1+\varepsilon_2}$ be the $(\varepsilon_1+\varepsilon_2)$-strengthening of $\mathcal{L}$. By the definition of strengthening a labeling function and Proposition 1, we have $\mathcal{L}_\varepsilon(x) \subseteq \mathcal{L}_{\varepsilon_1+\varepsilon_2}(x) \subseteq (\mathcal{L}_{\varepsilon_1})_{\varepsilon_2}(x)$ for all $x \in X$. Hence, by the semantics of $\text{LTL}_{\backslash \bigcirc}$, $(\varphi, (\mathcal{L}_{\varepsilon_1})_{\varepsilon_2})$ is realizable for $\mathcal{S}_{\delta_2}$ with a sampled-data control strategy with sampling period T.

By Proposition 2, $(\varphi, (\mathcal{L}_{\varepsilon_1})_{\varepsilon_2})$ is realizable for $\mathcal{S}_{\delta_2}$ with a sampled-data control strategy with sampling period τ and dwell-time N. By Proposition 3, $(\varphi, \mathcal{L}_{\varepsilon_1})$ is realizable for $\mathcal{T}_{\delta_2,\tau}$ with a dwell-time N control strategy, because $\varepsilon_2 \geq \frac{(M+\delta_2)\tau}{2}$ (indeed equal). Construct $\mathcal{T}$ by Theorem 1 so that $\mathcal{T}_{\delta_1,\tau} \preceq \mathcal{T} \preceq \mathcal{T}_{\delta_2,\tau}$. By Proposition 4, $(\varphi, \mathcal{L}_{\varepsilon_1})$ is realizable for $\mathcal{T}$ and hence also for $\mathcal{T}_{\delta_1,\tau}$ with a dwell-time N control strategy. By Proposition 3, $(\varphi, \mathcal{L})$ is realizable for $\mathcal{S}_{\delta_1}$ with a sampled-data control strategy with sampling period τ and dwell-time N, because $\varepsilon_1 \geq \frac{(M+\delta_1)\tau}{2}$. Finally, by Proposition 2 again, $(\varphi, \mathcal{L})$ is realizable for $\mathcal{S}_{\delta_1}$ with a sampled-data control strategy with sampling period T. One can algorithmically construct such a control strategy by synthesizing a dwell-time N controller strategy for the finite transition system $\mathcal{T}$. For the case there is not necessarily a proposition preserving partition, we can choose $\varepsilon_1 = \frac{(M+\delta_1)\tau+\eta}{2}$ and $\varepsilon_2 = \frac{(M+\delta_2)\tau+\eta}{2}$ to account for mismatch by an abstraction with granularity $\frac{\eta}{2}$. In this case, we can choose τ and η sufficiently small such that

$$\eta + \frac{(2M + \delta_1 + \delta_2)\tau}{2} = \varepsilon_1 + \varepsilon_2 \leq \varepsilon. \tag{15}$$

On the other hand, by this construction of $\mathcal{T}$, if $(\varphi, \mathcal{L}_{\varepsilon_1})$ is not realizable for $\mathcal{T}$, then we can conclude that $(\varphi, \mathcal{L}_\varepsilon)$ is not realizable for $\mathcal{S}_{\delta_2}$ with a sampled-data control strategy with sampling period T. $\square$

A decision diagram summarizing the argument in the proof of Theorem 2 can be found in the Appendix of [19]. When there is no *a prior* fixed sampling period for the decision process, we can formulate the robust decidability theorem as follows, where it is proved that the problem can be solved for all sufficiently small sampling periods. The proof follows exactly from the proof of Theorem 2 with $N = 1$.

Theorem 3 (Robust decidability II). *Given a temporal logic specification* φ, *any* $\delta_2 > \delta_1 \geq 0$, *and any* $\varepsilon > 0$. *Let* $\mathcal{L} : X \to 2^\Pi$ *be a labelling function and* $\mathcal{L}_\varepsilon$ *be an* ε-*strengthening of* $\mathcal{L}$. *Then there exists some* $\tau^* > 0$ *(and one can explicitly compute it) such that, for each* $\tau \in (0, \tau^*]$, *there exists a decision procedure that determines which one of the following holds:*

- *there exists (and one can algorithmically construct) a sampled-data control strategy with sampling period* τ *such that* $(\varphi, \mathcal{L})$ *is realizable for* $\mathcal{S}_{\delta_1}$; *or*
- $(\varphi, \mathcal{L}_\varepsilon)$ *is not realizable for* $\mathcal{S}_{\delta_2}$ *with a sampled-data control strategy with sampling period* τ.

Another version of robust decidability can be formulated as follows, which says that with one procedure, one can decide robust realizability by a sampled-data control strategy with *any* sampling period greater than a threshold value (e.g., a lower bound limited by the physical sampling frequency).

Theorem 4 (Robust decidability III). *Given a temporal logic specification* φ, *any* $\delta_2 > \delta_1 \geq 0$, $\varepsilon > 0$, *and* $\tau^* > 0$. *Let* $\mathcal{L} : X \to 2^\Pi$ *be a labelling function and* $\mathcal{L}_\varepsilon$ *be an* ε-*strengthening of* $\mathcal{L}$. *Then there exists some* $\tau > 0$ *(and one can explicitly compute it) and a decision procedure that determines which one of the following holds:*

- *there exists (and one can algorithmically construct) a sampled-data control strategy with sampling period* τ *such that* $(\varphi, \mathcal{L})$ *is realizable for* $\mathcal{S}_{\delta_1}$; *or*
- $(\varphi, \mathcal{L}_\varepsilon)$ *is not realizable for* $\mathcal{S}_{\delta_2}$ *with a sampled-data control strategy with a sampling period* $T \geq \tau^*$.

To prove Theorem 4, we need the following lemma, which shows that, if $\delta_2 > \delta_1$, then system $\mathcal{T}_{\delta_1, \tau}$ can be abstracted by $\mathcal{T}_{\delta_2, \tau'}$ despite a slight mismatch between the sampling periods τ and τ'.

Lemma 1. *Given any* $\tau^* > 0$ *and* $\delta_2 > \delta_1 \geq 0$, *there exists* $r^* > 0$ *such that* $\mathcal{T}_{\delta_1, T} \preceq_{id_X} \mathcal{T}_{\delta_2, T+r}$ *for all* $T \geq \tau^*$ *and all* $|r| \leq r^*$, *where* $id_X \subseteq X \times X$ *is the identity relation.*

Proof. Choose any $x \in X$ and $u \in U$. Let $x_1 \in \mathrm{Post}_{\mathcal{T}_{\delta_1, T}}(x, u)$. We show that $x_1 \in \mathrm{Post}_{\mathcal{T}_{\delta_2, T+r}}(x, u)$. By definition, there exists a trajectory $\mathbf{x}$ such that $\mathbf{x}(0) =$

x, $\mathbf{x}(T) = x_1$, and $\mathbf{x}'(s) \in f(\mathbf{x}(s), u) + \delta_1 \mathbb{B}$ for all $s \in [0, T]$. Let $\mathbf{z}(s) = \mathbf{x}(\frac{T}{T+r}s)$ for $s \in [0, T]$. Then $\mathbf{z}(0) = x$, $\mathbf{z}(T+r) = x_1$ and

$$\mathbf{z}'(s) = \frac{T}{T+r}\mathbf{x}'(\frac{T}{T+r}s) \in \frac{T}{T+r}f(\mathbf{z}(s), u) + \frac{T}{T+r}\delta_1\mathbb{B}$$

$$\subseteq f(\mathbf{z}(s), u) - \frac{r}{T+r}f(\mathbf{z}(s), u) + \delta_1\mathbb{B}$$

$$\subseteq f(\mathbf{z}(s), u) + (\frac{|r|M}{\tau^* - |r|} + \delta_1)\mathbb{B},$$

where we assumed $|r|$ is sufficiently small so that $|r| \leq \tau^*$. Clearly, since $\delta_1 < \delta_2$, we can choose $r^* > 0$ so that $\frac{|r|M}{\tau^*-|r|} + \delta_1 < \delta_2$ for all $|r| \leq r^*$. Hence, $\mathbf{z}'(s) \in f(\mathbf{z}(s), u) + \delta_2\mathbb{B}$ and $x_1 = \mathbf{z}(T+r) \in \text{Post}_{\mathcal{T}_{\delta_2, T+r}}(x, u)$.   □

Now we can present the proof of Theorem 4.

Proof (Proof of Theorem 4).
    Let ε_1 and ε_2 be as defined in the proof for Theorem 2. Choose δ_3 such that $\delta_2 > \delta_3 > \delta_1$. Let τ^*, η^*, and μ^* be chosen so that (13) and (14) (or (13) and (15) if a proposition preserving partition is not used), with δ_3 replacing δ_2 in (13), hold for all $\tau \leq \tau^*$, $\eta \leq \eta^*$, and $\mu \leq \mu^*$.
    Suppose that $(\varphi, \mathcal{L}_\varepsilon)$ is realizable for $\mathcal{S}_{\delta_2}$ with a sampled-data control strategy with sampling period T. Without loss of generality, assume $\frac{\tau^*}{2} < T \leq \tau^*$. Otherwise, one can divide T by a positive integer number N so that $\frac{T}{N} \in (\tau^*/2, \tau^*]$ and $(\varphi, \mathcal{L}_\varepsilon)$ is realizable for $\mathcal{S}_{\delta_2}$ with a sampled-data control strategy with sampling period T/N (with dwell-time N).
    Construct, by Theorem 1, $\mathcal{T}$ so that

$$\mathcal{T}_{\delta_3, T} \preceq \mathcal{T} \preceq \mathcal{T}_{\delta_2, T}. \tag{16}$$

Let $\tau \leq \frac{\tau^*}{2}$ be chosen (guaranteed by Lemma 1) so that

$$\mathcal{T}_{\delta_1, T+r} \preceq_{\text{id}_X} \mathcal{T}_{\delta_3, T}. \tag{17}$$

for all $|r| \leq \tau$.
    Let $\mathcal{L}_{\varepsilon_1}$, $(\mathcal{L}_{\varepsilon_1})_{\varepsilon_2}$ and $\mathcal{L}_{\varepsilon_1+\varepsilon_2}$ be as defined in the proof for Theorem 2. By Proposition 3, $(\varphi, \mathcal{L}_{\varepsilon_1})$ is realizable for $\mathcal{T}_{\delta_2, T}$, because $\varepsilon_2 \geq \frac{(M+\delta_2)T}{2}$. By Proposition 4 and (16), $(\varphi, \mathcal{L}_{\varepsilon_1})$ is realizable for $\mathcal{T}$ and hence also for $\mathcal{T}_{\delta_3, T}$. Let m be the largest integer such that $m\tau \leq T$. Then $|m\tau - T| \leq \tau$. By (17), we obtain $\mathcal{T}_{\delta_1, m\tau} = \mathcal{T}_{\delta_1, T+(m\tau-T)} \preceq_{\text{id}_X} \mathcal{T}_{\delta_3, T}$. By Proposition 4 again, $(\varphi, \mathcal{L}_{\varepsilon_1})$ is realizable for $\mathcal{T}_{\delta_3, m\tau}$. By Proposition 3, $(\varphi, \mathcal{L})$ is realizable for $\mathcal{S}_{\delta_1}$ with a sampled-data control strategy with sampling period $m\tau$, because $\varepsilon_1 \geq \frac{(M+\delta_1)m\tau}{2}$. Finally, by Proposition 2, $(\varphi, \mathcal{L})$ is realizable for $\mathcal{S}_{\delta_1}$ with a sampled-data control strategy with sampling period τ. One can algorithmically construct such a control strategy by synthesizing a control strategy for $\mathcal{T}$ to realize $(\varphi, \mathcal{L}_{\varepsilon_1})$.   □

Remark 3. Theorem 4 is sharp in the sense that, if one does not impose a lower bound on the sampling period, it is possible to show that a one-dimensional continuous-time control system can robustly simulate any Turing machine. Since the undecidable Halting problem can be encoded as a reachability problem, one cannot expect to have a general decision procedure in this setting. Details can be found in the Appendix of [19].

4.3   Dealing with Arbitrary Control Signals

As mentioned in Remark 2, we formulated the problem only for sampled-data control strategies. In this section, we prove a lemma that shows this is assumption is without loss of generality. An input $\mathbf{u} : \mathbb{R}^+ \to U$ is called a sampled-data input with period $\tau > 0$ if there exists $t_0 = 0, \cdots, t_i, \cdots$ such that it is constant on each $[t_i, t_{i+1})$ and $t_{i+1} - t_i = \tau$.

Lemma 2. *Let* $\mathbf{u} : [0,T] \to U$ *be a measurable signal. Then for* $\mu > 0$, *there exists some* $\tau > 0$, *a finite subset of* $[U]_\mu$ *of* U, *and a sampled-data input* $\mathbf{v} : [0,T] \to [U]_\mu$ *with period greater than* τ *such that* $\int_0^T |\mathbf{u}(s) - \mathbf{v}(s)|\, ds \leq \mu$.

Proof. Since U is compact, $\mathbf{u} \in L^1([0,T], U)$. The conclusion follows from the fact that step functions defined on rational partitions and taking rational values are dense in $L^1([0,T], U)$ (see, e.g., [29, p. 152, Chap. 7]).   □

4.4   Completeness via Controllability

In this subsection, we show that under a suitable notion of local controllability around a trajectory that realizes a given temporal logic specification on the nominal control system (1), we can always construct a robust abstraction to find a sampled-data control strategy to robustly realize the same specification (subject to an ε-strengthening of the labeling function for an arbitrarily small ε). In other words, local controllability suffices to remove the robustness relaxation in our notion of completeness. We refer the readers to [9,23] for sufficient conditions on local controllability around a closed orbit [23] or reference trajectory [9].

Definition 4. *Let* $\mathcal{O} \subseteq X$ *be an open connected set. Let* $T \geq 0$. *A point* X_T *is* $\mathcal{O}$-reachable from $x_0 \in X$ at time T *if there exists a trajectory* $(\mathbf{x}, \mathbf{u})$ *such that* $\mathbf{x}(0) = x_0$, $\mathbf{x}(T) = x_T$, *and* $\mathbf{x}(t) \in \mathcal{O}$ *for all* $t \in [0,T]$ *and* $\mathbf{u} : [0,T] \to U$ *is a measurable signal. The set of all points* X_T *that are* $\mathcal{O}$-reachable from x_0 *at time* T *is denoted by* $\mathcal{R}(x_0, T, \mathcal{O})$. *Let* $\mathcal{R}(x_0, \mathcal{O}) = \cup_{T \geq 0} \mathcal{R}(x_0, T, \mathcal{O})$. *We say the control system (1) is controllable on* $\mathcal{O}$ *if* $\mathcal{R}(x_0, \mathcal{O}) = \mathcal{O}$.

Theorem 5 (Robust realizability via controllability). *Let* φ *be a temporal logic specification and* $\mathcal{L} : X \to 2^\Pi$ *be a labelling function. For any* $\varepsilon > 0$, *if there exists a trajectory* $(\mathbf{x}, \mathbf{u})$ *for (1) such that* $\mathbf{x}$ *satisfies* $(\varphi, \mathcal{L}_\varepsilon)$ *and (1) is controllable on an open set* $\mathcal{O}$ *containing* $\mathbf{x}$, *then there exists some* $\delta > 0$ *and a sampled-data control strategy for* $\mathcal{S}_\delta$ *to realize* $(\varphi, \mathcal{L})$.

Proof. For any $\varepsilon > 0$, if $\mathbf{x}$ satisfies $(\varphi, \mathcal{L}_\varepsilon)$, we can easily show that state trajectories that are ε-close to $\mathbf{x}$ satisfy $(\varphi, \mathcal{L})$. Hence, we only need to show that there exists a sampled-data control strategy for trajectories of $\mathcal{S}_\delta$ to stay in an ε-neighborhood of $\mathbf{x}$.

By the compactness of X, assume, without loss of generality, that the ε-neighborhood of the image of $\mathbf{x}$ is contained in $\mathcal{O}$. We construct a finite resolution sampled-data control strategy for $\mathcal{S}_\delta$ as follows. For any $x \in X$, let q be a grid point in $[X]_\eta$ such that $|x - q| \leq \frac{\eta}{2}$. Suppose that q is in an $\frac{\varepsilon}{2}$-ball around some point p on $\mathbf{x}$. Let $\mathbf{u}_1$ be a control signal that steers q to some q' on $\mathbf{x}$ at some time $T > 0$ according to dynamics of (1) without leaving an ε-ball of γ. This is always possible under the local controllability assumption. By Lemma 2, there exists a sampled-data signal $\mathbf{u}_2$ with period greater than some $\tau > 0$ such that $\int_0^T |\mathbf{u}_1(s) - \mathbf{u}_2(s)|\, ds \leq \mu$. We estimate the state trajectories of $\mathcal{S}_\delta$ under control of $\mathbf{v}$ as follows. Let $\mathbf{x}_1$ be the trajectory of the nominal system $\mathcal{S}$ under $\mathbf{u}_1$ starting from q and ending at q'. Let $\mathbf{x}_2$ be a trajectory of $\mathcal{S}_\delta$ starting from x. For $t \in [0, T]$, we have

$$\begin{aligned}|\mathbf{x}_1'(t) - \mathbf{x}_2'(t)| &\leq |f(\mathbf{x}_1(t), \mathbf{u}_1(t)) - f(\mathbf{x}_2(t), \mathbf{u}_2(t))| + \delta \\ &\leq |f(\mathbf{x}_1(t), \mathbf{u}_1(t)) - f(\mathbf{x}_2(t), \mathbf{u}_1(t))| \\ &\quad + |f(\mathbf{x}_2(t), \mathbf{u}_1(t)) - f(\mathbf{x}_2, \mathbf{u}_2(t))| + \delta \\ &\leq L|\mathbf{x}_1(t) - \mathbf{x}_2(t)| + L|\mathbf{u}_1(t) - \mathbf{u}_2(t)| + \delta.\end{aligned} \tag{18}$$

By Gronwall's inequality (see, e.g., [2, p. 120]), we have

$$|\mathbf{x}_1(t) - \mathbf{x}_2(t)| \leq |x - q|\, e^{Lt} + \int_0^t (L|\mathbf{u}_1(s) - \mathbf{u}_2(s)| + \delta) e^{L(t-s)} ds$$

$$\leq \frac{\eta}{2} e^{Lt} + \frac{\delta}{L}(e^{Lt} - 1) + L\mu e^{Lt}, \quad \forall t \in [0, T].$$

From this estimate, we can see that for any fixed $T > 0$, we can choose η, $\delta > 0$, and $\mu > 0$ sufficient small such that the right-hand side of the above inequality is less than $\frac{\varepsilon}{2}$. It follows that the state trajectory $\mathbf{x}_2$ of $\mathcal{S}_\delta$ remains in a ε-neighborhood of $\mathbf{x}$ and, at $t = T$, is within a $\frac{\varepsilon}{2}$-neighborhood of q'. Since there is only a finite number of grid points of granularity $\frac{\eta}{2}$ in a compact domain, the choice of sampling period τ for the signals satisfying Lemma 2 can be fixed. Therefore, there exists a sampled-data control strategy for state trajectories of $\mathcal{S}_\delta$ to stay in an ε-neighborhood of $\mathbf{x}$, as long as they start in an $\frac{\varepsilon}{2}$-neighborhood of $x_0 = \mathbf{x}(0)$. Since $\mathbf{x}$ satisfies $(\varphi, \mathcal{L}_\varepsilon)$, all trajectories of $\mathcal{S}_\delta$ starting from the $\frac{\varepsilon}{2}$-neighborhood of x_0 satisfy $(\varphi, \mathcal{L})$. $\qquad\square$

Remark 4. It is clear from the proof of Theorem 5 that the robust realizability result does not depend on the reference trajectory $\mathbf{x}$ satisfying (1), but on the path induced by the trajectory. Therefore, if system (1) has a control neighborhood that contains a path parameterizable by any trajectory satisfying the specification, the conclusion still holds. As a result, if a system is controllable in a neighborhood $\mathcal{O}$ and a specification is satisfiable by a path in $\mathcal{O}$, then the specification is robustly realizable by a sampled-data control strategy.

Combining the robust realizability result Theorem 5 and the result on robust completeness proved in previous sections, we can show that controllability implies completeness of discrete abstractions in the following sense.

Corollary 1 (Completeness via controllability). *Given a temporal logic specification φ and any $\varepsilon > 0$, let $\mathcal{L} : X \to 2^{\Pi}$ be a labelling function and $\mathcal{L}_\varepsilon$ be an ε-strengthening of $\mathcal{L}$. Suppose that $(\varphi, \mathcal{L}_\varepsilon)$ is satisfiable by a trajectory of (1) contained in a controllable neighborhood. Then, for any $\varepsilon' \in (0, \varepsilon)$, there exists $\delta > 0$, $\tau > 0$, and a finite transition system $\mathcal{T}$ such that $\mathcal{T}_\tau \preceq \mathcal{T} \preceq \mathcal{T}_{\delta,\tau}$ and $(\varphi, \mathcal{L}_{\varepsilon'})$ is realizable for $\mathcal{T}$. Moreover, a control strategy synthesized using $\mathcal{T}$ for $(\varphi, \mathcal{L}_{\varepsilon'})$ can be refined as a sampled-data control strategy for $\mathcal{S}$ that realizes $(\varphi, \mathcal{L})$.*

Proof. Choose any ε_1 and ε_2 such that $\varepsilon' < \varepsilon_1 < \varepsilon_2 < \varepsilon$. By Theorem 5, there exists $\delta > 0$ and $\tau > 0$ such that $(\varphi, \mathcal{L}_{\varepsilon_2})$ is realizable for $\mathcal{S}_\delta$. Suppose that τ is also chosen sufficiently small according to conditions of Proposition 3. Then $(\varphi, \mathcal{L}_{\varepsilon_1})$ is realizable for $\mathcal{T}_{\delta,\tau}$. The existence of $\mathcal{T}$ follows from Theorem 1. By Propositions 4, $(\varphi_{\varepsilon'}, \mathcal{L})$ is realizable for $\mathcal{T}$, provided that the time discretization τ and space discretization η (in the case of non-proposition preserving abstraction) are chosen sufficiently small. Continuing this reasoning for $\mathcal{T}_\tau$ and $\mathcal{S}$, we obtain that $(\varphi, \mathcal{L})$ is realizable for $\mathcal{S}$ with a sampled-data control strategy synthesized from the abstraction $\mathcal{T}$.

Remark 5. The completeness result Corollary 1 is stated with respect to the nominal system (1). It is clear from the reasoning in the proof that under the same assumption we can synthesize a robust sampled-data control strategy for $\mathcal{S}$ from the abstraction $\mathcal{T}$.

5   Conclusions

In this paper, we proved two sets of theoretical results on completeness of abstraction-based nonlinear control. First, we show that control synthesis for sampled-data nonlinear systems with temporal logic specifications is robustly decidable in the sense that if a robust control strategy exists, then a robust control strategy can be found using a sufficiently fine discretization. Second, we show that, under the assumption of nonlinear controllability around a trajectory that realizes a given specification, it is always possible to construct a sampled-data control strategy via a sufficiently fine discrete abstraction.

We see the main theoretical contributions of this work as showing the existence of robustly complete abstractions for continuous-time nonlinear control systems and that nonlinear controllability implies completeness. It is hoped that this work will motivate further research on computing tight abstractions of nonlinear control systems. In this regard, Theorem 1 on robust completeness can be viewed as a potential metric on closeness of abstractions and Corollary 1 can help provide assurance that control synthesis via discrete abstractions always works for controllable systems.

References

1. Angeli, D.: A lyapunov approach to incremental stability properties. IEEE Trans. Autom. Control **47**(3), 410–421 (2002)
2. Aubin, J.P., Cellina, A.: Differential Inclusions: Set-valued Maps and Viability Theory. Springer, Heidelberg (2012). https://doi.org/10.1007/978-3-642-69512-4
3. Baier, C., Katoen, J.P.: Principles of Model Checking. MIT Press, Cambridge (2008)
4. Belta, C., Yordanov, B., Aydin Gol, E.: Formal Methods for Discrete-Time Dynamical Systems. SSDC, vol. 89. Springer, Cham (2017). https://doi.org/10.1007/978-3-319-50763-7
5. Clarke, E.M., Grumberg, O., Peled, D.: Model Checking. MIT Press, Cambridge (1999)
6. Fainekos, G.E., Girard, A., Kress-Gazit, H., Pappas, G.J.: Temporal logic motion planning for dynamic robots. Automatica **45**(2), 343–352 (2009)
7. Fainekos, G.E., Pappas, G.J.: Robustness of temporal logic specifications for continuous-time signals. Theor. Comput. Sci. **410**(42), 4262–4291 (2009)
8. Grädel, E., Thomas, W., Wilke, T. (eds.): Automata Logics, and Infinite Games. LNCS, vol. 2500. Springer, Heidelberg (2002). https://doi.org/10.1007/3-540-36387-4
9. Hermes, H.: On local and global controllability. SIAM J. Control **12**(2), 252–261 (1974)
10. Kloetzer, M., Belta, C.: Temporal logic planning and control of robotic swarms by hierarchical abstractions. IEEE Trans. Robot. **23**(2), 320–330 (2007)
11. Koiran, P., Cosnard, M., Garzon, M.: Computability with low-dimensional dynamical systems. Theor. Comput. Sci. **132**(1–2), 113–128 (1994)
12. Kress-Gazit, H., Wongpiromsarn, T., Topcu, U.: Correct, reactive, high-level robot control. IEEE Robot. Autom. Mag. **18**(3), 65–74 (2011)
13. Li, Y., Liu, J.: Invariance control synthesis for switched nonlinear systems: an interval analysis approach. IEEE Trans. Autom. Control **63**(7), 2206–2211 (2018)
14. Li, Y., Liu, J.: Robustly complete reach-and-stay control synthesis for switched systems via interval analysis. In: Proceedings of ACC (2018)
15. Li, Y., Liu, J.: Rocs: A robustly complete control synthesis tool for nonlinear dynamical systems. In: Proceedings of HSCC, pp. 130–135 (2018)
16. Li, Y., Liu, J.: Robustly complete synthesis of memoryless controllers for nonlinear systems with reach-and-stay specifications. IEEE Trans. Autom. Control **66**(3), 1199–1206 (2021)
17. Li, Y., Sun, Z., Liu, J.: A specification-guided framework for temporal logic control of nonlinear systems. arXiv preprint arXiv:2104.01385 (2021).
18. Liu, J.: Robust abstractions for control synthesis: completeness via robustness for linear-time properties. In: Proceedings of HSCC, pp. 101–110. ACM (2017)
19. Liu, J.: Closing the gap between discrete abstractions and continuous control: Completeness via robustness and controllability. In: Proceedings of FORMATS (2021). https://www.math.uwaterloo.ca/~j49liu/papers/2021/liu2021closing.pdf
20. Liu, J., Ozay, N., Topcu, U., Murray, R.: Synthesis of reactive switching protocols from temporal logic specifications. IEEE Trans. Autom. Control **58**(7), 1771–1785 (2013)
21. Liu, J., Ozay, N.: Abstraction, discretization, and robustness in temporal logic control of dynamical systems. In: Proceedings of HSCC, pp. 293–302 (2014)

22. Liu, J., Ozay, N.: Finite abstractions with robustness margins for temporal logic-based control synthesis. Nonlinear Anal. Hybrid Syst. **22**, 1–15 (2016)
23. Nam, K., Arapostathis, A.: A sufficient condition for local controllability of nonlinear systems along closed orbits. IEEE Trans. Autom. Control **37**(3), 378–380 (1992)
24. Nilsson, P., Ozay, N., Liu, J.: Augmented finite transition systems as abstractions for control synthesis. Discrete Event Dyn. Syst. **27**(2), 301–340 (2017)
25. Ozay, N., Liu, J., Prabhakar, P., Murray, R.M.: Computing augmented finite transition systems to synthesize switching protocols for polynomial switched systems. In: Proceedings of ACC, pp. 6237–6244 (2013)
26. Pnueli, A.: The temporal logic of programs. In: Proceedings of FOCS, pp. 46–57. IEEE (1977)
27. Pola, G., Girard, A., Tabuada, P.: Approximately bisimilar symbolic models for nonlinear control systems. Automatica **44**(10), 2508–2516 (2008)
28. Reissig, G., Weber, A., Rungger, M.: Feedback refinement relations for the synthesis of symbolic controllers. IEEE Trans. Autom. Control **62**(4), 1781–1796 (2017)
29. Royden, H., Fitzpatrick, P.: Real Analysis. Printice-Hall, Boston (2010)
30. Tabuada, P.: Verification and Control of Hybrid Systems: A Symbolic Approach. Springer, Heidelberg (2009). https://doi.org/10.1007/978-1-4419-0224-5
31. Tabuada, P., Pappas, G.J.: Linear time logic control of discrete-time linear systems. IEEE Trans. Autom. Control **51**(12), 1862–1877 (2006)
32. Zamani, M., Pola, G., Mazo, M., Tabuada, P.: Symbolic models for nonlinear control systems without stability assumptions. IEEE Trans. Autom. Control **57**(7), 1804–1809 (2012)

An Integer Static Analysis for Better Extrapolation in Uppaal

Sebastian Lund(ID), Jesper van Diepen, Kim G. Larsen, Marco Muñiz$^{(\boxtimes)}$(ID),
Tobias Ringholm Jørgensen, and Tobias Skaarup Daa Andersen

Department of Computer Science, Aalborg University, Aalborg, Denmark
muniz@cs.aau.dk

Abstract. Extended Timed Automata (XTA) is a widely used formalism to show the correctness of industrial applications. The decidability results and current extrapolations for XTA are based on constants in the automaton. However, in the case of XTA such bounds depend on integer variables or variable expressions. Since computing such bounds can be as expensive as the verification task, tools such as UPPAAL over-approximate the bounds by values given in the type definitions. These values are excessively large and can yield huge state spaces. In this paper we outline a targeted static analysis to efficiently over-approximate location based invariants (and thereby ranges) of integer variables. We have implemented our analysis in UPPAAL where the new tighter bounds are available to all currently implemented extrapolation operations. Our experiments show an exponential reduction in the state space of several models. In addition, the computation overhead introduced by the integer static analysis is negligible.

1 Introduction

Software systems are ubiquitous in every day life. Some of these systems are safety-critical systems. Malfunctioning or unexpected behavior on a safety-critical system can have catastrophic economical losses or even cost human lives. Thus ensuring correct behavior of safety-critical systems is a prime concern. A successfully approach towards correctness is that of model checking. In model checking, the underlying system is formalized using a suitable model, e.g., Timed Automata [1]. Similarly, the system requirements are formalized using a suitable logic. Finally, the model checker, e.g., UPPAAL [2] systematically and exhaustively explores the state space induced by the model to show if the model satisfies the given requirement.

The model checker UPPAAL has been successful for showing correctness in a number of industrial case studies, e.g. [3,4]. The success of the tool is given by several factors, including an efficient implementation using dedicated data structures, efficient extrapolation/abstraction techniques (*only for clocks*), and a rich formalism for describing the behavior of timed systems. UPPAAL models are Extend Timed Automata (XTA) which are Timed Automata augmented with

© Springer Nature Switzerland AG 2021
C. Dima and M. Shirmohammadi (Eds.): FORMATS 2021, LNCS 12860, pp. 84–99, 2021.
https://doi.org/10.1007/978-3-030-85037-1_6

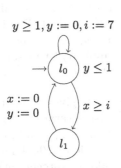

$y \geq 1, y := 0, i := 7$

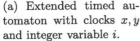

$x := 0$
$y := 0$

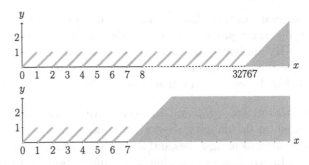

(a) Extended timed automaton with clocks x, y and integer variable i.

(b) Symbolic states computed for the XTA from Figure 1a (top) UPPAAL uses the maximal value for integer type, resulting in over 32000 states. (bot) UPPAAL uses 7 with the maximal constant abstraction.

Fig. 1. Maximal constant abstraction on simple automaton with integer variables.

discrete variables, function calls, arrays, expressions, etc. Integer variables can strongly influence the performance of UPPAAL by both increasing discrete states or by affecting abstraction techniques, e.g., extrapolation techniques. In order to produce a finite system UPPAAL implements extrapolation techniques such as [5–7]. However, these methods assume that in the timed automata clocks are merely compared to natural numbers (constants). Unfortunately, in some UPPAAL models, clocks are compared to nonconstant expressions. In such situations the maximum value of the expression is currently derived from type information and defaults to impractically large integer values.

In this work we contribute to the verification of extended timed automata by computing tighter bounds on the values of integer variables involved in integer expressions. We then use the new computed bounds in current extrapolation methods implemented in UPPAAL which result in much better extrapolation (with significantly fewer symbolic states). Our main task involves over-approximating integer bounds in large networks of XTA. To make our approach scalable a number of steps are needed. These steps include, finding dependencies among variables, splitting the networks of XTA to perform local analysis, applying the abstract interpretation framework [8], etc. For evaluation purposes, we have implemented our approach in UPPAAL, we run the implementation on a number of case studies. Experiments show exponential savings in several models. In addition for all models, the overhead introduced by the static analysis is negligible.

Example 1. Consider the XTA in Fig. 1a, it contains clocks x, y and integer variable i. The guard $x \geq i$ in the edge from location l_0 to location l_1 compares the value of clock x with the integer variable i. By taking the edge from location l_0 to location l_0 the automaton resets the value of clock y, whereas the value of x keeps increasing. In this XTA there is no maximal constant for the value of x, but the maximal attainable value of variable i can be used to perform, e.g., maximal constant abstraction to ensure a finite state system. Currently to verify an invariant property in this XTA UPPAAL generates 32772 states c.f. Fig. 1b top. By applying our static analysis we can conclude that the maximal value for variable i is 7 and the maximal constant abstraction can be applied at this value c.f. Fig. 1b bot. With our method UPPAAL generates only 12 states.

Related Work. Maximal constant abstraction using regions [1] gives the fundamental decidability results for timed automata. There exist several efficient abstractions using zones and location based maximal constants, e.g., [6] and further improvements using lower and upper bounds LU-extrapolation [7,9]. These methods rely on constants appearing in guards, but do not address integer variables. Our method thus supplements these existing techniques. Integer static analysis has been of particular interest the context of program verification and relevant existing techniques include abstract interpretation [8]. In [10] abstract interpretation has been applied to determine invariant linear inequalities in linear hybrid systems, their method differs from ours in that they only consider *Interrupts* as interaction between systems which differs from the semantics of XTA.

The structure of the paper is as follows. Section 2 gives the foundations of our work. Section 3 describes a local abstract interpretation for over-approximating bounds of integer variables for single XTA. Section 4 describes how to apply our local analysis to network of XTA. In Sect. 5 we present experimental results on a number of case studies. Finally in Sect. 6 we present our conclusion and future work.

2   Preliminaries

This section presents the underlying theories and formalisisms used in our work. Section 2.1 presents Extended Timed Automata which describe the formal models used in UPPAAL. Section 2.2 presents Abstract Interpretation which is the mathematical framework in which we formulate our static analsys.

2.1   Extended Timed Automata (XTA)

Our formal model is *extended timed automata* which extends timed automata [1] by adding discrete variables and expressions for such variables. XTA is an abstract representation of modeling formalism used in the tool UPPAAL [2]. The following definitions follow the style from [11].

Clocks and Discrete Variables. Let X be a set of *clocks*. A *clock valuation* is a function $\mu : X \to \mathbb{R}_{\geq 0}$. We use $\mathcal{V}(X)$ to denote the set of all valuations for clocks in X. Let V be a set of *discrete variables*. The function D assigns to each variable $v \in V$ a finite domain $D(v)$. A *variable valuation* is a function $\nu : V \to \bigcup_{v \in V} D(v)$ that maps variables to values such that $\nu(v) \in D(v)$. We use $\mathcal{V}(V)$ to denote the set of all variable valuations. We let μ_0 (resp., ν_0) to denote the valuation that maps every clock (resp., variable) to the value 0.

Expressions. We use expr to denote an expression over V. We assume that expressions are well typed and for expression expr we use $D(\text{expr})$ to denote its domain. Given a variable valuation ν and an expression expr, we use $\text{expr}^\nu \in D(\text{expr})$ to denote the value of expr under ν. We use $V(\text{expr}) \in 2^V$ to denote the set of variables in expr such that for all $\nu, \nu' \in \mathcal{V}(V)$ and for all $v \in V(\text{expr})$ if $\nu(v) = \nu'(v)$ then $\text{expr}^\nu = \text{expr}^{\nu'}$.

Constraints. The set $B(X)$ is the set of *clock constraints* generated by the grammar $\phi ::= x \bowtie \text{expr} \mid \phi_1 \wedge \phi_2$, where $x \in X$, $D(\text{expr})$ is inside the domain of all natural numbers $\mathbb{N}$ and $\bowtie \in \{<, \leq, \geq, >\}$. The set $B(V)$ is a set of *Boolean variable constraints* over V. The set $B(X, V)$ of constraints comprises $B(X)$, $B(V)$, and conjunctions over clock and variable constraints. Given a constraint $\phi \in B(X, V)$, we use $X(\phi)$ to denote the set of clocks in ϕ, and $V(\phi)$ to denote the set of variables in ϕ. We define the evaluation of a constraint $\phi \in B(X, V)$ as ϕ^ν where expressions in ϕ are evaluated under ν.

Updates. A *clock update* is of the form $x := \text{expr}$ where $x \in X$, and $D(\text{expr}) \subseteq \mathbb{N}$. A *variable update* is of the form $v := \text{expr}$ where $v \in V$ and $D(\text{expr}) \subseteq D(v)$. The set $U(X, V)$ of *updates* contains all finite, possibly empty sequences of clock and variable updates. Given clock valuation $\mu \in \mathcal{V}(X)$, variable valuation $\nu \in \mathcal{V}(V)$, and update $r \in U(X, V)$, we use r^ν to denote the update resulting after evaluating all expressions in r under ν, we use $X(r)$ to denote the set of clocks written to in r, and $V(r)$ to denote the set of variables written or read in r. We let $[\![r^\nu]\!] : \mathcal{V}(X) \cup \mathcal{V}(V) \to \mathcal{V}(X) \cup \mathcal{V}(V)$ be a map from valuations to valuations. We use $\mu[r^\nu]$ to denote the updated clock valuation $[\![r^\nu]\!](\mu)$. Analogously, for variable valuation ν', we use $\nu'[r^\nu]$ to denote the updated variable valuation $[\![r^\nu]\!](\nu')$.

Channels. Given a set C of *channels*, the set $H(C)$ of synchronizations over channels is generated by the grammar $h ::= c[\text{expr}]! \mid c[\text{expr}]? \mid \tau$, where $c \in C$, $D(\text{expr}) \subseteq \mathbb{N}$, and τ represents an internal action. Given a variable valuation ν, for synchronization h of the form $c[\text{expr}]!$ we use h^ν to denote $c[\text{expr}^\nu]!$, and similar for synchronizations of the form $c[\text{expr}]?$.

Definition 1 (Extended Timed Automata XTA). *An* extended timed automaton $\mathcal{A}$ *is a tuple* $(L, L^u, L^c, l_0, X, V, H(C), E, I)$ *where: L is a set of locations, $L^u \subseteq L$ denotes the set of urgent locations in L, $L^c \subseteq L$ denotes the set of committed locations in L and $L_u \cap L_c = \emptyset$, $l_0 \in L$ is the initial location, X is a nonempty set of clocks, V is the set of variables, $H(C)$ is a set of channel expressions for set of channels C, $E \subseteq L \times H(C) \times B(X) \times B(V) \times U(X, V) \times L$ is a set of edges between locations with a channel expressions, a clock guard, a variable guard, an update set, and $I : L \to B(X)$ assigns clock invariants to locations.*

Definition 2 (Network of XTA). *A network $\mathcal{N}$ of XTA consists of a finite sequence $\mathcal{A}_1, \ldots, \mathcal{A}_n$ of XTA, where $\mathcal{A}_i = (L_i, L_i^u, L_i^c, l_i^0, X_i, V_i, H(C)_i, E_i, I_i)$*

for $1 \leq i \leq n$. *Locations are pairwise disjoint, i.e.,* $L_i \cap L_j = \emptyset$ *for* $1 \leq i, j \leq n$ *and* $i \neq j$. *The set of locations is* $L = \cup_{i=1}^n L_i$, *analogously for urgent* L^u *and committed* L^c *locations. The set of clocks is* $X = \cup_{i=1}^n X_i$ *and the set of variables is* $V = \cup_{i=1}^n V_i$. *The set of channel expressions is* $H(C) = \cup_{i=1}^n H(C)_i$. *The set of edges is* $E = \cup_{i=1}^n E_i$. *A location vector is a vector* $\vec{l} = (l_1, \ldots, l_n)$, *and* $\vec{l}_0 = (l_1^0, \ldots, l_n^0)$ *is the initial location vector. The invariant function over location vectors is* $I(\vec{l}) = \bigwedge_i I_i(l_i)$.

We write $\vec{l}[l_i'/l_i]$ to denote the vector where the i-th element l_i of $\vec{l}$ is replaced by l_i'. We write $\vec{l}^i$ to denote the i-th element of $\vec{l}$.

Definition 3 (Semantics of a Network of XTA). *Let* $\mathcal{N} = \mathcal{A}_1, \ldots, \mathcal{A}_n$ *be a network of TA. Its semantics is defined as a transition system* $(Q, q_0, \rightarrow)$, *where* $Q \subseteq (L_i \times \cdots \times L_n) \times \mathcal{V}(X) \times \mathcal{V}(V)$ *is the set of states comprising a location vector, a clock valuation, and a variable valuation,* $q_0 = (\vec{l}_0, \mu_0, \nu_0)$ *is the initial state, and* $\rightarrow \subseteq S \times (2^E \cup \mathbb{R}_{\geq 0}) \times S$ *is the transition relation defined by the following transitions:*

- *delay,* $(\vec{l}, \mu, \nu) \xrightarrow{\delta} (\vec{l}, \mu + \delta, \nu)$ *if* $\vec{l}^i \notin L_i^u \cup L_i^c$ *for* $1 \leq i \leq n$, *and* $\delta \in \mathbb{R}_{\geq 0}.\mu + d \models I(\vec{l})^\nu$,

- *internal,* $(\vec{l}, \mu, \nu) \xrightarrow{\{e_i\}} (\vec{l}[l_i'/l_i], \mu', \nu')$ *if* $e_i = (l_i, \tau, \phi, \psi, r, l_i') \in E_i$ *s.t.* $\nu' = \nu[r^\nu]$, $\nu \models \psi^\nu$, $\mu \models \phi^\nu$ $\mu' = \mu[r^\nu]$, $\mu' \models I(\vec{l}[l_i'/l_i])^{\nu'}$), *and if* $\vec{l}^k \in L_k^c$ *for some* $1 \leq k \leq n$ *then* $l_i \in L_i^c$,

- *handshake,* $(\vec{l}, \mu, \nu) \xrightarrow{\{e_i, e_j\}} (\vec{l}[l_j'/l_j, l_i'/l_i], \mu', \nu')$ *if* $e_i = (l_i, h_i!, \phi_i, \psi_i, r_i, l_i') \in E_i$ *and* $e_j = (l_j, h_j?, \phi_j, \psi_j, r_j, l_j') \in E_j$ *s.t.* $h_i^\nu = h_j^\nu$, *and* $\nu \models (\psi_i^\nu \wedge \psi_j^\nu)$, $\mu \models (\phi_i^\nu \wedge \phi_j^\nu)$, $\nu' = \nu[r_i^\nu][r_j^\nu]$, $\mu' = \mu[r_i^\nu][r_j^\nu]$, $\mu' \models I(\vec{l}[l_j'/l_j, l_i'/l_i])^{\nu'}$), *and if* $\vec{l}^k \in L_k^c$ *for some* $1 \leq k \leq n$ *then* $l_i \in L_i^c$ *or* $l_j \in L_j^c$.

Since clocks are real valued, the semantics of XTA yield an infinite transition system. The decidability results in timed automata is based on the notions of *regions* and *region equivalence* over clock valuations [1]. While this result is an important theoretical result, in practice the number of regions is too large, thus current approaches use the notion of *zones* together with different extrapolation operations [7]. When using these techniques the number of regions or zones in the resulting system depends on, e.g., the maximal constant value in the automaton. While detecting the maximal constant values is trivial in timed automata, XTA contains integer variables and expressions, which make finding the maximal values as hard as the verification task. Currently UPPAAL has no static analysis to infer integer bounds in expressions and it defaults to the maximal integer, which can severely affect the verification task.

2.2 Abstract Interpretation

The framework of abstract interpretation developed by Patrick and Radhia Cousot [8], formalizes sound approximations of systems. In abstract interpretation the semantics of XTA and their approximation is defined in terms of lattice-theoretical domains. Given an XTA $\mathcal{A}$, our analysis presented in Sect. 3 uses the abstract interpretation framework to over-approximate bounds in integer variables in $\mathcal{A}$. In this section we will define the lattice-theoretic terms that we will make use of in rest of the paper. Our presentation follows the style from [12] with slight modifications.

Definition 4 (Partially Ordered Set). *A set S with a binary relation $\leq$ is called a partially ordered set if and only if the following three conditions hold:*

1. *$\leq$ is reflexive: $\forall x \in S. \; x \leq x$,*
2. *$\leq$ is transitive: $\forall x, y, z \in S. \; x \leq y$ and $y \leq z$ implies $x \leq z$,*
3. *$\leq$ is antisymmetric: $\forall x, y \in S. \; x \leq y$ and $y \leq x$ implies $x = y$.*

A partially ordered set is denoted by $S(\leq)$. An element $x \in S$ is a lower bound of $X \subseteq S$ if and only if $\forall x' \in X. \; x \leq x'$. A lower bound x of $X \subseteq S$ is called greatest lower bound if and only if for all lower bounds $x' \in S$ of X we have $x' \leq x$. Conversely, $x \in S$ is an upper bound of $X \subseteq S$ if and only if $\forall x' \in X. \; x' \leq x$. An upper bound x of $X \subseteq S$ is called least upper bound if and only if for all upper bounds $x' \in S$ of X we have $x \leq x'$.

Definition 5 (Lattice). *A partially ordered set $L(\leq)$ is called a lattice if and only if for all $x, y \in L$ there exists a least upper bound $x \vee y$ and a greatest lower bound $x \wedge y$ of x and y in L. A lattice is denoted by $L(\leq, \vee, \wedge)$. We call $\vee$ the join and $\wedge$ the meet operation of the lattice.*

Definition 6 (Complete Lattice). *A lattice $L(\leq, \vee, \wedge)$ is called complete if for all $X \subseteq L$ there exists a least upper bound $\bigvee X$ and a greatest lower bound $\bigwedge X$ of X in L. In particular, L has a greatest element $\top = \bigvee L$ and a least element $\bot = \bigwedge L$. A complete lattice is denoted by $L(\leq, \vee, \wedge, \top, \bot)$.*

Definition 7 (Galois Connection). *Let $L_1(\sqsubseteq_1)$ and $L_2(\sqsubseteq_2)$ be partially ordered sets. The pair (α, γ) is called a Galois connection, or a pair of adjoint functions if and only if $\alpha \in L_1 \to L_2, \gamma \in L_2 \to L_1$ and: $\forall x \in L_1, y \in L_2.\alpha(x) \sqsubseteq_2 y \iff x \sqsubseteq_1 \gamma(y)$. We denote a Galois connection by $(L_1, \sqsubseteq_1) \underset{\alpha}{\overset{\gamma}{\rightleftarrows}} (L_2, \sqsubseteq_2)$.*

Definition 8 (Widening). *A widening operator is a function $\nabla : L \times L \to L$ such that for all $x, y \in L, x \leq x \nabla y, y \leq x \nabla y$ and for all increasing chains $(x_0 \leq x_1 \leq \ldots)$, the increasing chain defined as $y_0 = x_0, \ldots, y_{i+1} = y_i \nabla x_{i+1}$ is not strictly increasing.*

Definition 9 (Convex Polyhedra). *A convex polyhedron is the convex closure of a system of generators; a set of vertices $\mathsf{Vert}(P)$ and a set of rays $\mathsf{Ray}(P)$ of n-vectors such that, $P = \{\sum_{v_i \in \mathsf{Vert}(P)} \alpha_i \cdot v_i + \sum_{r_j \in \mathsf{Ray}(P)} \beta_j \cdot r_j | \alpha_i \geq 0, \beta_j \geq 0, \sum_i \alpha_i = 1\}$. We use $\mathcal{P}_V$ to denote the set of all convex polyhedra.*

Alternatively a convex polyhedron P can be represented as the set of solutions to a system of linear inequalities: $P = \{X | AX \geq B\}$ where A is an $m \times n$ matrix and B is an m-vector; we refer to the set of linear inequalities by $\mathsf{Ineq}(P)$. Finally, given a set of points S we use $\mathsf{ConvexCl}(S)$ to denote its convex closure.

3   Abstract Interpretation over Integer Variables

In this section we present our approach to over-approximating the bounds of integer variables using the abstract interpretation framework. In general our input is a network of XTA. However, performing a static analysis on the product of the network is too inefficient. For this reason our analysis is applied at the component level. In later sections we describe how can we apply our analysis on networks of XTA.

The first step of our analysis consists of defining our concrete domain and the collecting semantics. In the rest of this section we consider a network $\mathcal{N}$ consisting of a single automaton $\mathcal{A} = (L, L^u, L^c, l_0, X, V, H(C), E, I)$. Recall that by Definition 3 the semantics of $\mathcal{N}$ induces a transition system $(Q, q_0, \rightarrow)$.

Definition 10 (Concrete Domain). *Our concrete domain S is given by the power set of the set of states from the underlying transition system, i.e., $S = 2^Q$. Given a state $s \in S$ the posterior is defined as $\mathsf{Post}(s) = \{q' | q \in s, q \rightarrow q'\}$. Our concrete domain forms a complete lattice with order $\subseteq$. It follows from constructive versions of Tarski's theorem [13] that the set of reachable states can be computed as $S_R = \bigcup \{\mathsf{Post}^n(\{q_0\}) | n \in \mathbb{N}\}$.*

Next we address time constraints in $\mathcal{A}$, for this we over-approximate the behavior of $\mathcal{A}$ by assuming that all clock constraints are satisfied. This first over-approximation makes our analysis simpler and more efficient at the cost of some precision on the bounds of the integer variables.

We now need an abstract domain to efficiently represent and compute bounds of integer variables. In addition, many maximal constant abstractions benefit from location based bounds, e.g., LU-extrapolation [7]. For this we choose as an abstract domain the set of functions from locations to convex polyhedra.

Definition 11 (Abstract Domain). *Our abstract domain $S^\#$ is the set of functions from locations to convex polyhedra, i.e., $S^\# = L \rightarrow \mathcal{P}_V \cup \emptyset$. Given $s_1^\#, s_2^\# \in S^\#$ we define the join operator as $s_1^\# \sqcup s_2^\# = \{l \mapsto \mathsf{ConvexCl}(s_1^\#(l) \cup s_2^\#(l)) \mid l \in L\}$, the meet operator as $s_1^\# \sqcap s_2^\# = \{l \mapsto s_1^\#(l) \cap s_2^\#(l) \mid l \in L\}$, the ordering as $s_1^\# \sqsubseteq s_2^\#$ iff $\forall l \in L.s_1^\#(l) \sqsubseteq s_2^\#(l)$, the greatest element as $\top_S^\# = \{l \mapsto \mathbb{R}^{|V|} \mid l \in L\}$, and the least element as $\bot_S^\# = \{l \mapsto \emptyset \mid l \in L\}$.*

Lemma 1. *$S^\#(\sqsubseteq, \bot^\#, \top^\#, \sqcup, \sqcap)$ is a complete lattice.*

The next step is to define the abstraction and concretization functions. Intuitively, the abstraction α abstracts away time and forms a convex polyhedron over the integer variable valuations in each location. The concretization γ extracts the variable valuations from the polyhedron in each location and combines them with all possible clock valuations.

Definition 12 (Abstraction and Concretization). *The abstraction $\alpha : S \rightarrow S^\#$ is defined by $\alpha(s) = \{l \mapsto \mathsf{ConvexCl}(\{\nu \mid (l, \mu, \nu) \in s\}) \mid l \in L\}$, and the concretization $\gamma : S^\# \rightarrow S$ is defined by $\gamma(s^\#) = \{(l, \mu, \nu) \mid l \in L, \mu \in \mathcal{V}(X), \nu(v) \in s^\#(l) \text{ for } v \in V\}$.*

The following lemma lay out the foundations for the correctness of our approach.

Lemma 2. (α, γ) *is a Galois connection between* $(S, \subseteq)$ *and* $(S^\#, \sqsubseteq)$.

3.1 Efficient Posterior Computation

At this stage we are ready to define our abstract posterior $\mathsf{Post}^\#$ based on α and γ. However, this can be impractical to compute. In the following, we describe an efficient procedure to compute $\mathsf{Post}^\#$. By the semantics of XTA c.f. Definition 3 there are delay, internal, and handshake transitions. We have already over-approximated time by assuming that all clock guards are satisfied. In a similar way for a single automaton, we over-approximate its behavior by assuming that all synchronizations are possible by considering all $h!$ and $h?$ as τ. Therefore, we only need to consider transitions induced by single edges.

In order to define $\mathsf{Post}^\#$ for abstract state $s^\#$ for automaton $\mathcal{A}$ with edges E we need to consider operations involving convex polyhedra and edges containing variable constraints and variable updates.

Convex Polyhedra and Variable Constraints. The variable valuations satisfying variable constraint ψ from a convex polyhedron P is given by the intersection of P with the values satisfying ψ. We have the requirement for the resulting polyhedron to be convex. In practice many variable constraints are linear expressions and can be directly used in the intersection. On the contrary in the presence of non-linear expressions, we over-approximate them by their full domain. In the following, we will denote the intersection of a convex polyhedron P with a variable constraint ψ by $P \sqcap \psi$.

Convex Polyhedra and Variable Updates. Given polyhedron P and an update r we need to define its image after applying the discrete variable updates. Our approach is to transform the updates into linear transformations which can be applied to P.

Definition 13 (Linear Assignments on Polyhedra). *Given a polyhedron* P *and a linear assignment* $(\boldsymbol{A}, \boldsymbol{b}) \subseteq \mathbb{Q}^{|V| \times |V|} \times \mathbb{Q}^{|V|}$ *the image of* P *is given by* $P' = \{\boldsymbol{A}x + \boldsymbol{b} | x \in P\}$. *The generators of the image* P' *can be computed from the generators of* P *by transforming the vertices and rotating the rays:* $\mathsf{Vert}(P') = \{\boldsymbol{A}v + \boldsymbol{b} | v \in \mathsf{Vert}(P)\}$ *and* $\mathsf{Ray}(P') = \{\boldsymbol{A}r | r \in \mathsf{Ray}(P)\}$.

While a variable update $v := \mathsf{expr}$ in r is not always a linear assignment, it can always be converted into a lower and upper bound linear assignments such that $\mathbf{A}_L x + \mathbf{b}_L \leq \mathsf{expr}(x) \leq \mathbf{A}_U x + \mathbf{b}_U$. The image of P can then be computed by $P' = \mathsf{ConvexCl}(P'_L \cup P'_U)$ where P'_π for $\pi \in \{L, U\}$ is the image of P under $(\mathbf{A}_\pi, \mathbf{b}_\pi)$. In the worst case the assignment is bounded by the intersection of the domains $D(v)$ and $D(\mathsf{expr})$. In practice most expressions are already linear or easily bounded. We denote the successive application of all variable updates in r on a polyhedron P by $P' = P[r]$.

Example 2. Consider a polyhedron with a single point $P = \{(i = 0, j = 1, k = 2)\}$. The non-linear update $i := j\%10 + k$ can be converted into the lower bound linear assignment $i := 0 + k$ and upper bound $i := 10 + k$. The image is then a polyhedron P' with two generator points $\mathsf{Vert}(P') = \{(i = 2, j = 1, k = 2), (i = 12, j = 1, k = 2)\}$

With the above operations we are ready to define $\mathsf{Post}^{\#}$. Given an abstract state $s^{\#}$ the successor is computed by accumulating all the variable information in $s^{\#}$ together with the new information obtained from guards and updates in all edges. Formally:

Definition 14 (Abstract posterior). *Given automaton $\mathcal{A}$ with edges E, the posterior of abstract state $s^{\#} \in S^{\#}$ is obtained as follows:*

$$\mathsf{Post}^{\#}(s^{\#}) = s^{\#} \sqcup \bigsqcup \{\bot^{\#}\left[l' \mapsto (s^{\#}(l) \sqcap \psi)[r]\right] | (l, h, \phi, \psi, r, l') \in E\}$$

where $[]$ applied to $\bot^{\#}$ denotes function update.

Theorem 1. $\mathsf{Post}^{\#}$ *is an over-approximation, i.e.,* $\mathsf{Post}^{\#} \sqsupseteq \alpha \circ \mathsf{Post} \circ \gamma$.

3.2 Accelerating Analysis with Widening

By Lemma 1 our abstract domain forms a complete lattice and we can over-approximate the set of reachable states by $S_R^{\#} = \bigsqcup \{\mathsf{Post}^{\#^n}(\alpha(s_0)) | n \in \mathbb{N}\}$. Further, the fix point can be reached in a finite number of steps because the domains of discrete variables are bound. Alas, the analysis has to be fast to be useful in practice. To accelerate towards a fixed-point we employ *widening* c.f. Definition 8. The so-called *standard widening* operator on polyhedra [14] is $P' = P \nabla Q$ where P' is defined by the subset of inequalities in $\mathsf{Ineq}(P)$ that are satisfied by all points in Q. The intuition is that if an increasing chain $(Q_1, \ldots, Q_n)$ breaks an inequality at some Q_i, it will do so again even if the inequality is loosened to encompass Q_i, so the inequality should be removed entirely. The standard widening is often imprecise; just imagine the common case where a variable iterates up to a constant. This has led to the formulation of several more precise widening operators [10,15]. In this paper we employ the widening *up to* method from [10]. We consider the operator ∇^M over $S^{\#}$ where we widen *up to* a set of linear inequalities M.

Definition 15. *Given $s_1^{\#}, s_2^{\#} \in S^{\#}$ and $M = (M_{l_0}, \cdots, M_{l_n})$ where M_l is a finite set of linear inequalities, the widening $s_1^{\#} \nabla^M s_2^{\#}$ is for all $l \in L$ the intersection of the standard widening $s_1^{\#}(l) \nabla s_2^{\#}(l)$ and all inequalities in M_l that are satisfied by both $s_1^{\#}(l)$ and $s_2^{\#}(l)$.*

We keep a distinct M_l for each location $l \in L$. We consider simple cycles, cycles involving each location at most once, from l to itself and compute their invariants by applying guard intersection and linear assignments on the universe polyhedra $\mathbb{R}^{|V|}$ in edge order. M_l is the union of the invariant inequalities for all simple

---

Algorithm 1. Variable Bounds Analysis XTA

Require: $\mathcal{A} = \{L, L^u, L^c, V, X, H(C), E, \ell_0, I\}$ and abstract state $s^\#$
1: **procedure** BOUNDS_ANALYSIS($\mathcal{A}, s^\#$)
2:     Compute cycle invariants M for all locations.
3:     **do**
4:         $s_{old}^\# \leftarrow s^\#$
5:         $s^\# \leftarrow s^\# \nabla^M \mathsf{Post}^\#(s^\#)$
6:     **while** $s_{old}^\# \sqsubseteq s^\#$ ▷ until fixed-point
7:     **return** $s^\#$ ▷ $s^\#$ contains location based variable bounds for $\mathcal{A}$
8: **end procedure**

---

cycles from l to itself. Note that M_l should not be considered as a system of linear inequalities; they may be contradictory. They should instead be considered a set of guesses, that may be proven wrong in future iterations. The intuition is that if a cycle is enabled once it can be fired until reaching some cycle invariant, so we widen up to the tightest available guess.

It is easy to see that $s_1^\# \nabla^M s_2^\#$ is a widening operator: It must contain the union of $s_1^\#$ and $s_2^\#$, and an increasing chain will eventually run out of linear inequalities in M and stabilize by standard widening. This further implies $s^\# \nabla^M \mathsf{Post}^\#(s^\#) \sqsupseteq \mathsf{Post}^\#(s^\#)$ so we know by Theorem 1 that it is also an over-approximation. With $\mathsf{Post}^\#$ and our widening operator defined we can perform the variable bounds analysis in an XTA as described in Algorithm 1.

4 Integer Bounds in Network of XTA

In practice, industrial applications are modeled as networks of XTA. Networks include shared variables and synchronizations among automata, and such interactions can affect the bounds of shared variables. Therefore, in order to apply our analysis presented in Sect. 3, which works at the component level, we need to consider the interactions among automata in the network.

Our approach consists of building a directed graph induced by variable dependencies. If the resulting graph contains cycles, we break the cycles by relaxing the bounds on involved variables to their domains. Finally, we can correctly compute the integer bounds at every component by applying Algorithm 1 in a topological order induced by the acyclic graph.

Definition 16 (Discrete Variable Reads and Writes). *Given an automaton $\mathcal{A}$ with discrete variables V, the set $\mathsf{R}(\mathcal{A}) \subseteq V$ denotes the variables that are being read in updates in $\mathcal{A}$. Similarly the set $\mathsf{W}(\mathcal{A}) \subseteq V$ denotes the variables that are being written in updates in $\mathcal{A}$.*

Definition 17 (Dependency Graph). *Given a network $\mathcal{N} = \mathcal{A}_1, \ldots, \mathcal{A}_n$, its dependency graph $\mathcal{G}(\mathcal{N}) = (\mathfrak{N}, \mathfrak{E})$ is such that $\mathfrak{N} = \{\mathcal{A}_1, \ldots, \mathcal{A}_n\}$ and edges $\mathfrak{E} \subseteq \mathfrak{N} \times \mathfrak{N}$ with $(\mathcal{A}_i, \mathcal{A}_j) \in \mathfrak{E}$ iff. $\mathsf{W}(\mathcal{A}_i) \cap \mathsf{R}(\mathcal{A}_j) \neq \emptyset$.*

Example 3. Fig. 2 shows a dependency graph for a network with 5 automata. We observe that there is read write dependency between $\mathcal{A}_2$ and $\mathcal{A}_4$ because $W(\mathcal{A}_4) \cap R(\mathcal{A}_2) = \{i, j\}$. In addition, there is a cyclic dependency among components $\mathcal{A}_2, \mathcal{A}_3, \mathcal{A}_4$. To break the cycle we must either over-approximate $\{k\}$, $\{m\}$ or $\{i, j\}$ to their full domains. As heuristic, we prioritize removing the edge with the least total amount of variables. Once the cycle has been resolved, we can fix a topological order on the dependency graph and use Algorithm 1 to compute bounds at the component level.

Computing Bounds. Algorithm 2 gives a high level overview of our UPPAAL implementation. The algorithm takes as input a network $\mathcal{N} = (\mathcal{A}_1, \ldots, \mathcal{A}_n)$ and returns an n-tuple of functions from which location-based variable bounds can be obtained. The algorithm maintains a map $\mathcal{B}$ from variables in V to closed intervals $[a, b]$ where a and b are integers. Line 2 constructs the dependency graph $\mathcal{G}(\mathcal{N})$ representing variable dependencies. The for loop in Line 3 eliminates dependency cycles, updates the edges in $\mathfrak{E}$, and stores the eliminated variables in $\bar{V}$.

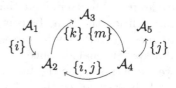

Fig. 2. Dependency graph.

These variables will be over-approximated in Line 7 to the rational bounds $[a, b]$ obtained from finite domain $D(v)$. Using the updated acyclic dependency graph $\mathcal{G}(\mathcal{N})$, Line 8 computes a topological order $\preccurlyeq$ for the automata in $\mathcal{N}$. The for loop from Line 9 iterates over $\mathcal{N}$ using the ordering $\preccurlyeq$. Because variables may be read in guards too, Line 10 ensures that these are

---

Algorithm 2. Bounds Analysis in Network of XTA

Require: A network of XTA $\mathcal{N} = (\mathcal{A}_1, \ldots, \mathcal{A}_n)$
1: $\bar{V} \leftarrow \emptyset; \mathcal{B} \leftarrow \emptyset$
2: construct dependency graph $\mathcal{G}(\mathcal{N}) = (\mathfrak{N}, \mathfrak{E})$
3: **for all** minimal dependency cycles $\mathfrak{E}' \subseteq \mathfrak{E}$ **do**
4:     pick $(\mathcal{A}_i, \mathcal{A}_j) \in \mathfrak{E}'$ and $\mathfrak{E} \leftarrow \mathfrak{E} \setminus \{(\mathcal{A}_i, \mathcal{A}_j)\}$
5:     $\bar{V} \leftarrow \bar{V} \cup (W(\mathcal{A}_i) \cap R(\mathcal{A}_j))$
6: **end for**
7: for all $v \in \bar{V}$ update $\mathcal{B}(v)$ with $[a, b]$ obtained from $D(v)$
8: fix a topological ordering $\preccurlyeq$ from $\mathcal{G}(\mathcal{N})$
9: **for all** $\mathcal{A}_i$ in $\mathcal{N}$ using order $\preccurlyeq$ **do**
10:     remove guards ψ in $\mathcal{A}_i$ such that $\mathcal{A}_i \preccurlyeq \mathcal{A}_j$ and $W(\mathcal{A}_j) \cap V(\psi) \neq \emptyset$
11:     create abstract state $s^\#$ with known bounds in $\mathcal{B}$
12:     $s^\#_{\mathcal{A}_i} \leftarrow$ BOUNDS_ANALYSIS$(\mathcal{A}_i, s^\#)$ ▷ Algorithm 1
13:     for $v \in W(\mathcal{A}_i) \setminus \bar{V}$ obtain $(v, [a, b])$ from $s^\#_{\mathcal{A}_i}$ and merge with $\mathcal{B}$
14: **end for**
15: update $s^\#_{\mathcal{A}_i}$ with bounds in $\mathcal{B}$ for variables in $W(\mathcal{A}_i) \cap W(\mathcal{A}_j)$ for $i, j \leq n$ and $j \neq i$
16: **return** $(s^\#_{\mathcal{A}_1}, \ldots, s^\#_{\mathcal{A}_n})$

over-appoximated by removing guards that depend on writes in automata further down in the $\preccurlyeq$ order. Line 11 creates an abstract state $s^{\#}$ with known bounds in $\mathcal{B}$, this ensures that any write-read dependency is over-approximated. Line 12 executes Algorithm 1 in the modified automaton starting at $s_0^{\#}$. In Line 13 the global variable ranges in $\mathcal{B}$ for v are updated by the possible range of v in the union of all polyhedra in $s_{\mathcal{A}_i}^{\#}$. Finally, Line 15 propagates the global variable bounds in $\mathcal{B}$ to over-approximate write-write dependencies in location bounds for all automata in $\mathcal{N}$.

5 Evaluation

As a first application we use the bounds resulting from the analysis to improve the different extrapolation techniques implemented in UPPAAL. We consider domains where timed automata is often used as the underlying modeling formalism. These domains include scheduling and communication protocols.

Preemptive CPU Scheduler. A CPU scheduler decides which processes should be executed on a set of CPUs. We model a simple scheduling algorithm as a distributed system where the scheduler assigns processes to CPUs through handshake transitions. The scheduler maintains a timer for each running process with a timeout. A timeout results in a clock interrupt forcing the process off the CPU to let a new process run. Processes are able to perform asynchronous I/O operations with I/O system calls (traps) yielding control back to the scheduler. The scheduler varies the timeout based on how many processes are forced to yield by clock interrupts as opposed to yielding early with I/O interrupts. This results in a scheduler assigning large time intervals when few processes require compute resources, reducing the overhead of switching between processes frequently. The model is complex making use of essentially all language features in UPPAAL; functions in assignments and guards, forall-, exists- and select-statements in expressions and arrays of clocks, variables and channels.

Transmission Control Protocol. We modify the Transmission Control Protocol UPPAAL model from [16] to be more true to the specification of TCP [17] by increasing the timeout at each retransmission attempt. Unfortunately, when modelling by exponential backoff as per the specification, we are unable to reduce maximal constants due to the non-linear relations. We instead model it by linear backoff, which is more accurate than no backoff at all. Additionally, we modify the system by adding a *User* trying to open TCP client connections every few seconds through handshake transitions.

5.1 Experimental Results

We have implemented our approach in UPPAAL using the Parma Polyhedra Library [18] for operations on convex polyhedra. Our experiments are run on an Ubuntu machine with 32GB of RAM and 64 AMD Opteron 6376 @ 2.3GHz processors. We consider different models, extrapolation methods, and queries.

Models. We consider the models `Simple-i` where i is the value of the discrete variable i in automaton from Fig. 1a. The Preemptive CPU Scheduler models `Sched-Ni-Pj` described above where variable i is the number of CPUs and j is the number of running processes. The Transmission Control Protocol models `TCP-Ni-Rj` described above where variable i is the number of clients and j is the server table size. The Time-Triggered Protocol for SAE class A sensor/actuator networks [19] `TTPA-i` model where variable i is the number of nodes. The Timed Triggered Architecture protocol [20] `TTAC-i` where variable i is the number of nodes.

Extrapolation Methods. In order to ensure termination, UPPAAL implements different extrapolation methods. Our implementation improves these methods by using tighter bounds. We consider the following extrapolation methods clock difference `DIF` [5], local maximal constant `MAX` [6], and local lower upper bound `LU` [7].

Table 1 shows our results. Column "without analysis" corresponds to the current UPPAAL implementation where extrapolation uses bounds that are extracted from variable type definitions. Column "with analysis" corresponds to our UPPAAL implementation where extrapolation uses bounds resulting from our analysis. The time includes the run time of our analysis. The query AGnotdeadlock verifies absence of deadlocks, query EAllEstablished verifies whether all TCP connections can be established at once.

For the `Simple` models we observe a linear state space reduction. For the `Sched` models we observe a reduction exponential in the number of clocks. We do also observe exponential savings for the satisfied queries in the `TCP` model. In the case of the `TTPA` and `TTAC` models our analysis produces tighter bounds, but no state reduction is achieved. This is because additional invariants prevent clocks to reach the bounds. Nevertheless, we observe that the computation time required for the static analysis is negligible, and thus the static analysis should always be enabled. Finally, the table shows that our analysis can improve all extrapolations currently implemented in UPPAAL.

Accuracy of Variable Bounds. We assert that the bounds identified by our analysis are in fact an over-approximation. Toward this goal, for a given discrete variable i and bounds $[a, b]$, we check the invariant $\forall \Box a \leq i \leq b$. Table 2 shows verified variable bounds. Additionally, we can verify whether bounds are exact when the query $\forall \Box i < b$ is not satisfied. We observe that all bounds are over-approximations and most are exact. It is worth noting that the run time of our analysis is linear in the number of components and has been less than 1 s for all models. In contrast model checking each query requires exploring an exponential number of states induced by the components, which requires several minutes in UPPAAL.

Table 1. Experiments with and without analysis for improved integer bounds. Queries marked with * are not satisfied. States are total states explored.' T.O.indicates a time-out after 2 h.

Model	Query	Extrap.	Without analysis		With analysis		Reduction ratio	
			States	Time sec.	States	Time sec.	States	Time
Simple-7	AGnotdeadlock	MAX	32771	0.32	11	0.05	2979	6.4
Simple-100	AGnotdeadlock	MAX	32771	0.32	104	0.06	315	5.3
Simple-1000	AGnotdeadlock	MAX	32771	0.32	1004	0.07	32.5	4.6
Sched-N1-P2	AGnotdeadlock	MAX	2571	0.14	1326	0.18	1.94	0.76
Sched-N1-P3	AGnotdeadlock	MAX	41080	1.75	9971	0.59	4.12	2.99
Sched-N1-P4	AGnotdeadlock	MAX	361633	97	41883	2.03	8.63	47.58
Sched-N1-P5	AGnotdeadlock	MAX	1945457	2460	126470	15.2	15.38	161.64
Sched-N1-P6	AGnotdeadlock	MAX	-	T.O.	327855	115	-	-
Sched-N1-P8	AGnotdeadlock	MAX	-	T.O.	1716827	5234	-	-
Sched-N1-P2	AGnotdeadlock	DIF	3361	15.5	1777	12.2	1.89	1.27
Sched-N1-P3	AGnotdeadlock	DIF	151901	49.5	48937	17.3	3.10	2.86
Sched-N1-P4	AGnotdeadlock	DIF	-	T.O.	1599344	2618	-	-
TCP-N2-R1	EAllEstablished*	LU	1363973	1531	8424	0.66	161.92	2316.44
TCP-N3-R1	EAllEstablished*	LU	-	T.O.	310240	9.26	-	-
TCP-N4-R1	EAllEstablished*	LU	-	T.O.	10673159	1352	-	-
TCP-N2-R2	EAllEstablished	LU	611	0.1	593	0.47	1.03	0.21
TCP-N3-R3	EAllEstablished	LU	51803	1.46	45718	1.48	1.13	0.98
TCP-N4-R4	EAllEstablished	LU	5968585	352	4441036	151	1.34	2.32
TTPA-6	AGnotdeadlock	MAX	1916683	16	1916683	17	1	0.94
TTPA-7	AGnotdeadlock	MAX	10049328	104	10049328	105	1	0.99
TTAC-4	AGnotdeadlock	MAX	18865320	190	18865320	191	1	0.99

Table 2. Correctness check of computed lower and upper bounds. Bounds marked with † are exact. All bound queries are satisfied.

Model	Var	Bounds	Model	Var	Bounds	Model	Var	Bounds
TTPA-6	PS	$[0,24]^\dagger$	TTAC-3	DeltaRound	$[0,1200]^\dagger$	TTAC-4	DeltaRound	$[0,1500]^\dagger$
	TT	$[0,42]^\dagger$		MEDL.date	$[0,2399]$		MEDL.date	$[0,2999]$
	PR	$[0,18]^\dagger$		BusGuardian0.date	$[0,562]^\dagger$		BusGuardian0.date	$[0,562]^\dagger$
TTPA-7	PS	$[0,28]^\dagger$		BusGuardian1.date	$[0,862]^\dagger$		BusGuardian1.date	$[0,862]^\dagger$
	TT	$[0,49]^\dagger$		BusGuardian2.date	$[0,1162]^\dagger$		BusGuardian2.date	$[0,1162]^\dagger$
	PR	$[0,21]^\dagger$		BusGuardian3.date	$[0,1462]^\dagger$		BusGuardian3.date	$[0,1462]^\dagger$
							BusGuardian4.date	$[0,1762]^\dagger$

6 Conclusion and Future Work

Networks of Extended Timed Automata are extensively used to show the correctness of industrial systems. The decidability results for model checking using XTA are based on extrapolations which use constants appearing in guards in the underlying automata. In practice model checkers like UPPAAL use richer languages and allow for integer variables and expressions. Currently UPPAAL will use the type definitions to obtain integer variable bounds, these bounds are often unnecessary large and have a negative effect in the verification process.

We present an abstract interpretation for computing tighter integer bounds for integer variables. To make the approach scalabe the static analysis is performed at the component level. We lift our analysis to networks of XTA by detecting variable dependencies and over-approximating some involved variables. The new bounds computed by our analysis are available to all extrapolation operations implemented in UPPAAL, which include local maximal constants, lower upper bound, and clock difference abstractions. Our experiments show promising results, we observe that the above mentioned extrapolation operations greatly profit from the tighter bounds. Additionally, in cases where there is no state space reduction, we observe that the overhead of the static analysis is insignificant, thus it should always be enabled.

Future Work. Recent work in [11] presents Urgent Partial Order Reduction (UPOR) for XTA. Since integer bounds were not available before in UPPAAL, the current implementation over-approximates integer variables by removing integer guards and relaxing clock constraints. This introduces a number of dependencies which prevent the application of UPOR. We plan to refine the UPOR analysis using the results from this paper. In addition, in [21] an abstraction method based in constants for Priced Timed Automata and priced zones is presented. In similar ways as for XTA, the analysis presented in this paper can be extended to support and improve such existing abstraction techniques.

References

1. Alur, R., Dill, D.L.: A theory of timed automata. Theor. Comput. Sci. **126**(2), 183–235 (1994)
2. Behrmann, G., David, A., Larsen, K.G.: A tutorial on UPPAAL. In: Bernardo, M., Corradini, F. (eds.) SFM-RT 2004. LNCS, vol. 3185, pp. 200–236. Springer, Heidelberg (2004). https://doi.org/10.1007/978-3-540-30080-9_7
3. Feo-Arenis, S., Westphal, B., Dietsch, D., Muñiz, M., Andisha, S., Podelski, A.: Ready for testing: ensuring conformance to industrial standards through formal verification. Formal Aspects Comput. **28**(3), 499–527 (2016). https://doi.org/10.1007/s00165-016-0365-3
4. Havelund, K., Skou, A., Larsen, K.G., Lund, K.: Formal modeling and analysis of an audio/video protocol: an industrial case study using UPPAAL. In: Proceedings Real-Time Systems Symposium, pp. 2–13 (1997). https://doi.org/10.1109/REAL.1997.641264
5. Bengtsson, J., Yi, W.: On clock difference constraints and termination in reachability analysis of timed automata. In: Dong, J.S., Woodcock, J. (eds.) ICFEM 2003. LNCS, vol. 2885, pp. 491–503. Springer, Heidelberg (2003). https://doi.org/10.1007/978-3-540-39893-6_28
6. Behrmann, G., Bouyer, P., Fleury, E., Larsen, K.G.: Static guard analysis in timed automata verification. In: Garavel, H., Hatcliff, J. (eds.) TACAS 2003. LNCS, vol. 2619, pp. 254–270. Springer, Heidelberg (2003). https://doi.org/10.1007/3-540-36577-X_18
7. Behrmann, G., Bouyer, P., Larsen, K.G., Pelánek, R.: Lower and upper bounds in zone-based abstractions of timed automata. Int. J. Softw. Tools Technol. Transf. **8**(3), 204–215 (2006). https://doi.org/10.1007/s10009-005-0190-0. ISSN: 1433-2787

8. Cousot, P., Cousot, R.: Abstract interpretation: a unified lattice model for static analysis of programs by construction or approximation of fixpoints. In: Proceedings of the 4th ACM SIGACT-SIGPLAN Symposium on Principles of Programming Languages, POPL 1977, pp. 238–252. Association for Computing Machinery, Los Angeles (1977). ISBN: 9781450373500. https://doi.org/10.1145/512950.512973

9. Herbreteau, F., Srivathsan, B., Walukiewicz, I.: Better abstractions for timed automata. In: 2012 27th Annual IEEE Symposium on Logic in Computer Science, pp. 375–384 (2012). https://doi.org/10.1109/LICS.2012.48

10. Halbwachs, N., Proy, Y.-E., Roumanosff, P.: Verification of real-time systems using linear relation analysis. Formal Methods Syst. Des. **11**, 157–185 (1997). https://doi.org/10.1023/A:1008678014487

11. Larsen, K.G., Mikučionis, M., Muñiz, M., Srba, J.: Urgent partial order reduction for extended timed automata. In: Hung, D.V., Sokolsky, O. (eds.) ATVA 2020. LNCS, vol. 12302, pp. 179–195. Springer, Cham (2020). https://doi.org/10.1007/978-3-030-59152-6_10 ISBN: 978-3-030-59152-6

12. Wies, T.: Symbolic shape analysis. PhD thesis. University of Freiburg (2009). http://www.freidok.uni-freiburg.de/volltexte/6972/

13. Cousot, P., Cousot, R.: Constructive versions of tarski's fixed point theorems. English (US). Pac. J. Math. **82**(1), 43–57 (1979). https://doi.org/10.2140/pjm.1979.82.43. ISSN: 0030–8730

14. Cousot, P., Halbwachs, N.: Automatic discovery of linear restraints among variables of a program. In: Proceedings of the 5th ACM SIGACT-SIGPLAN Symposium on Principles of Programming Languages, pp. 84–96 (1978)

15. Bagnara, R., Hill, P.M., Ricci, E., Zaffanella, E.: Precise widening operators for convex polyhedra. Sci. Comput. Program. **58**(1–2), 28–56 (2005)

16. Saini, S., Fehnker, A.: Evaluating the stream control transmission protocol using uppaal. In: Electronic Proceedings in Theoretical Computer Science, vol. 244, March 2017, pp. 1–13. https://doi.org/10.4204/eptcs.244.1

17. Paxson, V., Allman, M., Chu, J., Sargent, M.: Computing TCP's retransmission timer. Technical report rfc 2988, November (2000)

18. Bagnara, R., Hill, P.M., Zaffanella, E.: The Parma polyhedra library: toward a complete set of numerical abstractions for the analysis and verification of hardware and software systems. Sci. Comput. Program. **72**(1), 3–21 (2008). https://doi.org/10.1016/j.scico.2007.08.001. http://www.sciencedirect.com/science/article/pii/S0167642308000415. Special Issue on Second issue of experimental software and toolkits (EST). ISSN: 0167–6423

19. Steiner, W., Elmenreich, W.: Automatic Recovery of the TTP/A Sensor/Actuator Network, October 2003

20. Godary, K.: Validation temporelle de réseaux embarqués critiques etfiables pour l'automobile. PhD thesis. Institut National des Sciences Appliquées de Lyon (2005)

21. Bouyer, P., Colange, M., Markey, N.: Symbolic optimal reachability in weighted timed automata. In: Chaudhuri, S., Farzan, A. (eds.) CAV 2016, Part I. LNCS, vol. 9779, pp. 513–530. Springer, Cham (2016). https://doi.org/10.1007/978-3-319-41528-4_28 ISBN: 978-3-319-41528-4

Explaining Safety Violations in Real-Time Systems

Thomas Mari[1,2]([✉]), Thao Dang[2], and Gregor Gössler[1]

[1] Univ. Grenoble Alpes, INRIA, CNRS, Grenoble INP, LIG, 38000 Grenoble, France
`gregor.goessler@inria.fr`
[2] CNRS/VERIMAG, Grenoble, France

Abstract. We tackle the problem of explaining faults in real-time systems. Intuitively, an explanation of the violation of a safety property by an execution is a concise excerpt of the faulty execution that retains only the elements that were relevant for entailing the violation, thus exhibiting how causes accumulate over time and propagate to entail the effect. Fault explanation therefore goes beyond the well-known concepts of fault diagnosis and localization.

We provide a formal definition of causal explanations on dense-time models, based on the well-studied formalisms of timed automata and zone-based abstractions. Our approach is able to account for limited observability of the faulty execution. We propose a symbolic formalization to effectively construct such explanations, which we have implemented in a prototype tool. We illustrate our approach on several examples.

1 Introduction

Embedded real-time systems have been part of our daily lives for several decades now, and the number of such devices is growing exponentially. There is a rich body of work on software engineering, formal verification, and certification of such systems. However, when looking at the headlines about failures and casualties caused by embedded systems, one may wonder whether we have learned to fully master their growing complexity.

As a complementary approach, accountability aims at constructing systems in such a way that the responsibilities for a failure can be identified and explained *post mortem* [15]. Intuitively, an explanation is a concise excerpt of the observed execution that retains only the elements that were relevant for entailing the violation. However, formalizing this objective is far from obvious, and different communities have tackled the problem under different angles.

A first challenge consists in conveying the "right" amount of information, *e.g.*, in order to help a human expert in quickly understanding the causes of the violation, or to automatically react to the failure by swapping a component

This work has been partially supported by the projects Univ. Grenoble Alpes IRS SEC, ANR DCore (ANR-18-CE25-0007), and ANR-CREST-JST CyphAI.

C. Dima and M. Shirmohammadi (Eds.): FORMATS 2021, LNCS 12860, pp. 100–116, 2021.
https://doi.org/10.1007/978-3-030-85037-1_7

or changing parameters. In this work we are interested in *causal* explanations that allow us to track the chains from cause to effect while eliminating irrelevant events from the explanation.

A second challenge is to devise explanations that satisfy the requirements of embedded systems. First, embedded real-time systems usually have an infinite state space, requiring reasoning on an appropriate abstraction. Nevertheless, research on reasoning about causation on abstractions is only in its infancy [2,7]. Second, explanations for embedded systems have to cope with the limited observability of state and events, which is again an issue that is hardly addressed in existing work on causation.

The work presented in this paper is part of an ongoing effort to construct explainable embedded real-time systems. We investigate how to construct, from a system model, a safety property, and an execution log that violates the property, a concise explanation of how the log brought about the violation of the property.

This paper makes the following contributions. We provide a formal definition of causal explanations on dense-time models, based on the well-studied formalism of timed automata. We propose a symbolic approach to effectively construct explanations. We illustrate our approach on several examples and a case study.

2   Related Work

Causal Explanations. Our construction of choice explanations is based on effective choice explanations for discrete-event systems [6]. The latter are, in turn, inspired by [11], which leverages game theory to explain counterexample traces from model-checking by exhibiting the portions of the trace in which the system could have avoided the violation of an expected property no matter how the environment behaves.

Several authors have proposed a construction of explanations for the satisfaction of a property P by an execution trace based on sub-sequences of the trace that are sufficient to entail P, such as explanatory diagnoses [17] and causal compression [4]. However, in contrast to our approach, sub-sequence explanations do not convey any information about the outcome produced by alternative branches in a non-deterministic system.

Static program slicing [22] determines a part ("slice") of a program that influences a set of variables at a given point. Dynamic slicing [14] computes a slice for a given computation, yielding a smaller slice. In contrast to slicing, our approach accounts for counterfactual runs that have not been taken in the actual execution.

Fault Diagnosis, Localization, and Repair. Counterfactual causation has been studied in many disciplines as a precise assessment of individual causes that contribute to bring about an effect, see e.g. the influential definition of *actual causality* in [9]. Some form of counterfactual reasoning has been used by many authors to diagnose, localize, and repair faults. We only cite some representative examples here. As these approaches exhibit individual causes rather than chains from cause to effect, they are less apt to explain how contributory causes accumulate over time and propagate to entail an effect. The seminal work of [19] proposes a framework of model-based fault diagnosis that defines a diagnosis as a minimal sets of components whose faults make the observations consistent with the system model. The use of a distance metric is explored in [8] to localize, based on an error trace, a possible fault as the difference between the error trace and a closest correct trace. Similarly, Delta debugging [24] starts from a failing and a passing input and finds a pair of a failing and a passing input with minimal distance. A variant of actual causality is used in [3] to over-approximate the set of causes for the first violation of an LTL formula by a trace. The goal of program repair is, given a program that violates an expected property P, to construct a syntactically close program that satisfies P, see e.g. [21] for the repair of reactive programs. Closer to our setting, [12] uses MaxSMT to repair clock bounds in a network of timed automata so as to ensure an expected property.

In contrast to the pieces of related work cited above that are based on some form of model to compare the actual execution with counterfactual traces, many recent techniques summarized under the umbrella term of *explainable AI* lack a model and hence, the possibility of counterfactual reasoning [18].

3   Preliminaries

Let C be a set of clock variables that take values in $\mathbb{R}^+$. A C-valuation is a function $C \to \mathbb{R}^+$. Let $\mathbf{0}$ denote the C-valuation assigning 0 to all clocks. An atomic constraint on C is an inequality $c \sim k$ or $c - c' \sim k$ where $c, c' \in C$, $\sim \in \{\leq, <, \geq, >\}$ and $k \in \mathbb{N}$. We say that a C-valuation v satisfies an atomic constraint $c \sim k$ (or $c - c' \sim k$) if $v(c) \sim k$ (or $v(c) - v(c') \sim k$). A C-constraint is a finite conjunction of all atomic constraints on C. Let $\mathbb{C}$ denote the set of C-constraints. By abuse of notation, we use a C-constraint interchangably with the sets of C-valuations that satisfy it.

Definition 1 (Timed Automaton). *A timed automaton (TA) $\mathcal{A}$ is a tuple $\mathcal{A} = \langle \Sigma, L, L_0, C, F, \mathcal{I}, E \rangle$ where*

- *Σ is a finite set of events;*
- *L is a finite set of locations;*
- *$L_0 \subseteq L$ is the set of initial locations;*
- *C is a set of clock variables;*
- *$F \subseteq L$ is a set of accepting locations;*
- *$\mathcal{I} : L \to \mathbb{C}$ specifies for each location an invariant;*
- *$E \subseteq L \times \mathbb{C} \times \Sigma \times 2^C \times L$ is a set of edges of the form $e = \langle \ell, g, \sigma, X, \ell' \rangle$ where ℓ and ℓ' are respectively source and target locations; σ is an event; g is the guard of e; and X is a set of clocks to be reset when the edge is traversed.*

To account for the fact that some events are not observable, the set Σ of events is partitioned into two subsets of observable and unobservable events.

We formalize the semantics of timed automata using labeled transition systems, or LTS. An LTS is a tuple $\langle \Sigma, \mathcal{V}, \mathcal{E}, \mathcal{V}^0, \mathcal{V}^F \rangle$ where Σ is the alphabet, $\mathcal{V}$ is a set of nodes, $\mathcal{E} \subseteq \mathcal{V} \times \Sigma \times \mathcal{V}$ is the set of labeled transitions, and $\mathcal{V}^0 \subseteq \mathcal{V}$ and $\mathcal{V}^F \subseteq \mathcal{V}$ are the sets of initial and accepting nodes, respectively. For $\nu \in \mathcal{V}$ let $\nu^\bullet = \{\nu' \in \mathcal{V} \mid \exists \sigma \in \Sigma : (\nu, \sigma, \nu') \in \mathcal{E}\}$ be the postset of ν. In the following we use the terms LTS and graph interchangeably.

Definition 2 (Semantic LTS). *The* semantic LTS *of a timed automaton* $\mathcal{A} = \langle \Sigma, L, L_0, C, F, \mathcal{I}, E \rangle$ *is the LTS* $sem(\mathcal{A}) = \langle \Sigma', \mathcal{V}, \mathcal{E}, \mathcal{V}^0, \mathcal{V}^F \rangle$ *where*

- $\Sigma' = \Sigma \cup \mathbb{R}^+$ *is the set of labels;*
- $\mathcal{V} = \{(\ell, v) \mid \ell \in L \wedge v \in \mathcal{I}(\ell)\}$, *i.e. the states of* $\mathcal{A}$ *are the pairs* (ℓ, v) *where* $v \in \mathcal{I}(\ell)$ *is a clock valuation that satisfies the invariant of the location* ℓ;
- $\mathcal{V}^0 = \{(\ell, v) \in \mathcal{V} \mid \ell \in L_0 \wedge v = \mathbf{0}\}$;
- $\mathcal{V}^F = \mathcal{V}$ *(indeed the accepting states do not matter);*
- *the set of transitions are of two types, discrete and time transitions:*

$$\mathcal{E} = \{((\ell, v), \sigma, (\ell', v')) \mid \exists g, X : \langle \ell, g, \sigma, X, \ell' \rangle \in E \wedge v' = v[X := 0] \wedge v' \in \mathcal{I}(\ell')\}$$
$$\cup \{((\ell, v), \delta, (\ell, v')) \mid \delta > 0 \wedge v' = v + \delta \wedge v' \in \mathcal{I}(\ell)\}$$

The states (ℓ', v') *and* (ℓ, v') *are respectively called e-successor δ-successor of* (ℓ, v).

As usual we write $(\ell, v) \xrightarrow{\cdot} (\ell', v')$ for $((\ell, v), \cdot, (\ell', v')) \in \mathcal{E}$. By abuse of notation we omit the curly braces in $\{\nu^0\}$ when there is a single initial state. Note that since δ is a real number, a time transition $(\ell, v) \xrightarrow{\delta} (\ell, v')$ can be split into an arbitrary number k of time transitions, that is, $(\ell, v) \xrightarrow{\delta_1} (\ell, v_1) \xrightarrow{\delta_2} (\ell, v_2) \ldots \xrightarrow{\delta_k} (\ell, v_k)$ such that $\delta = \delta_1 + \delta_2 + \ldots + \delta_k$.

Definition 3 (Runs and Traces). *Let* $G = \langle \Sigma, \mathcal{V}, \mathcal{E}, \mathcal{V}^0, \mathcal{V}^F \rangle$ *be an LTS.*

- *A* run *of* G *starting from* $\nu_1 \in \mathcal{V}$ *is a (finite or infinite) sequence of states and transitions:* $\rho = \nu_1 \xrightarrow{e_1} \nu_2 \xrightarrow{e_2} \ldots$. *We denote by* $\Upsilon(G)$ *the set of all runs of* G. *A state* ν *is* reachable *if there is a run from an initial state to* ν.
- *Given a run* $\rho \in \Upsilon(G)$, *the sequence of labels in* ρ *is called* trace. *We denote by* $\Psi(G)$ *the set of all traces of* G.

Definition 4 (Timed Log). *A* timed log *is a one-clock, deterministic and acyclic TA. In addition, all the events of the automaton are observable.*

An example of timed log is a timed automaton roughly depicted as follows: $l_0 \xrightarrow{x=t_0, a, \emptyset} l_1 \xrightarrow{x=t_1, b, \emptyset} l_2 \xrightarrow{x=t_2, a, \emptyset} l_3$, with l_3 as an accepting location and l_0 an initial location. The edge from the location l_0 to the location l_1 has the guard $x = t_0$; its event is a; and its set of clocks to be reset is empty.

As mentioned in the introduction, we are interested in explaining why a system, modeled as a timed automaton $\mathcal{A}$, violates a safety property. To this end, we define a *safety property observer* as a timed automaton with one sink state, to model the property violation of a timed log. In addition, this observer is required to be receptive with respect to all observable events of $\mathcal{A}$, as defined in the following. An LTS $\langle \Sigma, \mathcal{V}, \mathcal{E}, \mathcal{V}^0, \mathcal{V}^F \rangle$ is *receptive* over $\Sigma_1 \subseteq \Sigma$ if at every reachable state ν, all events in Σ_1 are enabled, that is, $\forall \sigma \in \Sigma_1 \; \exists \nu' : \nu \xrightarrow{\sigma} \nu'$. Given a timed log $\mathcal{L}$ and a safety property observer $\mathcal{P}$, we say that $\mathcal{L}$ violates the safety property at hand if each run of $\mathcal{L}$ is a run of $\mathcal{P}$ that reaches the sink state.

The sets of states and transitions of a timed automaton are infinite, and therefore, as in verification, finite abstractions can be used to construct explanations. In this work, we use time-abstracting bisimulations to abstract away the quantitative information about time lapses in the execution of a timed automaton. This leads to finite discrete abstractions of the original timed automata from which we can compute choice-based explanations [6]. The following definition is adapted from [20] so as to distingluish events, and accepting vs. non-accepting states.

Definition 5 (Strong bisimulations). *A binary relation $\sim$ on an LTS $G = \langle \Sigma, \mathcal{V}, \mathcal{E}, \mathcal{V}^0, \mathcal{V}^F \rangle$ is a* strong bisimulation *if for any pair of nodes p and q of G such that $p \sim q$, the following conditions hold:*

- $\forall \sigma \in \Sigma \; \forall p' \in \mathcal{V} : \left(p \xrightarrow{\sigma} p' \implies \exists q' : q \xrightarrow{\sigma} q' \wedge p' \sim q' \right);$
- *the above condition also holds when p and q are swapped;*
- $p \in \mathcal{V}^F \iff q \in \mathcal{V}^F.$

When G is the semantic LTS of a TA, the relation $\sim$ is a strong time-abstracting bisimulation *(STAB) if for any pair of nodes $p = \langle \ell_1, v_1 \rangle$ and $q = \langle \ell_2, v_2 \rangle$ of G such that $p \sim q$, the following conditions hold:*

- $\ell_1 = \ell_2;$
- $\forall \sigma \in \Sigma \setminus \mathbb{R}^+ \; \forall p' \in \mathcal{V} : \left(p \xrightarrow{\sigma} p' \implies \exists q' : q \xrightarrow{\sigma} q' \wedge p' \sim q' \right);$
- $\forall \delta > 0 \; \forall p' \in \mathcal{V} : \left(p \xrightarrow{\delta} p' \implies \exists \delta' > 0 \; \exists q' : q \xrightarrow{\delta'} q' \wedge p' \sim q' \right);$
- *the above conditions also hold when p and q are swapped;*
- $p \in \mathcal{V}^F \iff q \in \mathcal{V}^F.$

We use STAB, implemented in Minim [20], to construct a finite symbolic abstraction of TA. We then reduce the latter with respect to strong bisimulation so as to merge bisimilar states involving different locations.

4   Explanations

Our goal is to explain, for a TA $\mathcal{A}$ modelling a system, an observer $\mathcal{P}$ of a safety property, and a timed log $\mathcal{L}$ of observable events of $\mathcal{A}$ that violates $\mathcal{P}$, how the violation came to happen. More precisely, in this work, we focus on *non-deterministic choices* in the execution that entailed the failure, where different choices would have helped to avoid it. Prominent of such failures are "concurrency bugs" that only occur in certain interleavings of threads, and deadline misses due to bad scheduling decisions in real-time systems.

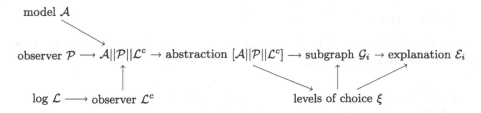

Fig. 1. Overview of the approach.

To construct such explanations for real-time systems, we lift the *effective choice explanations* formalized in [6] to timed automata. The main steps of our construction, as shown in Fig. 1, are the following.

1. Construct a timed *log observer* $\mathcal{L}^c$ from $\mathcal{L}$ that tracks, for any run ρ of $\mathcal{L}^c$, whether the observable behavior of ρ produces $\mathcal{L}$.
2. Compose $\mathcal{A}$, $\mathcal{P}$, and $\mathcal{L}^c$ to form a timed automaton $\mathcal{A}||\mathcal{P}||\mathcal{L}^c$, where $||$ is the standard parallel composition of timed automata, see *e.g.* [23].
3. Construct a discrete abstraction $[\mathcal{A}||\mathcal{P}||\mathcal{L}^c]$ of the continuous-time semantics of $\mathcal{A}||\mathcal{P}||\mathcal{L}^c$, using a time-abstracting bisimulation.
4. Compute the *levels of choice* on $[\mathcal{A}||\mathcal{P}||\mathcal{L}^c]$ that, intuitively, represent, for each equivalence class $q \in [\mathcal{A}||\mathcal{P}||\mathcal{L}^c]$, the number of *bad choices* $\xi(q)$ left before violating $\mathcal{P}$.
5. Extract, from $[\mathcal{A}||\mathcal{P}||\mathcal{L}^c]$, a sequence of subgraphs $\mathcal{G}_i$ representing the traces that will be condensed to an explanation of length i.
6. Abstract away, from each $\mathcal{G}_i$, all transitions that do not decrease ξ, in order to obtain the explanation $\mathcal{E}_i$ that retains only those (discrete or timed) transitions that contributed to the failure.

We will now discuss each of these steps.

Log Observer. Given an alphabet Σ and a timed log $\mathcal{L}$ over the observable alphabet $\Sigma^{obs} \subseteq \Sigma$, we construct a *log observer* that accepts all runs over Σ and enters an accepting *sink* state whenever an observed behavior is inconsistent with the log.

Definition 6 (Log observer). *The observer of a log* $\mathcal{L} = \langle \Sigma, L, L_0, C, F, \mathcal{I}, E \rangle$ *is the TA* $\mathcal{L}^c := \langle \Sigma, L', L_0, C, F, \mathcal{I}', E' \rangle$ *where*

- $L' = L \cup \{sink\}$ *where* $sink \notin L$ *is a fresh location;*
- $\mathcal{I}' = \mathcal{I} \cup \{sink \mapsto true\}$*;*
- $E' = E \cup E_1 \cup E_2$ *where*
  - $E_1 = \{\ell \xrightarrow{\mathcal{C}(\ell,\sigma),\sigma,\emptyset} sink \mid \ell \in L \wedge \sigma \in \Sigma\}$ *where* $\mathcal{C}(\ell,\sigma) = \neg \bigvee\{g \mid \exists \ell' \in L : \ell \xrightarrow{g,\sigma,\cdot} \ell'\}$.

- $E_2 = \{sink \xrightarrow{true,\sigma,\emptyset} sink \mid \sigma \in \Sigma\}.$

Intuitively, E_1 is the set of edges from a location in $\mathcal{L}$ that are not consistent with $\mathcal{L}$, used to make the log observer receptive with respect to Σ^{obs}.

Discrete Abstraction. To obtain discrete abstractions for the timed automaton $\mathcal{A}||\mathcal{P}||\mathcal{L}^c$, we use the STAB of Definition 5. Let us briefly recall the notion of time-abstracting quotient graph [20]. Given a TA over alphabet Σ with semantic LTS $G = \langle \Sigma \cup \mathbb{R}^+, \mathcal{V}, \mathcal{E}, \mathcal{V}^0, \mathcal{V}^F \rangle$ and a partition $\tilde{\mathcal{V}}$ of $\mathcal{V}$, the quotient of G with respect to $\tilde{\mathcal{V}}$ is the LTS $G/\tilde{\mathcal{V}} = \langle \Sigma', \tilde{\mathcal{V}}, \mathcal{E}', \tilde{\mathcal{V}}^0, \tilde{\mathcal{V}}^F \rangle$ where

- $\Sigma' = \Sigma \cup \{\delta\}$ where δ is a fresh symbol;
- $\mathcal{E}' = \{\tilde{\nu} \xrightarrow{\sigma} \tilde{\nu}' \mid (\nu, \sigma, \nu') \in \mathcal{E} \wedge \sigma \in \Sigma\} \cup \{\tilde{\nu} \xrightarrow{\delta} \tilde{\nu}' \mid \exists t > 0 : (\nu, t, \nu') \in \mathcal{E}\};$
- $\tilde{\mathcal{V}}^0 = \{\tilde{\nu} \mid \nu \in \mathcal{V}^0\}$ and $\tilde{\mathcal{V}}^F = \{\tilde{\nu} \mid \nu \in \mathcal{V}^F\}$

and for $\nu \in \mathcal{V}$, $\tilde{\nu}$ denotes the element of $\tilde{\mathcal{V}}$ for which $\nu \in \tilde{\nu}$.

In particular, we are interested in the quotient with respect to the equivalence classes of states, called symbolic states, induced by STAB. Let $[\mathcal{A}||\mathcal{P}||\mathcal{L}^c] := \mathcal{A}||\mathcal{P}||\mathcal{L}^c/\sim$ be the quotient graph with respect to STAB. This quotient graph can be computed by the existing timed automata model-checkers, such as UPPAAL and Kronos [16,23]. In this work, we use the tool Minim [20] integrated in Kronos.

Levels of Choice. In the following, we compute the level of choice on $[\mathcal{A}||\mathcal{P}||\mathcal{L}^c]$. Intuitively, the level of choice measures how close the system is to violating the required safety property.

Definition 7 (Level of choice). *Given an LTS $G = \langle \Sigma, \mathcal{V}, \mathcal{E}, \mathcal{V}^0, \mathcal{V}^F \rangle$, we say that $\xi : \mathcal{V} \to \mathbb{N} \cup \{\infty\}$ is the level of choice function if:*

1. *$\forall \nu \in \mathcal{V}^F : \xi(\nu) = 0$*
2. *$\forall \nu \in \mathcal{V}$ such that ν is not co-reachable, $\xi(\nu) = \infty$*
3. *for all other states $\nu \in \mathcal{V}$ let*

$$\xi(\nu) = \min^+ \left(\{\ell \mid \exists \nu' : \xi(\nu') = \ell \wedge \exists e \in \Sigma : \nu \xrightarrow{e} \nu'\} \right)$$

   where

$$\min^+(G) = \begin{cases} \min(G) & \text{if } |G| \leq 1 \\ 1 + \min(G) & \text{otherwise} \end{cases}$$

   and we set $\min \emptyset = \infty$.
4. *Maximality: ξ is maximal among the functions fulfilling the preceding conditions.*

Definition 8 (Effective choice). *Given an LTS $G = \langle \Sigma, \mathcal{V}, \mathcal{E}, \nu^0, \mathcal{V}^F \rangle$ and a level of choice function $\xi : \mathcal{V} \to \mathbb{N} \cup \{\infty\}$, a transition $s \xrightarrow{e} s' \in \mathcal{E}$ is an effective choice transition iff $\xi(s) = 1 + \xi(s')$ and $\exists \rho = s' \xrightarrow{e_0} s_1 \xrightarrow{e_1} ...s_n \in run(G)$ such that $\xi(s_n) = 0$ and $(\max_{s \in \rho} \xi(s)) = \xi(s')$. When such a transition exists, the state s is called an effective choice state.*

Intuitively, an effective choice transition is a transition that decrements the level of choice and is prefix of a run ρ violating $\mathcal{P}$ along which the level of choice no longer exceeds $\xi(s')$.

Theorem 1. *Given an LTS $G = \langle \Sigma, \mathcal{V}, \mathcal{E}, \mathcal{V}^0, \mathcal{V}^F \rangle$, a level of choice function ξ on G, and a strong bisimulation $\sim$ on $\mathcal{V}$, we have that $s \sim s' \implies \xi(s) = \xi(s')$.*

Proof (sketch). Let $n \in \mathbb{N}$ be the smallest level of choice such that two bisimilar states have different levels of choice.

$$\exists s, s' \in \mathcal{V} \times \mathcal{V}, (\xi(s) = n \vee \xi(s') = n) \wedge s \sim s' \wedge \xi(s) \neq \xi(s') \qquad \text{(P(n))}$$

Toward contradiction, we suppose that there exists a minimal $n \in \mathbb{N}$ such that the above formula $P(n)$ holds. For the case $n = 0$, we can notice that two states in $\mathcal{V}^F$ have the level of choice 0 by construction. We can reach a contradiction because from a state s with $\xi(s) > 0$ there is a path that avoids $\mathcal{V}^F$, while from the state s' with $\xi(s') = 0$ all paths lead to $\mathcal{V}^F$. The respective successors are also bisimilar but only one of them is in $\mathcal{V}^F$. For the case $n > 0$, we can reach a contradiction by proving that n is not minimal. For this case the proof is longer.

This theorem allows us to work on the LTS further reduced with respect to strong bisimulation instead of $[\mathcal{A}||\mathcal{P}||\mathcal{L}^c]$, as we know that bisimulation preserves the level of choice.

Once we have the abstraction $[\mathcal{A}||\mathcal{P}||\mathcal{L}^c]$ and labeling with levels of choice, we are ready to extract the explanations. The basic idea is to extract, from $[\mathcal{A}||\mathcal{P}||\mathcal{L}^c]$, a graph that retains only

- the states of $[\mathcal{A}||\mathcal{P}||\mathcal{L}^c]$ that are co-reachable from the final location of $\mathcal{L}^c$, *i.e.*, the states that are consistent with the observed log, and
- the edges along which the level of choice decreases, *i.e.*, the ones that bring the system closer to a violation of $\mathcal{P}$.

To this end we proceed as follows.

Graph Splitting. Given an acyclic graph $G = \langle \Sigma, \mathcal{V}, \mathcal{E}, \mathcal{V}^0, \mathcal{V}^F \rangle$ equipped with a level of choice function $\xi : \mathcal{V} \to \mathbb{N} \cup \{\infty\}$, we compute a split graph as follows. For any $\nu \in \mathcal{V}$ let

$$bounds(\nu) = \begin{cases} \{\max\{\xi(\nu), bounds(\nu')\} \mid \nu' \in \nu^\bullet\} & \text{if } \nu^\bullet \neq \emptyset \\ \{\xi(\nu)\} & \text{otherwise} \end{cases}$$

We define the split graph $\mathcal{G} = \langle \Sigma, \mathcal{V}', \mathcal{E}', (\mathcal{V}')^0, (\mathcal{V}')^F \rangle$ where

$$\mathcal{V}' = \{(\nu, b) \mid \nu \in \mathcal{V} \wedge b \in bounds(\nu)\}$$
$$\mathcal{E}' = \{((\nu, b), e, (\nu', b')) \mid (\nu, e, \nu') \in \mathcal{E} \wedge b = \max\{b', \xi(\nu)\}$$
$$(\mathcal{V}')^0 = \{(\nu, b) \in \mathcal{V}' \mid \nu \in \mathcal{V}^0\}$$
$$(\mathcal{V}')^F = \{(\nu, b) \mid \nu \in \mathcal{V}^F\}$$

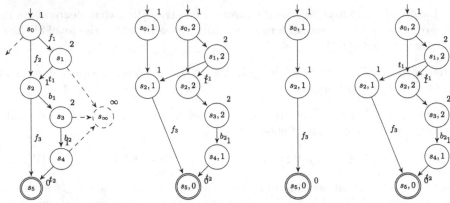

(a) Discrete graph with levels of choice.

(b) Split graph. Only labels of effective choice transitions are shown.

(c) Subgraph 1

(d) Subgraph 2

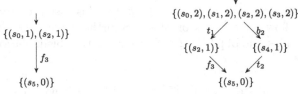

(e) Explanation $\mathcal{E}_1$. The shortest explanation of the system failure is the occurrence of event f_3.

(f) Explanation $\mathcal{E}_2$. The events that ultimately entailed the system failure are either $t_1; f_3$ or $b_2; t_2$.

Fig. 2. Splitting, sub-graph extraction, and explanations obtained after determinization. Dashed transitions are in the model but not consistent with the log.

That is, we duplicate the states according to the maximum levels of choice that may be encountered in the future, and update the edges so as to point to the matching copy. We extend ξ to the split graph by putting $\xi((\nu, b)) := \xi(\nu)$. Intuitively, $\mathcal{G}$ accepts the same traces as G, while ensuring that each state is either effective choice or not, independent of the future behavior.

Example 1. Consider the discrete graph shown in Fig. 2(a). From s_0 a fault f_1 or f_2 may occur, and f_1 may be coped with until a timeout t_1 occurs. From s_2, a second fault f_3 will entail a system failure. However, the initial fault can be handled by primary and secondary fallback mechanisms b_1 and b_2, until a timeout t_2 occurs. The split graph is shown in Fig. 2(b).

Subgraph Extraction. The explanations in the split graph are bounded in length by $[\xi(\nu_0), \max \xi]$. Our experiments suggest that explanations are easier to grasp when only explanations of the same length are presented simultaneously. We therefore extract, from the split graph $\mathcal{G} = \langle \Sigma, \mathcal{V}', \mathcal{E}', (\mathcal{V}')^0, (\mathcal{V}')^F \rangle$, for $l \in$

$[\xi(\nu_0), \max \xi]$, the graph $\mathcal{G}_l$ of explanations of length l by restricting the LTS $\langle \Sigma, \mathcal{V}'', \mathcal{E}'', (\mathcal{V}'')^0, (\mathcal{V}'')^F \rangle$ where

$$\mathcal{V}'' = \{(\nu, b) \in \mathcal{V}' \mid b \leq l\}$$
$$\mathcal{E}'' = \mathcal{E}' \cap (\mathcal{V}'' \times \Sigma \times \mathcal{V}'')$$
$$(\mathcal{V}'')^0 = \{(\nu, b) \in (\mathcal{V}')^0 \mid b = l\}$$
$$(\mathcal{V}'')^F = (\mathcal{V}')^F \cap \mathcal{V}''$$

to the states that are reachable from $(\mathcal{V}'')^0$, and from which some state in $(\mathcal{V}'')^F$ is reachable. Notice that $\mathcal{G}_l$ is the empty graph when there is no explanation of length l. We then construct, for each (non-empty) subgraph, an explanation by applying the standard determinization (τ-elimination) algorithm based on subset construction [1] to "collapse" the non-pertinent parts of the graph.

Example 2. From the split graph of Fig. 2(b), two sub-graphs of constant height, in terms of effective choice transitions, are extracted (Figs. 2(c) and 2(d)). By determinization we obtain the explanations $\mathcal{E}_1$ and $\mathcal{E}_2$ of Figs. 2(e) and 2(f) that highlight the decisive events for disjoint scenarios, with increasing complexity of the explanation.

Theorem 2. *For each trace $w \in \Psi(\mathcal{G})$ there exists $l \in [\xi(\nu_0), \max \xi]$ such that $w \in \mathcal{G}_l$.*

Proof (sketch). Let $w \in \Psi(\mathcal{G})$ and $\rho = \nu_0 \xrightarrow{e_1} \nu_1 \xrightarrow{e_2} \ldots \xrightarrow{e_n} \nu_n \in \Upsilon(\mathcal{G})$ such that $w = e_1 \ldots e_n$. Let $l = \max_{i \in [0,n]}(\xi(\nu_i))$ and $\langle b_0, b_1, \ldots, b_n \rangle \in \mathbb{N}^{n+1}$ such that $\forall i \in [0, n], b_i = max\{\xi(\nu_j) \mid j \in [i, n]\}$. Then the run $\rho' = (\nu_0, b_0) \xrightarrow{e_1} (\nu_1, b_1) \xrightarrow{e_1} \ldots \xrightarrow{e_n} (\nu_n, b_n)$ is in $\Upsilon(\mathcal{G}_l)$ by construction of $\mathcal{G}_l$.

This result means that any log-consistent violation is contained in some sub-graph after split and extraction.

4.1 Further Improvements

Compressing δ-sequences and Estimating Time Delays. Our explanations may still encompass sequences of discretized time delays whose intermediate states are distinguished by the bisimulation. Our motivation for eliminating such sequences of delays is twofold. First, to construct a more concise explanation. In the case study, compressing δ-sequences allows us to reduce the number of transitions in the explanation from 21 to 7. Second, compressing sequences of time delays allows us to quantitatively estimate the possible time delays of the concrete runs that are summarized by the explanation.

Given a sub-graph $\mathcal{G}_l = \langle \Sigma, \mathcal{V}, \mathcal{E}, \mathcal{V}^0, \mathcal{V}^F \rangle$, a δ^+-*sequence* is an atomic sequence of transitions $\sigma = \nu_1 \xrightarrow{\delta} \nu_2 \xrightarrow{\delta} \ldots \xrightarrow{\delta} \nu_{n+1}$, that is,

$$\forall i \in \{1, \ldots, n\} \ \forall e \in \Sigma \ \forall \nu' \in \mathcal{V} : \left(\nu_i \xrightarrow{e} \nu' \implies e = \delta \wedge \nu' = \nu_{i+1}\right)$$

such that $\nu_1 \xrightarrow{\delta} \nu_2$ is an effective choice transition.

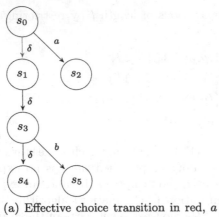
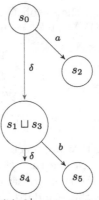

(a) Effective choice transition in red, a and b are discrete events, the transitions in black are either effective choice or not.

(b) δ^+-compression.

Fig. 3. Compression of sequences of discretized time delays. (Color Figure online)

As illustrated in Fig. 3, we replace each maximal δ^+-sequence σ with a single transition $\nu_1 \xrightarrow{\delta} \nu_{n+1}$. The second condition requires the first transition of the sequence to be effective choice, which ensures the information about effective choice states, used in the sequel, to be preserved.

In order for the explanation to convey quantitative timing information, we estimate, for each abstract time transition $\nu \xrightarrow{\delta} \nu'$, the range of concrete delays represented by the transition, given the location invariants in ν and ν'. For each state s and clock c, there exists the constants $\inf_c^s, \sup_c^s \in \mathbb{N} \cup \{\infty\}$ such that in s, $\inf_c^s \leq c \leq \sup_c^s$. If s' is a time successor of s then we can estimate the delay to be between $\delta_{\inf} = \max_{c \in C}(\inf_c^{s'} - \sup_c^s)$ and $\delta_{\sup} = \min_{c \in C}(\sup_c^{s'} - \inf_c^s)$. In the case where $\delta_{\inf}$ is negative it is set to 0.

Safe Alternatives. The rationale of our construction of explanations is to highlight the events that contributed to the violation of a safety property. Complementary to this information, and equally crucial for understanding how the property was violated, is the question "how could the outcome have been avoided?". Providing this information is the goal of *safe alternatives*.

Definition 9 (Safe alternative). *A transition $\nu \xrightarrow{e} \nu'$ of an LTS $\mathcal{G}_l$ is a safe alternative iff ν is an effective choice state and $\xi(\nu') \geq \xi(\nu)$.*

Intuitively, given a choice state, a safe alternative is a transition that would have contributed to avoiding the violation by not decreasing the level of choice.

State Constraints. So far we have focused our attention on the *events* of a failing run. The complementary information crucial for understanding the outcome, is in which *states* some relevant event took place. In this section, let us assume the TA to be equipped with a function $\pi : L \rightarrow 2^{\Pi}$ that labels each location with a set of atomic propositions. A straight-forward approach for displaying the states in the explanation would be to compute, for each aggregate state of the determinized graph consisting of a set Q of locations, the disjunction of the invariants (resp. of the atomic proposition) of the locations in L. This would, however, lead to unreadably complex expressions.

We therefore make the design choice to label each state $q = \{\nu_1, ..., \nu_k\} \in Q$ returned by determinization, with a *convex* predicate of the form $\nu_1 \sqcup \cdots \sqcup \nu_k :=$ $\hat{C}(q) \wedge SP(q)$, where $\hat{C}(q)$ is the weakest convex clock constraint that is implied by the invariants of the locations of all effective choice states in q. It is straight-forward to compute this clock constraint from the DBMs of the involved location invariants.

Similarly, for the function SP that aggregates, for a state q, atomic propositions of the states in q, multiple definitions are possible. We settle for the conjunction of the atomic propositions that hold in all effective choice states in q. This set is therefore obtained as:

$$SP(q) = \bigcap_{\nu_i \in q: \ \nu_i \text{ is an effective choice state}} \bigcap_{\ell \in \nu_i} \pi(\ell)$$

An example of the obtained state predicates is shown in Fig. 7.

5   Implementation and Case Study

We have implemented our results in a tool written in Python. It relies on Kronos [23] for the composition of timed automata, Minim for the generation of the quotient graph, and CADP [5] for reductions up to bisimulation.

We illustrate our approach on the dual-chamber implantable pacemaker model of [10]. It is a multi-component system where components are timed automata communicating over channels [16]. We use the model of [13] that we have translated into the Kronos format. The model consists of 5 timed automata for the components of the pacemaker and 2 timed automata that model its environment, that is, the atrial and ventricular behavior of a heart. Whenever delays between sensed atrial or ventricular events exceed a threshold, the pacemaker produces an AP (atricular pace) or VP (ventricular pace) event.

Among the safety properties discussed in [10] we focus on the requirement that the time between two ventricular events (sensed or paced) never exceeds 1000 ms. The safety property observer is shown in Fig. 5. If the heart model is safe then the system is also safe. We have therefore modified the parameters of the pacemaker so as to allow for unsafe behaviors.

Figure 4(a) shows the model of the ventricular behavior, with a frequency between $Vminwait = 500$ ms and $Vmaxwait = 1100$ ms, so as to allow a for fault. On the pacemaker model we increase the upper rate interval $TURI$ from 400 ms to 1600 ms. This parameter determines the minimum delay between two

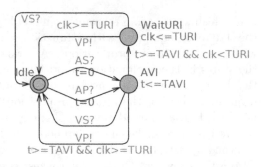

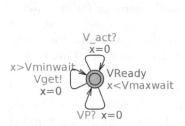

(a) Heart ventricular component.   (b) Pacemaker ventricular component *AVI*.

Fig. 4. Two components of the model.

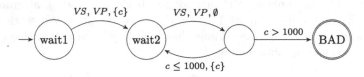

Fig. 5. Safety property observer.

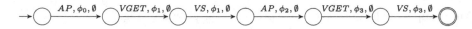

Fig. 6. Timed log. All location invariant are *true*, $\phi_0 = (x = 850)$, $\phi_1 = (850 \leq x \leq 1000)$, $\phi_2 = (1700 \leq x \leq 1800)$, $\phi_3 = (1850 \leq x \leq 2200)$.

ventricular events *VP* in the *AVI* component shown in Fig. 4(b). In order to compare our results, we have taken the same parameters as in [13].

We fix the set of observable events as the set $\Sigma^{obs} = \{VP, VS, AS, AGET, AP, VGET\}$ of signals exchanged between components, whereas we consider all internal events of the components as unobservable. We use Uppaal to obtain a witness trace for the violation of the property, from whose projection on the observable events we construct the timed log shown in Fig. 6.

Let us now apply our approach to explain the causes of the violation. The sizes of the timed automata, discrete abstractions, and explanation are shown in Table 1.

1. The first step is to generate the log observer, which consists of 8 locations and 60 transitions.
2. We invoke Kronos to compose the components, the safety property observer, and the log observer.
3. We use Minim to compute the quotient graph with respect to strong time-abstracting bisimulation.
4. The levels of choice and safe alternatives are computed.

Table 1. Sizes of the timed automata (number of locations), discrete abstractions, and resulting explanation.

Automaton	#states	#transitions
$\mathcal{A}\|\mathcal{P}$	96	296
$\mathcal{L}$	7	6
$\mathcal{L}^c$	8	60
$\mathcal{A}\|\mathcal{P}\|\mathcal{L}^c$	117	332
$\mathcal{A}\|\mathcal{P}\|\mathcal{L}^c$	117	274
$[\mathcal{A}\|\mathcal{P}\|\mathcal{L}^c]$	1817	5041
$[\mathcal{A}\|\mathcal{P}\|\mathcal{L}^c]$	2145	5870
$[\mathcal{A}\|\mathcal{P}\|\mathcal{L}^c]/\sim$	1763	4931
Log-consistent	50	52
Split	50	49
δ^+-compression	35	34
Explanation	8	7

5. We remove the states that are not consistent with the log or the property violation. The difference in size is important because the observed behavior is only a small part of the behavior of the model.
6. In this case study the effective choice states are not ambiguous, therefore splitting does not change the graph. Similarly, the extracted sub-graph amounts to the full graph here.
7. Two maximal δ^+-sequences of length 11 (resp. 6) are found, encompassing 10 (resp. 6) effective choice transitions. After δ^+-compression, the quantitative time delays along the abstract delay transitions (called "time_succ" in our implementation) are computed.
8. After determinization we obtain the explanation shown in Fig. 7.

In our case, the explanation is a sequence of discrete and δ-transitions. Each of them moves the system closer to the violation of the safety property, in spite of safe alternatives (shown as transitions without a target state) that would have avoided the violation. In our case the safe alternatives are mostly events sent by the heart model. This is logical because we know that *VGET* from the heart induces immediately a ventricular event in the *PVRP* component (not shown here) that would have avoided the violation. In order to understand why the pacemaker failed to adjust the ventricular events rate, we need to look at the state predicates. If we focus on the last three transitions, we see that the pacemaker waits 150 ms and takes an internal transition *I_AVI*. If we look at the model of the *AVI* component, we see that this event could only occur because we increased *TURI*. From this point the violation becomes unavoidable after a further delay of 400 ms.

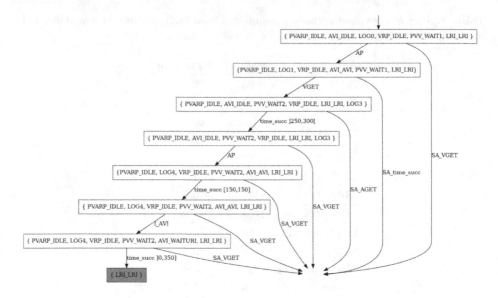

Fig. 7. Pacemaker explanation

Comparison with TarTar [13]. We use the same model as in [13], up to the fact that we have increased the parameters *Aminwait* and *Vminwait* (the minimal atrial and ventricular rate of the heart model, respectively) from 1 ms to 500 ms in order to reduce the size of the quotient graph to a size that can be managed by Minim. This modification does not impact the safety violation we are interested in.

TarTar focuses on fixing time delay parameters in order to repair safety violations, and proposes a repair of the bounds on *TURI*. Our approach is more general in the sense that it does not restrict its attention to time delays. On the other hand, it does not propose a repair. In particular, our explanations are useful to explain failures caused by nondeterministic behavior, or when there are no admissible repairs but one still wants to understand the causes of a violation.

6   Discussion

We have proposed a novel approach to explain the violation of a safety property by a real-time system. In essence, an explanation is formed by the parts of the behaviors that are consistent with the log, that jointly contributed to move the system into the failure state.

This work is a first step in constructing explainable cyber-physical systems. Much work remains to be done though towards this long-term goal. In particular, we need to establish formal properties of our explanations, such as soundness and completeness. We will also investigate how to construct explanations online, and how to extend our analysis to more general classes of hybrid systems.

Acknowledgment. The authors thanks Stavros Tripakis and Sergio Yovine for their help in using Kronos.

References

1. Aho, A.V., Sethi, R., Ullman, J.D.: Compilers - Principles, Techniques, and Tools. Addison Wesley, Boston (1986)
2. Beckers, S., Eberhardt, F., Halpern, J.Y.: Approximate causal abstractions. In: Adams, R.P., Gogate, V. (eds.) Proceedings of The 35th Uncertainty in Artificial Intelligence Conference, Proceedings of Machine Learning Research, vol. 115, pp. 606–615. PMLR, 22–25 Jul 2020 (2020)
3. Beer, I., Ben-David, S., Chockler, H., Orni, A., Trefler, R.J.: Explaining counterexamples using causality. Formal Methods Syst. Des. **40**(1), 20–40 (2012)
4. Danos, V., et al.: Graphs, rewriting and pathway reconstruction for rule-based models. In D'Souza, D., Kavitha, T., Radhakrishnan, J. (eds.) IARCS Annual Conference on Foundations of Software Technology and Theoretical Computer Science (FSTTCS 2012), Leibniz International Proceedings in Informatics (LIPIcs), vol. 18, pp. 276–288. Schloss Dagstuhl - Leibniz-Zentrum fuer Informatik (2012)
5. Garavel, H., Lang, F., Mateescu, R., Serwe, W.: CADP 2011: a toolbox for the construction and analysis of distributed processes. Int. J. Softw. Tools Technol. Transf. **15**(2), 89–107 (2013)
6. Gössler, G., Mari, T., Pencolé, Y., Travé-Massuyès, L.: Towards causal explanations of property violations in discrete event systems. In: DX 2019 - 30th International Workshop on Principles of Diagnosis, pp. 1–8, November 2019
7. Gössler, G., Stefani, J.-B.: Causality analysis and fault ascription in component-based systems. Theoret. Comput. Sci. **837**, 158–180 (2020)
8. Groce, A., Chaki, S., Kroening, D., Strichman, O.: Error explanation with distance metrics. STTT **8**(3), 229–247 (2006)
9. Halpern, J.Y., Pearl, J.: Causes and explanations: a structural-model approach. Part I: causes. Br. J. Philos. Sci. **56**(4), 843–887 (2005)
10. Jiang, Z., Pajic, M., Moarref, S., Alur, R., Mangharam, R.: Modeling and verification of a dual chamber implantable pacemaker. In: Flanagan, C., König, B. (eds.) TACAS 2012. LNCS, vol. 7214, pp. 188–203. Springer, Heidelberg (2012). https://doi.org/10.1007/978-3-642-28756-5_14
11. Jin, H., Ravi, K., Somenzi, F.: Fate and free will in error traces. STTT **6**(2), 102–116 (2004)
12. Kölbl, M., Leue, S., Wies, T.: Clock bound repair for timed systems. In: Dillig, I., Tasiran, S. (eds.) CAV 2019. LNCS, vol. 11561, pp. 79–96. Springer, Cham (2019). https://doi.org/10.1007/978-3-030-25540-4_5
13. Kölbl, M., Leue, S., Wies, T.: TarTar: a timed automata repair tool. In: Lahiri, S.K., Wang, C. (eds.) CAV 2020. LNCS, vol. 12224, pp. 529–540. Springer, Cham (2020). https://doi.org/10.1007/978-3-030-53288-8_25
14. Korel, B., Laski, J.: Dynamic program slicing. IPL **29**(3), 155–163 (1988)
15. Küsters, R., Truderung, T., Vogt, A.: Accountability: definition and relationship to verifiability. In: ACM Conference on Computer and Communications Security, pp. 526–535 (2010)
16. Larsen, K.G., Pettersson, P., Yi, W.: Uppaal in a nutshell. Int. J. Softw. Tools Technol. Trans. **1**(1–2), 134–152 (1997)

17. McIlraith, S.A.: Explanatory Diagnosis: Conjecturing Actions to Explain Observations, pp. 155–172. Springer, Berlin, Heidelberg (1999). https://doi.org/10.1007/978-3-642-60211-5_13
18. Pearl, J.: Theoretical impediments to machine learning with seven sparks from the causal revolution. In: Proceedings of Eleventh ACM International Conference on Web Search and Data Mining (WSDM 2018), pp. 3–3. ACM (2018)
19. Reiter, R.: A theory of diagnosis from first principles. Artif. Intell. **32**(1), 57–95 (1987)
20. Tripakis, S., Yovine, S.: Analysis of timed systems using time-abstracting bisimulations. Formal Methods Syst. Des. **18**(1), 25–68 (2001)
21. von Essen, C., Jobstmann, B.: Program repair without regret. Formal Methods Syst. Des. **47**(1), 26–50 (2015)
22. Weiser, M.: Program slicing. IEEE Trans. Softw. Eng. **10**(4), 7 (1984)
23. Yovine, S.: KRONOS: a verification tool for real-time systems. Softw. Tools Technol. Trans. **1**(1+2), 123–133 (1997)
24. Zeller, A.: Why Programs Fail. Elsevier, New York (2009)

DiffRNN: Differential Verification
of Recurrent Neural Networks

Sara Mohammadinejad$^{(\boxtimes)}$, Brandon Paulsen, Jyotirmoy V. Deshmukh,
and Chao Wang

University of Southern California, Los Angeles, CA, USA
{saramoha,bpaulsen,jdeshmuk,wang626}@usc.edu

Abstract. Recurrent neural networks (RNNs) such as Long Short Term
Memory (LSTM) networks have become popular in a variety of applications such as image processing, data classification, speech recognition,
and as controllers in autonomous systems. In practical settings, there
is often a need to deploy such RNNs on resource-constrained platforms
such as mobile phones or embedded devices. As the memory footprint
and energy consumption of such components become a bottleneck, there
is interest in compressing and optimizing such networks using a range
of heuristic techniques. However, these techniques do not guarantee the
safety of the optimized network, e.g., against adversarial inputs, or equivalence of the optimized and original networks. To address this problem,
we propose DIFFRNN, the first differential verification method for RNNs
to certify the equivalence of two structurally similar neural networks.
Existing work on differential verification for *ReLU*-based feed-forward
neural networks does not apply to RNNs where nonlinear activation
functions such as *Sigmoid* and *Tanh* cannot be avoided. RNNs also pose
unique challenges such as handling sequential inputs, complex feedback
structures, and interactions between the gates and states. In DIFFRNN,
we overcome these challenges by bounding nonlinear activation functions
with linear constraints and then solving constrained optimization problems to compute tight bounding boxes on non-linear surfaces in a high-
dimensional space. The soundness of these bounding boxes is then proved
using the *dReal* SMT solver. We demonstrate the practical efficacy of our
technique on a variety of benchmarks and show that DIFFRNN outperforms state-of-the-art RNN verification tools such as POPQORN.

Keywords: Recurrent neural networks · Resource-constrained
platforms · Compression techniques · Differential verification

1 Introduction

Deep neural networks, and in particular, recurrent neural networks (RNNs), have
been successfully used in a wide range of applications including image classification, speech recognition, and natural language processing. However, their rapid

J. V. Deshmukh and C. Wang—Equal contribution.

© Springer Nature Switzerland AG 2021
C. Dima and M. Shirmohammadi (Eds.): FORMATS 2021, LNCS 12860, pp. 117–134, 2021.
https://doi.org/10.1007/978-3-030-85037-1_8

growth in safety-critical applications such as autonomous driving [3] and aircraft collision avoidance [19] is accompanied by safety concerns [25]. For example, neural networks are known to be vulnerable to adversarial inputs [14,45], which are security exploits designed to fool the neural networks [23,31,32,54].

In addition, trained neural networks typically go through changes before deployment, thus raising concerns that the changes may introduce new behaviors. Specifically, since neural networks are computationally and memory intense, they are difficult to deploy on resource-constrained devices [5,16]. Network compression techniques (such as edge pruning, weight quantization, and neuron removal) are often needed to reduce the network's size [5]. Compression techniques typically use mean-squared error over sampled inputs as a performance measure to test equivalence. Such a measure is statistical, and does not provide formal worst-case guarantees on the deviation between behaviors of two networks.

While there are recent efforts on applying differential testing [26,36,46] and fuzzing [33,52,53] techniques to neural networks, they can only increase the confidence that the networks behave as expected for some of the inputs. However, they cannot prove the equivalence of the networks for all inputs. To the best of our knowledge, RELUDIFF [34] and NEURODIFF [35] are the only tool that aims to prove the equivalence of two neural networks for all inputs, which takes as input two feed-forward neural networks with piecewise linear activation functions known as rectified linear units (*ReLU*). The *ReLU* activation essentially allows the neural network to be treated as a piecewise linear (PWL) function (with possibly many facets/pieces).

Such tools exploit the PWL nature of activations, and hence cannot natively handle non-PWL activation functions like *Sigmoid*, *Tanh*, and *ELU*, let alone the more complex operations of LSTMs, which take the *product* of these non-linear functions, e.g. *Sigmoid* × *Tanh*. This poses significant limitations because popular libraries "hardcode" *Tanh* and *Sigmoid* for some, or all of the activation functions in the network. Thus, for RNNs, we need a technique that can handle these challenging and arbitrary nonlinearities. In addition, we face several other unique challenges when considering RNNs, including how to *soundly and efficiently* handle (1) sequential inputs, (2) the complex feedback structures, and (3) interactions between the gates and states.

To overcome these challenges, we propose DIFFRNN, the first differential verification technique for bounding the difference of two structurally similar RNNs. Formally, given two RNNs that only differ in numerical values of their edge weights, denoted $\mathbf{y} = f(\mathbf{x})$ and $\mathbf{y}' = f'(\mathbf{x})$, where $\mathbf{x} \in X$ is an input, X is an input region of interest, and $\mathbf{y}, \mathbf{y}'$ are the outputs, DIFFRNN aims to prove that $\forall \mathbf{x} \in X$. $|f'(\mathbf{x}) - f(\mathbf{x})| < \epsilon$, where ϵ is a reasonably small number.

Figure 1a shows the high-level flow of DIFFRNN, whose input consists of two networks, RNN and RNN', an input region, X, and a small difference bound ϵ. It produces two possible outcomes: *Proved*, or *Unknown*. Internally, DIFFRNN uses symbolic interval arithmetic to compute linear bounds on both the output values of each network's neurons and the *differences* between the neurons of the two networks. We compute these linear bounds *efficiently* in a layer-by-layer

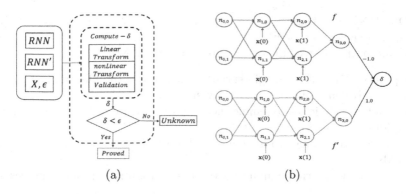

Fig. 1. (a) The differential verification flow of DIFFRNN. (b) Naïve differential verification of RNNs.

fashion, that is, using the bounds of the previous layer to compute the bounds of the current layer. If the bounds on the final output difference satisfy ϵ, DIFFRNN returns *Proved*, otherwise it returns *Unknown*.

To compute the output difference *accurately*, we bound nonlinear activation functions with linear constraints and then solve constrained optimization problems to obtain tight bounding boxes on nonlinear surfaces in a high-dimensional space. We also prove the soundness of these bounding boxes using *dReal* [11], which is an off-the-shelf *delta-sat* SMT solver[1] that supports nonlinear constraints.

While one could try and adapt an existing single-network verification tool to solve our problem, in practice, the bounds computed by this approach are too loose, since existing tools are not designed to exploit the relationships between neurons in two RNNs. To confirm this observation, we constructed the following experiment. We took two *identical* networks $f(\mathbf{x})$ and $f'(\mathbf{x})$, i.e., with the same network topology and edge weights. We then constructed a new network $f''(\mathbf{x}) = f'(\mathbf{x}) - f(\mathbf{x})$, illustrated in Fig. 1b. Then, we took POPQORN, a state-of-the-art RNN verification tool, and attempted to prove $f''(\mathbf{x}) < \epsilon$ for all $\mathbf{x}$. While POPQORN could not prove this for any $\epsilon < 2.0$, DIFFRNN could prove it easily for any $\epsilon > 0$.

We have implemented our proposed method and evaluated it on a variety of differential verification tasks involving networks for handwritten digit recognition (MNIST) [24] and human activity recognition [1]. Our results show that DIFFRNN is efficient and effective in certifying the functional equivalence of RNNs after compression techniques are applied. We also compared DIFFRNN with POPQORN [22], the state-of-the-art RNN verification tool. Our results show

---

[1] *dReal* is implemented based on delta-complete decision procedures; it returns either unsat or delta-sat on the given input formulas, where delta is a user-defined error bound [11].

that DIFFRNN significantly outperforms POPQORN [22]: On average DIFFRNN is 8X more accurate and 40% faster.

To summarize, our main contributions are as follows:

- We propose DIFFRNN, a differential verification method for proving the functional equivalence of two structurally similar RNNs.
- We develop techniques to handle the recursive nature of RNNs and nonlinear functions such as *Sigmoid* and *Tanh*.
- We develop techniques to handle both Vanilla RNNs and the more complex LSTMs.
- We formally verify the soundness of our linear approximation techniques using *dReal* [11].
- We experimentally demonstrate that our method significantly outperforms the state-of-the-art techniques.

2   Background

In this section, we review the basics of recurrent neural networks (RNNs), including Vanilla RNNs and LSTMs[2], and interval bound propagation (IBP), a technique for bounding the network's output values for all input values.

2.1   Recurrent Neural Networks

Vanilla RNNs. A vanilla recurrent neural network is a function that maps time-indexed *input sequences* to *output sequences*. Let X be a compact subset of $\mathbb{R}^m$, where m is the number of input values at each time step. An input sequence $\mathbf{x}$ is a function from time $\{0, 1, \ldots, T\}$ to input space X, where $T \in \mathbb{N}$, and $\mathbf{x}(j) \in X$ denotes the jth entry in the time-indexed input sequence. An output sequence is a similar function that maps to an output space $Y \subseteq \mathbb{R}^p$.

The structure of a vanilla RNN is as follows. It consists of a single layer of ℓ neurons, and its output $\mathbf{h}$ at time t depends on (a) the output $\mathbf{h}$ at time $t-1$, and (b) the input $\mathbf{x}$ at time t, as shown below:

$$\mathbf{a}(t) = W_{\mathbf{hh}} \cdot \mathbf{h}(t-1) + W_{\mathbf{hx}} \cdot \mathbf{x}(t) + \mathbf{b_h} \tag{1}$$

$$\mathbf{h}(t) = \sigma(\mathbf{a}(t)) \tag{2}$$

$$\mathbf{y}(t) = W_{\mathbf{hy}} \cdot \mathbf{h}(t) + \mathbf{b_y} \tag{3}$$

Here, $\mathbf{a}(t)$ is an intermediate variable that we introduce to represent the affine transformation of the current input $\mathbf{x}(t)$ and previous state $\mathbf{h}(t-1)$. The weight matrices $W_{\mathbf{hh}}$ and $W_{\mathbf{hx}}$ have dimensions $\ell \times \ell$ and $\ell \times m$ respectively. The bias term $\mathbf{b_h}$ is an $\ell \times 1$ matrix. σ is the nonlinear component-wise *activation function* from $\mathbb{R}^\ell$ to $\mathbb{R}^\ell$. We assume that $\mathbf{h}(0)$ is a fixed initial state of the RNN at time

---

[2] Gated recurrent units (GRUs) are structurally very similar to LSTMs, and differential verification hurdles for GRUs are the same as LSTMs; thus, we omit explaining GRUs in this paper for brevity.

0; it is a vector of size $\ell \times 1$. Finally, the output of the RNN at time t, $\mathbf{y}(t)$ is defined as a linear transformation of $\mathbf{h}(t)$, using the weight matrix $W_{\mathbf{hy}}$ and bias term $\mathbf{b_y}$.

Thus, each multiplication above is a matrix multiplication, and for all time steps t, $\mathbf{h}(t)$ and $\mathbf{x}(t)$ are ℓ- and m-length vectors, respectively. The activation function σ may be the sigmoid activation (σ_S) or the hyperbolic tangent activation (tanh)[3].

In differential verification, there is a second RNN whose parameters are denoted by $\mathbf{a'}$, $\mathbf{h'}$, $\mathbf{y'}$, $W'_{\mathbf{hh}}$, $W'_{\mathbf{hx}}$, $W'_{\mathbf{hy}}$, $\mathbf{b'_h}$ and $\mathbf{b'_y}$ respectively. The two RNNs under comparison are *structurally similar*, i.e., they only differ in the values of the edge weights, and have the same activation functions. We also introduce $\boldsymbol{\delta^a}$, $\boldsymbol{\delta^h}$, and $\boldsymbol{\delta^y}$ to represent the differences: $\boldsymbol{\delta^a}(t) = \mathbf{a'}(t) - \mathbf{a}(t)$, $\boldsymbol{\delta^h}(t) = \mathbf{h'}(t) - \mathbf{h}(t)$, and $\boldsymbol{\delta^y}(t) = \mathbf{y'}(t) - \mathbf{y}(t)$[4].

LSTMs. Long short-term memory networks (LSTMs) were introduced to overcome the limitation of Vanilla RNNs in learning long term sequential dependencies [43]. Refer to Appedix for details on LSTMs.

2.2   Interval Bound Propagation (IBP)

To soundly compute the output values of a neural network for all input values, we represent these values as intervals, and use interval arithmetic to compute their bounds.

Linear Operations. Given two intervals, e.g., $p \in [a, b]$ and $q \in [c, d]$, the resulting intervals of linear operations such as addition $(p+q)$, subtraction $(p-q)$, and scaling $(p \cdot c$, where c is a constant) are well defined. That is,

$$[a, b] + [c, d] = [a + c, b + d]$$
$$[a, b] - [c, d] = [a - d, b - c]$$
$$[a, b] \cdot c = \begin{cases} [a \cdot c, b \cdot c], & c \geq 0 \\ [b \cdot c, a \cdot c], & c < 0 \end{cases}$$

While the results are sound over-approximations, they may be overly conservative. For example, when $p = 5x$, $q = 4x$ and $x \in [-1, 1]$, since $p - q = 5x - 4x = x$, we know that $(p - q) \in [-1, 1]$, but interval subtraction returns $(p - q) = [-5, 5] - [-4, 4] = [-5 - 4, 5 - (-4)] = [-9, 9]$.

A technique for improving accuracy is the use of symbolic inputs. For example, instead of using the concrete intervals $p \in [-5, 5]$ and $q \in [-4, 4]$, we may

---

[3] For a scalar input u, $\sigma_S(u) = \frac{e^u}{1+e^u}$, and $\tanh(u) = \frac{e^u - e^{-u}}{e^u + e^{-u}}$.

[4] A many-to-one vanilla RNN differs from the Vanilla RNN model shown above in one small way. For an input sequence of length T, the output is computed only at time T, i.e., the final output of the network is defined as $\mathbf{y}(T)$ (see Fig. 6 in the Appendix of the arXiv version).

use the symbolic upper and lower bounds $p \in [5x, 5x]$ and $q \in [4x, 4x]$, leading to $(p - q) = [5x - 4x, 5x - 4x] = [x, x]$. As a result, we have $(p - q) = [-1, 1]$ after concertizing the symbolic bounds.

In this work, we represent the *symbolic* lower and upper bounds of p as $L(p)$ and $U(p)$, and the concrete lower and upper bounds as $\underline{p}$ and $\overline{p}$, respectively.

Non-linear Operations. Sound intervals may also be defined for outputs of *Sigmoid* (σ_S) and *Tanh* (tanh) activation functions. Since both functions are *monotonically increasing*, given a concrete input interval $p = [a, b]$, we have $\sigma(p) \in [\sigma(a), \sigma(b)]$. However, for a symbolic input interval, soundly approximating the output is challenging. In an existing verification tool named CROWN [55], e.g., this is solved by computing linear bounds on the output of each activation function. For LSTMs, the problem is even more challenging because it involves the *product* of nonlinear operations, such as $z = \sigma_S(x) \cdot \tanh(y)$ and $z = x \cdot \sigma_S(y)$. In POPQORN [22], for example, the output is bounded by searching for linear bounding planes of the form $\alpha x + \beta y + \gamma$, where α, β and γ are computed using gradient descent.

In this work, we build upon techniques from CROWN and POPQORN for bounding the output *values* of network f's neurons, to solve the new problem of bounding the *differences* between two networks f and f'.

3   Overview

In this section, we use an example to illustrate the high-level idea of our method and the shortcomings of state-of-the-art single-network verification techniques for differential verification.

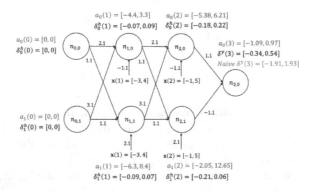

Fig. 2. Interval analysis of a recurrent neural network with Sigmoid activation function.

Figure 2 shows a *many-to-1* Vanilla RNN, f, where all neurons use the *Sigmoid* activation. The entire RNN has 1 hidden layer of 2 neurons, receives a sequence of 2 inputs, and returns a single output. For ease of presentation, the unrolled version of this RNN is shown in Fig. 2 for an input sequence of length 2. Thus, $n_{t,i}$ denotes the ith node in the tth sequence (time step). The initial values in $\mathbf{a}(0)$ and $\boldsymbol{\delta^h}(0)$ are set to 0. The goal is to bound $\boldsymbol{\delta^y}(3)$, the difference between outputs of the original RNN f and a modified RNN f'; here, $\boldsymbol{\delta^y}(3) = |f'(\mathbf{x}(1), \mathbf{x}(2)) - f(\mathbf{x}(1), \mathbf{x}(2))|$. In this example, the second RNN, f', is derived from the original RNN f by rounding its edge weights to the nearest whole numbers.

The naïve approach is to leverage an existing verification tool, originally designed to quantify the robustness of a single RNN (e.g., POPQORN [22]). As shown for the network in Fig. 1b, we can use POPQORN to bound the output of the combined network. For our running example, the bounds computed by POPQORN are $\boldsymbol{\delta^y}(3) = [-1.91, 1.93]$. However, as our analysis shows in this paper, the bounds are overly conservative. The reason is because, to soundly compute the difference $\boldsymbol{\delta^y}(3) = [f'_{low}, f'_{up}] - [f_{low}, f_{up}] = [f'_{low} - f_{up}, f'_{up} - f_{low}]$, POPQORN has to introduce significant approximation error.

DIFFRNN, in contrast, overcomes this problem by pairing neurons and edges of the first network with their counterparts of the second network, and directly computing the difference intervals layer by layer. By directly computing the differences as opposed to the output bounds of the corresponding neurons, we hope to obtain much tighter bounds. However, there are unique challenges in directly bounding the differences. While bounding the non-linear activation function $y = \sigma(x)$ for a single neuron is relatively easy [55], doing so for a pair of neurons at the same time is more difficult because we must bound $z = \sigma(x') - \sigma(x)$, which involves two variables. While we could bound the individual terms $\sigma(x')$ and $\sigma(x)$, and then subtract their bounds, doing so introduces too much approximation error.

To solve the problem, we propose the following new technique. First, we rewrite the difference as $z = \sigma(x + \delta_x) - \sigma(x)$, where x is the value of neuron's output in network f and $\delta_x = (x' - x)$ is the difference between the outputs of two corresponding neurons in f and f'. Given the intervals of x and δ_x, we then examine all possible combinations of their upper and lower bounds, and match these combinations with a set of pre-defined patterns, to soundly compute the interval of z.

For LSTMs, directly bounding the difference $z = x' \cdot \sigma_S(x') - x \cdot \sigma_S(x)$ or $z = \tanh(x') \cdot \sigma_S(x') - \tanh(x) \cdot \sigma_S(x)$ is even more challenging. To the best of our knowledge, no existing verification tool for neural networks can compute tight linear bounds for such functions. Our solution is to formulate them as constrained optimization problems and solve these problems using global optimization tools [37]. In addition, we prove the soundness of these bounds using dReal, an off-the-shelf delta-sat SMT solver that supports nonlinear constraints.

For the running example, our method would be able to compute the bounds $\boldsymbol{\delta^y}(3) = [-0.34, 0.54]$, which is more than 3X tighter than the bounds computed by POPQORN. The complete results of our experimental comparison with POPQORN will be presented in Sect. 5.

Algorithm 1: Differential Verification of Vanilla RNNs.

Input: *network f, network f', input region X*
Output: $\delta^y(T)$

1 **Init:** Initialize $[L(\mathbf{h}(0)), U(\mathbf{h}(0))]$ and $[\underline{\delta^h}(0), \overline{\delta^h}(0)]$ to 0
2 **for** *t : 1 to T* **do**
   | // affine transformer
3 | Compute $[L(\mathbf{a}(t)), U(\mathbf{a}(t))]$ and $[\underline{\delta^a}(t), \overline{\delta^a}(t)]$;
   | // nonlinear transformer (Algo. 2 in the arXiv version)
4 | Compute $[L(\mathbf{h}(t)), U(\mathbf{h}(t))]$ and $[\underline{\delta^h}(t), \overline{\delta^h}(t)]$;
5 Compute $[\underline{\delta^y}(T), \overline{\delta^y}(T)]$;

---

4 Directly Computing the Difference Interval

Our method for verifying Vanilla RNNs is shown in Algorithm 1. It takes two networks f and f', the input region X, and a small ϵ as input. After initializing the hidden state and the difference interval, it computes $\mathbf{h}(t)$ and $\delta^h(t)$ of the subsequent layers by applying the affine transformation (i.e., multiplying by the edge weights) followed by performing the non-linear transformation, whose details will be presented in Algorithm 2 in the arXiv version (due to lack of space). This is repeated layer by layer, until the output layer is reached. In the end, it computes the final difference interval from $\delta^h(T)$ and $\mathbf{h}(T)$. As mentioned earlier, we leverage the existing tool POPQORN [22] to compute the intervals $\mathbf{h}(t)$, while focusing on computing tight bounds on the differences $\delta^a(t)$ and $\delta^h(t)$.

4.1 Affine Transformer

For Vanilla RNNs, the affine transformation computes each $\delta^a(t)$ in two parts. The first part is caused by the differences between the edge weights in W_{hx}, denoted W_{hx}^Δ, for edges connecting the current input to neurons: $\delta_t(W_{hx}) = W_{hx}' \cdot \mathbf{x}(t) - W_{hx} \cdot \mathbf{x}(t) = W_{hx}^\Delta \cdot \mathbf{x}(t)$. The second part is caused by the differences between the edge weigths in W_{hh}, denoted W_{hh}^Δ, for edges connecting the previous hidden states to current hidden states, as well as the differences included in the previous hidden states, denoted $\delta^h(t-1)$.

$\delta_t(W_{hh}) = W_{hh}' \cdot \mathbf{h}'(t-1) - W_{hh} \cdot \mathbf{h}(t-1)$. Adding $W_{hh}' \cdot \mathbf{h}(t-1)$ to the first term and subtracting it from the second term, we get:

$$\delta_t(W_{hh}) = W_{hh}' \cdot \mathbf{h}'(t-1) - W_{hh} \cdot \mathbf{h}(t-1)$$
$$+ (W_{hh}' \cdot \mathbf{h}(t-1) - W_{hh}' \cdot \mathbf{h}(t-1))$$
$$= (W_{hh}' \cdot \mathbf{h}'(t-1) - W_{hh}' \cdot \mathbf{h}(t-1))$$
$$+ (W_{hh}' \cdot \mathbf{h}(t-1) - W_{hh} \cdot \mathbf{h}(t-1))$$
$$= W_{hh}' \cdot \delta^h(t-1) + W_{hh}^\Delta \cdot \mathbf{h}(t-1)$$

$\delta^{\mathbf{a}}(t)$ is then the sum of these two parts: $\delta^{\mathbf{a}}(t) = \delta_t(W_{\mathbf{hx}}) + \delta_t(W_{\mathbf{hh}})$. For LSTMs, the high-level verification procedure is similar to Algorithm 1 and is formalized in Algorithm 3 in the Appendix of arXiv version. The differences for gate $v \in \{\mathbf{i}, \mathbf{f}, \mathbf{g}, \mathbf{o}\}$ within each LSTM cell is computed as follows: $\delta^v(t) = \delta_t(W_{v\mathbf{x}}) + \delta_t(W_{v\mathbf{h}})$.

4.2 Nonlinear Transformer

Vanilla RNN. Here, we define the activation function transformations to compute $\delta^{\mathbf{h}}(t)$ from $\delta^{\mathbf{a}}(t)$. We do so by rewriting the following equation, using the definition of $\delta^{\mathbf{h}}(t)$ as follows: $\delta^{\mathbf{h}}(t) = \mathbf{h}'(t) - \mathbf{h}(t) = \sigma(\mathbf{a}'(t)) - \sigma(\mathbf{a}(t)) = \sigma(\mathbf{a}(t) + \delta^{\mathbf{a}}(t)) - \sigma(\mathbf{a}(t))$, where σ is the nonlinear activation function. While RELUDIFF [34] solves this problem for $\sigma = ReLU$, by exploiting the piece-wise linearity of $ReLU$, we propose new techniques for $\sigma = Sigmoid$ or $Tanh$, as well as composite nonlinear operations built upon them. Note that the technique can be used for other types of monotonic functions as well.

To obtain the tightest linear bounds on $\delta^{\mathbf{h}}(t)$, we formulate this problem as two optimization problems:

$$\underline{\delta^{\mathbf{h}}}(t) = \underset{\mathbf{a}(t), \delta^{\mathbf{a}}(t)}{\text{minimize}} \quad \sigma_S(\mathbf{a}(t) + \delta^{\mathbf{a}}(t)) - \sigma_S(\mathbf{a}(t))$$

$$\text{subject to} \quad \mathbf{a}(t) \in [\underline{\mathbf{a}}(t), \overline{\mathbf{a}}(t)], \ \delta^{\mathbf{a}}(t) \in [\underline{\delta^{\mathbf{a}}}(t), \overline{\delta^{\mathbf{a}}}(t)]$$

$$\overline{\delta^{\mathbf{h}}}(t) = \underset{\mathbf{a}(t), \delta^{\mathbf{a}}(t)}{\text{maximize}} \quad \sigma_S(\mathbf{a}(t) + \delta^{\mathbf{a}}(t)) - \sigma_S(\mathbf{a}(t))$$

$$\text{subject to} \quad \mathbf{a}(t) \in [\underline{\mathbf{a}}(t), \overline{\mathbf{a}}(t)], \ \delta^{\mathbf{a}}(t) \in [\underline{\delta^{\mathbf{a}}}(t), \overline{\delta^{\mathbf{a}}}(t)]$$

These are two-variable optimization problems of the form $f(x, d) = \sigma_S(x + d) - \sigma_S(x)$, which are expensive to solve at run time. To reduce the computational cost, we propose to reduce them first to single-variable optimization problems, by leveraging the fact that $f(x, d)$ is monotonic with respect to d. Our goal is to compute the maximum and minimum of $f(x, d) = \sigma_S(x + d) - \sigma_S(x)$, where $x \in [x_l, x_u]$ and $d \in [d_l, d_u]$. Due to the monotonicity of $f(x, d)$ with respect to d, we know that the minimum always occurs when $d = d_l$ and the maximum occurs when $d = d_u$. Thus, the problem is reduced to finding the maximum and minimum of $f(x, d)$ for a fixed $d = d_l$ or $d = d_u$.

Depending on the actual value of d being either positive or negative, the function $f(x, d)$ will be one of the two forms illustrated in Fig. 3.

Thus, to compute the minimum of $f(x, d)$, there are three cases to consider when d_l is positive, and another three cases to consider when d_l is negative. For instance, when $d_l \leq 0$ (Fig. 3a), if $x_l \leq x_u \leq -d_l/2$, since $f(x, d_l)$ is monotonically decreasing in this region, we have $\min(f(x, d_l)) = f(x_u, d_l)$; if $x_l \leq -d_l/2 \leq x_u$, we have $\min(f(x, d_l)) = f(-d_l/2, d_l)$; and if $-d_l/2 \leq x_l \leq x_u$ (monotonically increasing), we have $\min(f(x, d_l)) = f(x_l, d_l)$. The main advantage is that, by plugging in the bounds of x and d, we get the bounds of $f(x, d)$ immediately, without the need to solve any optimization problem at run time.

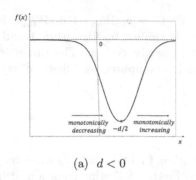
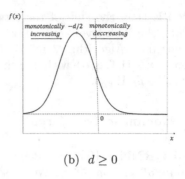

(a) $d < 0$ (b) $d \geq 0$

Fig. 3. $f(x) = \sigma_S(x + d) - \sigma_S(x)$. (a) shows $f(x)$ for $d < 0$ and (b) shows $f(x)$ for $d \geq 0$.

To compute $\underline{\delta^h}(t)$ and $\overline{\delta^h}(t)$, there are 12 cases in total, the details of which are formalized in Algo. 2 in the arXiv version. For $Tanh$ (tanh), the 12 cases are exactly the same as those for $Sigmoid$ (σ_S); thus, we omit them for brevity[5].

The final difference interval for Vanilla RNNs is computed from $\delta^h(T)$ and $h(T)$ as follows: $\delta^y = W'_{hy} \cdot \delta^h(T) + W^\Delta_{hy} \cdot h(T)$.

LSTM. Next, we consider computing $\delta^h(t)$ for LSTMs. All the computations for LSTMs are provided in the Appendix of the arXiv version due to lack of space.

5   Experiments

Benchmarks. Our benchmarks are 12 feed-forward neural networks with $Sigmoid$ and $Tanh$ activations[6], 12 Vanilla RNNs, and 6 LSTMs trained using the MNIST[7] [24] and Human Activity Recognition (HAR) [1] data sets. Detailed description of each benchmark is provided in Appendix. From each network f, we produce f' by rounding the edge weights of f from 32-bit floats to 16-bit floats, and then pruning edges with weights close to 0 (<0.001). There are three mainstream compression techniques: (1) weight quantization, (2) edge pruning, and (3) neuron removal, all of which can be handled by our method. Popular tools including TensorFlow and PyTorch train in float-32 and then can quantize

---

[5] For non-monotonic activation functions we can compute the maximum and minimum using off-the-shelf global optimization tools and then validate the computed bounds using SMT solvers.

[6] One of our evaluation objectives is to extend the results of RELUDIFF to general activation functions instead of $ReLUs$. This also allows us to validate our methodology in the relatively simpler world of feedforward networks before tackling RNNs.

[7] We took the same MNIST benchmarks used by previous work (POPQORN) for verification of single RNNs, to have a fair comparison. Based on the previous work, it seems to be a challenging benchmark set, due to the high input-dimensionality.

(upon request) to float-16 (or lower) automatically. Edges/neurons are pruned if the corresponding weights are close to 0. Thus, in practice, the two networks (f and f') are indeed structurally similar. While they are expected to be also functionally equivalent, no other tool (except our DIFFRNN) can formally prove it. We generate the input regions for differential verification using global perturbation [41] or targeted pixel perturbation [15]. We randomly take 100 test inputs, and for each one, we allow each of the inputs to be perturbed $-/+1\%$ of the whole range (*global* perturbation), or we randomly pick *3 inputs* and set their range to the whole range (targeted perturbation). Given an input region, the goal is to verify the difference of at most ϵ between the outputs of f and f'. The value of ϵ is specified for each benchmark separately as 10% of its output range.

Experimental Evaluation. We run the experiments on an Intel Core-i7 Macbook Pro with 2.7 GHz processors and 16 GB RAM. Timeout for each verifcation problem is set to 30 min. We compare the results of feed-forward networks with CROWN [55] which is the state-of-the-art verification tool for a single feedforward neural network. Among the existing tools for verifying a single RNN [18,40], we find empirically that POPQORN is significantly more accurate than those from [18,40]: the bounds computed by [18,40] often have too much approximation error, and hence would give too many false positives for the differential verification problem. Therefore, we compare our experimental results on RNNs with POPQORN, which leverages gradient descent techniques to compute linear bounds on nonlinear surfaces $x \cdot \sigma_S(y)$ and $\sigma_S(x) \cdot \tanh(y)^8$.

Results. In the 3000 differential verification problems that we consider, DIFFRNN can verify 2671 out of 3000 problems and is faster than CROWN and POPQORN in 90% of the cases. CROWN and POPQORN in total can verify only 1120 out of 3000 problems. DIFFRNN returns *Unknown* for other 329 verification problems that cannot verify.

Table 1 shows the results of differential verification of feed-forward neural networks with *Sigmoid* activation trained on MNIST data set. The networks have 3 structures 3×128 (3 hidden layers of 128 neurons), 2×512 (2 hidden layers of 512 neurons) and 4×1024 (4 hidden layers of 1024 neurons). Thus, the networks have 2, 3 and 4 layers in addition to input and output layers. The goal is to verify the difference of at most 1 ($\epsilon = 1$) between the outputs of f and f'. Among the 600 verification problems shown in Table 1, DIFFRNN verified all of them while CROWN verified only 224. Table 2 shows the results of differential verification of feed-forward neural networks with *Tanh* activation and three types of structures: 3×128, 2×1024 and 4×512 on the HAR data set. DIFFRNN verified 591 of the 600 cases for $\epsilon = 2$ as apposed to the 282 cases verified by CROWN.

---

[8] As POPQORN evaluates bounds using numerical tools based on gradient descent, while the approach is sound in theory, it is susceptible to numerical precision issues. Hence, we added an extra validation step using *dReal* to ensure numerical precision of the bounds computed by POPQORN.

Table 1. Number of verified problems from 100 verification problems, Avg δ and Avg verification time (seconds) $\cdot, \cdot, \cdot$ of DiffRNNand Crownon MNIST for DNN with Sigmoid activation and $\epsilon = 1$.

DNN benchmark	DiffRNN(New)	Crown [25]	Avg. speedup
3x128-global	100, 0.01, 21.0 s	1, 4.45, 29.2 s	1.39
2x512-global	100, 0.01, 61.5 s	7, 1.77, 67.4 s	1.09
4x1024-global	100, 0.22, 270.6 s	0, 13.29, 350.0 s	1.29
3x128-3-inputs	100, 0.00, 17.3 s	79, 0.71, 21.3 s	1.23
2x512-3-inputs	100, 0.00, 59.5 s	100, 0.30, 58.6 s	0.98
4x1024-3-inputs	100, 0.02, 240.8 s	37, 2.18, 273.5 s	1.13

Table 2. Number of verified problems from 100 verification problems, Avg δ and Avg verification time (seconds) $\cdot, \cdot, \cdot$ of DiffRNNand Crownon HAR for DNN with Tanh activation and $\epsilon = 2$.

DNN benchmark	DiffRNN(New)	Crown [25]	Avg. speedup
3x128-global	100, 0.07, 18.4 s	51, 1.93, 23.9 s	1.29
2x1024-global	100, 0.18, 150.9 s	33, 2.07, 184.3 s	1.22
4x512-global	0, 8.56, 172.3 s	0, 55.09, 272.8 s	1.58
3x128-3-inputs	100, 0.03, 17.17 s	98, 0.61, 20.6 s	1.19
2x1024-3-inputs	100, 0.09, 122.5 s	100, 0.59, 157.4 s	1.28
4x512-3-inputs	0, 4.21, 142.5 s	0, 27.11, 173.25 s	1.21

Table 3 shows the results of verifying Vanilla RNNs with $\epsilon = 1$ on the MNIST data set. The network structures are 4×128 (4 sequences of 128 neurons), 7×32 (7 sequences of 32 neurons) and 14×8 (14 sequences of 8 neurons). Among the 600 verification problems, DiffRNN verified 473 while Popqorn only verified 136. Table 4 shows the results of verifying Vanilla RNNs on the HAR data set. The networks are 3×32, 3×128 and 11×8 and $\epsilon = 2$. DiffRNN was faster than Popqorn in all cases and also verified more properties (598/600), while Popqorn only verified 478 properties. Finally, Table 5 shows the results of verifying LSTMs trained on the HAR data set for structures 3×32, 3×64 and 11×8 and $\epsilon = 0.2$. The results again show that DiffRNN was better: it verified all 600 cases while Popqorn can verify none of them. The bounds for LSTM networks (Table 5) are computed at run time, using global optimizers and then proved by the dReal SMT solver. In contrast, the bounds for DNNs and Vanilla RNNs are computed at the design time, which has less computational overhead.

Table 3. Number of verified problems from 100 verification problems, Avg δ and Avg verification time (seconds) $\cdot, \cdot, \cdot$ of DIFFRNNand POPQORNon MNIST for Vanilla RNN with Tanh activation and $\epsilon = 1$.

Vanilla RNN benchmark	DIFFRNN(New)	POPQORN [22]	Avg. speedup
4x128-global	100, 0.12, 617.2 s	0, 4.76, 1188.1 s	1.92
7x32-global	34, 1.26, 77.6 s	0, 16.72, 143.7 s	1.85
14x8-global	50, 3.68, 14.8 s	15, 6.64, 25.9 s	1.75
4x128-3-inputs	100, 0.03, 636.2 s	53, 0.98, 1121.2 s	1.76
7x32-3-inputs	96, 0.25, 74.0 s	12, 6.37, 134.1 s	1.81
14x8-3-inputs	93, 0.51, 13.3 s	56, 1.94, 25.1 s	1.88

Table 4. Number of verified problems from 100 verification problems, Avg δ and Avg verification time (seconds) $\cdot, \cdot, \cdot$ of DIFFRNNand POPQORNon HAR for Vanilla RNN with Tanh activation and $\epsilon = 2$.

Vanilla RNN benchmark	DIFFRNN(New)	POPQORN [22]	Avg. speedup
3x32-global	100, 0.01, 41.7 s	60, 1.83, 70.5 s	1.69
3x128-global	100, 0.03, 487.4 s	74, 1.59, 911.4 s	1.86
11x8-global	100, 0.02, 12.6 s	62, 1.92, 17.3 s	1.37
3x32-3-inputs	100, 0.00, 40.1 s	99, 0.62, 66.7 s	1.66
3x128-3-inputs	100, 0.02, 518.7 s	98, 0.61, 931.3 s	1.79
11x8-3-inputs	98, 0.07, 10.1 s	85, 0.93, 16.9 s	1.67

Table 5. Number of verified problems from 100 verification problems, Avg δ and Avg verification time (seconds) $\cdot, \cdot, \cdot$ of DIFFRNNand POPQORNon HAR for LSTM and $\epsilon = 0.2$.

LSTM benchmark	DIFFRNN(New)	POPQORN [22]	Avg. speedup
3x32-global	100, 0.07, 16003.8 s	0, 0.49, 15285.4 s	0.95
3x64-global	100, 0.07, 21960.2 s	0, 0.63, 17778.6 s	0.8
11x8-global	100, 0.06, 33398.4 s	0, 1.86, 35400.1 s	1.05
3x32-3-inputs	100, 0.07, 11669.5 s	0, 0.30, 14062.2 s	1.20
3x64-3-inputs	100, 0.06, 16738.2 s	0, 0.45, 17082.3 s	1.02
11x8-3-inputs	100, 0.06, 23882.5 s	0, 1.34, 31462.3 s	1.31

5.1 Limitations

We applied differential verification to 3 LSTM structures 4×128, 7×32 and 14×8 on the MNIST data set. Neither DIFFRNN nor POPQORN could verify any of these problems. The reason behind the failure of DIFFRNN is that, after 2 sequences of propagation, the difference intervals start to get loose, resulting in poor performance of the *dReal* SMT solver. As *dReal* is an interval constraint based solver, bigger intervals requires *dReal* to reason over bigger regions of space. While POPQORN was actually faster than DIFFRNN in this experiment, the final differences it computed are too loose and cannot verify the equivalence of any two networks for $\epsilon \leq 20$. Thus, the results point to directions for future research.

While in general DIFFRNN achieves a significant performance gain compared to the state-of-the-art verification tools for a single RNN, such as POPQORN, it can only tightly bound similarity of two 1-layer RNNs with up to 20 input sequences. To the best of our knowledge, there is no existing technique based on IBP that can certify multi-layer RNNs with long input sequences. POPQORN, [18,40] that are tools for quantifying the robustness of a single RNN can only certify the robustness for 1-layer RNNs. The reason is because IBP starts to get loose as the number of sequences or layers increases. In DIFFRNN, we are dealing with two RNNs at the same time, thus, the problem is twice harder. For example, 2-variable optimization problems in POPQORN correspond to 4-variable optimization problems in DIFFRNN.

Verifying a single neural network is already hard (with scalability issues). Differential verification is even harder. Thus, the only hope is to intelligently exploit the network similarity – more similarity should lead to faster verification. While state-of-the-art tools (POPQORN) could not even verify the equivalence of two identical networks, our method can do it in seconds. That said, if the networks are not similar, our method is not expected to be effective either.

Increasing the size of input region and ϵ are other factors that can affect the performance of differential verification using our DIFFRNN tool as well as other tools such as CROWN and POPQORN.

6   Related Work

RELUDIFF [34] and NEURODIFF [35] are currently the only tools that can verify neural networks in the differential setting. However, unlike our approach, RELUDIFF and NEURODIFF do not solve the many challenges that are unique to RNNs. More generally, our work falls into the category of techniques for improving safety, security, and reliability in deep learning. Along this line, there has been a significant amount of research that we can classify into two broad categories: (1) techniques for discovering misbehaviors, and (2) techniques for proving the absence of misbehaviors, like DIFFRNN. We review a representative set of these works here.

Techniques along the first line are often geared towards finding *adversarial examples* [23,45]. There have been many works using machine learning techniques such as gradient-based optimization and even generative adversarial networks [14,31,32,54]. In addition, other techniques use white-box heuristics [26,27,33,36,44,46] such as neuron coverage or various black-box techniques [50,52,53]. While useful for discovering misbehavior they do not guarantee the absence of misbehavior, which we do.

Techniques along the second line usually aim to *prove the absence of* adversarial examples. For example, many works have developed exact and complete techniques that are guaranteed to *eventually* terminate with the correct result. They have used LP solvers [2,4,8,9,17,39], built specialized solvers for neural networks [15,20,21], or combined approximation techniques with refinement [42,47,48].

Others have focused solely on approximation techniques [12,25,41,49,55], which often use abstract domains [6], such as intervals [30], zonotopes [13], and polyhedra [7]. Only very recent works have attempted to verify RNNs [18,22,40], but, as we have shown, they do not perform well in the differential setting.

In addition, these techniques have been integrated into the training process to produce more robust and verifiable networks [10,28,29,38,51]. We believe a similar approach could be taken to produce networks more amenable to differential verification. We leave this as future work.

7   Conclusion

We have presented DIFFRNN, the first method for differential verification of two closely related recurrent neural networks. By reasoning about general nonlinear activiation functions, our work goes beyond previous approaches for differential verification such as RELUDIFF (that used only *ReLU* activiations). More crucially, we show how we can extend our approach to a more general class of NNs, known as recurrent neural networks. DIFFRNN leverages interval analysis to directly and more accurately compute difference in the values of neurons of the two networks from the input layer to output layer. At each step, the soundness of the computed differences is validated using a nonlinear *delta-sat* SMT solver. Our experimental comparison of DIFFRNN with state-of-the-art verification tools such as CROWN and POPQORN show that the proposed method not only is faster but also can verify significantly more properties.

Acknowledgments. We thank the anonymous reviewers for their comments. The authors also gratefully acknowledge the support by the National Science Foundation (NSF) under the Career Award SHF-2048094, the NSF FMitF award CCF-1837131, the NSF grant CNS-1813117, and a grant from Toyota R&D North America.

References

1. Anguita, D., Ghio, A., Oneto, L., Parra, X., Reyes-Ortiz, J.L.: A public domain dataset for human activity recognition using smartphones. In: ESANN (2013)
2. Bastani, O., Ioannou, Y., Lampropoulos, L., Vytiniotis, D., Nori, A.V., Criminisi, A.: Measuring neural net robustness with constraints. In: Annual Conference on Neural Information Processing Systems, pp. 2613–2621 (2016)
3. Bojarski, M., et al.: End to end learning for self-driving cars. arXiv preprint arXiv:1604.07316 (2016)
4. Carlini, N., Wagner, D.A.: Towards evaluating the robustness of neural networks. In: IEEE Symposium on Security and Privacy, pp. 39–57 (2017)

5. Cheng, Y., Wang, D., Zhou, P., Zhang, T.: A survey of model compression and acceleration for deep neural networks. arXiv preprint arXiv:1710.09282 (2017)
6. Cousot, P., Cousot, R.: Abstract interpretation: a unified lattice model for static analysis of programs by construction or approximation of fixpoints. In: ACM SIGACT-SIGPLAN Symposium on Principles of Programming Languages, pp. 238–252 (1977)
7. Cousot, P., Halbwachs, N.: Automatic discovery of linear restraints among variables of a program. In: ACM SIGACT-SIGPLAN Symposium on Principles of Programming Languages, pp. 84–96 (1978)
8. Dvijotham, K., Stanforth, R., Gowal, S., Mann, T.A., Kohli, P.: A dual approach to scalable verification of deep networks. In: International Conference on Uncertainty in Artificial Intelligence, pp. 550–559 (2018)
9. Ehlers, R.: Formal verification of piece-wise linear feed-forward neural networks. In: Automated Technology for Verification and Analysis - 15th International Symposium, ATVA 2017, Pune, India, 3–6 October 2017, Proceedings, pp. 269–286 (2017)
10. Fischer, M., Balunovic, M., Drachsler-Cohen, D., Gehr, T., Zhang, C., Vechev, M.T.: DL2: training and querying neural networks with logic. In: International Conference on Machine Learning, pp. 1931–1941 (2019)
11. Gao, S., Kong, S., Clarke, E.M.: dreal: An smt solver for nonlinear theories over the reals. In: International conference on automated deduction. pp. 208–214. Springer (2013)
12. Gehr, T., Mirman, M., Drachsler-Cohen, D., Tsankov, P., Chaudhuri, S., Vechev, M.T.: AI2: safety and robustness certification of neural networks with abstract interpretation. In: IEEE Symposium on Security and Privacy, pp. 3–18 (2018)
13. Ghorbal, K., Goubault, E., Putot, S.: The zonotope abstract domain taylor1+. In: International Conference on Computer Aided Verification. pp. 627–633. Springer (2009)
14. Goodfellow, I.J., Shlens, J., Szegedy, C.: Explaining and harnessing adversarial examples. In: International Conference on Learning Representations (2015)
15. Gopinath, D., Katz, G., Pasareanu, C.S., Barrett, C.W.: DeepSafe: a data-driven approach for assessing robustness of neural networks. In: Automated Technology for Verification and Analysis - 16th International Symposium, ATVA 2018, Los Angeles, CA, USA, 7–10 October 2018, Proceedings, pp. 3–19 (2018)
16. Han, S., Mao, H., Dally, W.J.: Deep compression: compressing deep neural network with pruning, trained quantization and Huffman coding. In: International Conference on Learning Representations (2016)
17. Huang, X., Kwiatkowska, M., Wang, S., Wu, M.: Safety verification of deep neural networks. In: International Conference on Computer Aided Verification, pp. 3–29 (2017)
18. Jia, R., Raghunathan, A., Göksel, K., Liang, P.: Certified robustness to adversarial word substitutions. arXiv preprint arXiv:1909.00986 (2019)
19. Julian, K.D., Kochenderfer, M.J., Owen, M.P.: Deep neural network compression for aircraft collision avoidance systems. Journal of Guidance, Control, and Dynamics 42(3), 598–608 (2019)
20. Katz, G., Barrett, C.W., Dill, D.L., Julian, K., Kochenderfer, M.J.: Reluplex: an efficient SMT solver for verifying deep neural networks. In: International Conference on Computer Aided Verification, pp. 97–117 (2017)
21. Katz, G., et al.: The Marabou framework for verification and analysis of deep neural networks. In: International Conference on Computer Aided Verification, pp. 443–452 (2019)

22. Ko, C.Y., Lyu, Z., Weng, T.W., Daniel, L., Wong, N., Lin, D.: Popqorn: quantifying robustness of recurrent neural networks. arXiv preprint arXiv:1905.07387 (2019)
23. Kurakin, A., Goodfellow, I.J., Bengio, S.: Adversarial examples in the physical world. In: International Conference on Learning Representations (2017)
24. LeCun, Y., Cortes, C.: MNIST handwritten digit database (2010). http://yann.lecun.com/exdb/mnist/
25. Lyu, Z., Ko, C.Y., Kong, Z., Wong, N., Lin, D., Daniel, L.: Fastened crown: tightened neural network robustness certificates. arXiv preprint arXiv:1912.00574 (2019)
26. Ma, L., et al.: Deepgauge: multi-granularity testing criteria for deep learning systems. In: IEEE/ACM International Conference On Automated Software Engineering, pp. 120–131. ACM (2018)
27. Ma, S., Liu, Y., Lee, W., Zhang, X., Grama, A.: MODE: automated neural network model debugging via state differential analysis and input selection. In: Proceedings of the 2018 ACM Joint Meeting on European Software Engineering Conference and Symposium on the Foundations of Software Engineering, ESEC/SIGSOFT FSE 2018, Lake Buena Vista, FL, USA, 04–09 November 2018, pp. 175–186 (2018)
28. Madry, A., Makelov, A., Schmidt, L., Tsipras, D., Vladu, A.: Towards deep learning models resistant to adversarial attacks. In: International Conference on Learning Representations (2018)
29. Mirman, M., Gehr, T., Vechev, M.T.: Differentiable abstract interpretation for provably robust neural networks. In: International Conference on Machine Learning, pp. 3575–3583 (2018)
30. Moore, R.E., Kearfott, R.B., Cloud, M.J.: Introduction to Interval Analysis, vol. 110. SIAM (2009)
31. Moosavi-Dezfooli, S., Fawzi, A., Frossard, P.: DeepFool: a simple and accurate method to fool deep neural networks. In: IEEE Conference on Computer Vision and Pattern Recognition, pp. 2574–2582 (2016)
32. Nguyen, A.M., Yosinski, J., Clune, J.: Deep neural networks are easily fooled: high confidence predictions for unrecognizable images. In: IEEE Conference on Computer Vision and Pattern Recognition, pp. 427–436 (2015)
33. Odena, A., Goodfellow, I.: Tensorfuzz: debugging neural networks with coverage-guided fuzzing. arXiv preprint arXiv:1807.10875 (2018)
34. Paulsen, B., Wang, J., Wang, C.: Reludiff: differential verification of deep neural networks. arXiv preprint arXiv:2001.03662 (2020)
35. Paulsen, B., Wang, J., Wang, J., Wang, C.: Neurodiff: scalable differential verification of neural networks using fine-grained approximation. arXiv preprint arXiv:2009.09943 (2020)
36. Pei, K., Cao, Y., Yang, J., Jana, S.: Deepxplore: automated whitebox testing of deep learning systems. In: ACM Symposium on Operating Systems Principles, pp. 1–18 (2017)
37. Price, Kenneth V.., Storn, Rainer M.., Lampinen, Jouni A..: Differential Evolution: A Practical Approach to Global Optimization. LNCS, Springer, Heidelberg (2005). https://doi.org/10.1007/3-540-31306-0
38. Raghunathan, A., Steinhardt, J., Liang, P.: Certified defenses against adversarial examples. In: International Conference on Learning Representations (2018)
39. Ruan, W., Huang, X., Kwiatkowska, M.: Reachability analysis of deep neural networks with provable guarantees. In: International Joint Conference on Artificial Intelligence, pp. 2651–2659 (2018)
40. Shi, Z., Zhang, H., Chang, K.W., Huang, M., Hsieh, C.J.: Robustness verification for transformers. arXiv preprint arXiv:2002.06622 (2020)

41. Singh, G., Gehr, T., Püschel, M., Vechev, M.T.: An abstract domain for certifying neural networks. In: ACM SIGACT-SIGPLAN Symposium on Principles of Programming Languages, pp. 41:1–41:30 (2019)
42. Singh, G., Gehr, T., Püschel, M., Vechev, M.T.: Boosting robustness certification of neural networks. In: International Conference on Learning Representations (2019)
43. Stérin, T., Farrugia, N., Gripon, V.: An intrinsic difference between vanilla rnns and gru models. COGNITIVE **2017**, 84 (2017)
44. Sun, Y., Wu, M., Ruan, W., Huang, X., Kwiatkowska, M., Kroening, D.: Concolic testing for deep neural networks. In: Proceedings of the 33rd ACM/IEEE International Conference on Automated Software Engineering, ASE 2018, Montpellier, France, 3–7 September 2018, pp. 109–119 (2018)
45. Szegedy, C., et al.: Intriguing properties of neural networks. arXiv preprint arXiv:1312.6199 (2013)
46. Tian, Y., Pei, K., Jana, S., Ray, B.: Deeptest: automated testing of deep-neural-network-driven autonomous cars. In: International Conference on Software Engineering, pp. 303–314 (2018)
47. Wang, S., Pei, K., Whitehouse, J., Yang, J., Jana, S.: Efficient formal safety analysis of neural networks. In: Annual Conference on Neural Information Processing Systems, pp. 6369–6379 (2018)
48. Wang, S., Pei, K., Whitehouse, J., Yang, J., Jana, S.: Formal security analysis of neural networks using symbolic intervals. In: USENIX Security Symposium, pp. 1599–1614 (2018)
49. Weng, T., et al.: Towards fast computation of certified robustness for relu networks. In: International Conference on Machine Learning, pp. 5273–5282 (2018)
50. Wicker, M., Huang, X., Kwiatkowska, M.: Feature-guided black-box safety testing of deep neural networks. In: International Conference on Tools and Algorithms for Construction and Analysis of Systems, pp. 408–426 (2018)
51. Wong, E., Kolter, J.Z.: Provable defenses against adversarial examples via the convex outer adversarial polytope. In: International Conference on Machine Learning, pp. 5283–5292 (2018)
52. Xie, X., et al.: Deephunter: a coverage-guided fuzz testing framework for deep neural networks. In: Proceedings of the 28th ACM SIGSOFT International Symposium on Software Testing and Analysis, pp. 146–157 (2019)
53. Xie, X., Ma, L., Wang, H., Li, Y., Liu, Y., Li, X.: Diffchaser: detecting disagreements for deep neural networks. In: Proceedings of the 28th International Joint Conference on Artificial Intelligence, pp. 5772–5778. AAAI Press (2019)
54. Xu, W., Qi, Y., Evans, D.: Automatically evading classifiers: a case study on PDF malware classifiers. In: Network and Distributed System Security Symposium (2016)
55. Zhang, H., Weng, T.W., Chen, P.Y., Hsieh, C.J., Daniel, L.: Efficient neural network robustness certification with general activation functions. In: Annual Conference on Neural Information Processing Systems, pp. 4939–4948 (2018)

Formal Abstraction and Synthesis
of Parametric Stochastic Processes

Andrea Peruffo[1]([⊠]) and Alessandro Abate[2]

[1] Delft Center for Systems and Control, TU Delft, Delft, The Netherlands
a.peruffo@tudelft.nl
[2] Department of Computer Science, University of Oxford, Oxford, UK
alessandro.abate@cs.ox.ac.uk

Abstract. Formal abstractions of stochastic difference equations (SDEs) translate continuous-space processes into finite-state Markov models that can be automatically model checked against probabilistic specifications. These formal procedures carry an abstraction error that can be used to refine the outcomes of the model checking procedure from the abstract model to the concrete SDE. Parameter synthesis techniques aim at finding (any or all) model parameters that ensure the validity of a given specification, and are currently investigated by and large for finite-state parametric Markov models. In this work instead, we consider classes of parametric SDEs, and develop specific abstraction procedures relating the parameters in the obtained finite-state models to those of the concrete SDEs; we further show how parameter synthesis on the abstract models can be used to assert the satisfaction of given formal properties on the original parametric SDEs.

1 Introduction

Formal methods encompass a suite of approaches for the verification of quantitative and qualitative properties of systems. Model checking concerns a specification of interest, which is usually encoded in some modal logic (e.g. LTL, CTL, PCTL), and the system under study expressed as a formal model, commonly either a transition model [10], a probabilistic model [23], a timed system [7] or hybrid automaton [8]. Stochastic models in particular describe systems involving random phenomena and probabilistic behaviours. Formal verification of stochastic models is an active area of investigation, which has witnessed the development of quite a few software tools. PRISM [23] and Storm [14] support a variety of numerical and symbolic solvers, whereas FAUST^2 [26, 35] compute formal abstractions of uncountable-state models, Modest [19] and StocHy [12] combine nondeterministic choices and continuous system dynamics. For an extensive summary of state-of-the-art probabilistic model checkers, the interested reader may refer to [2, 3, 16].

Formal abstractions are techniques to approximate complex models by simpler ones, which can then be automatically verified in place of the original complex systems. This work deals with Stochastic Difference Equations (SDE) with

© Springer Nature Switzerland AG 2021
C. Dima and M. Shirmohammadi (Eds.): FORMATS 2021, LNCS 12860, pp. 135–153, 2021.
https://doi.org/10.1007/978-3-030-85037-1_9

continuous variables, and expands on existing formal abstraction procedures [4] to generate finite Markov chains and to verify standard reachability/safety properties. This approach is equipped with an analytical formulation of the abstraction error that certifies the procedure: in particular, these abstraction procedures can be further refined to improve accuracy (namely, to decrease the error). Alternative techniques embed this error in the abstraction, thus generating models with non-determinism [25] - in this paper we work with the former methods.

In practice, precise models that exactly describe a system, possibly under several different environments, are hard (if at all possible) to develop. A parametric framework allows to encompass this modelling uncertainty. The goal of parameter synthesis is to find a subset (in particular, a single instance, or the maximal subset) of the allowed parameter space, such that the satisfaction of a specification can be guaranteed on the corresponding model(s). In particular, [13] presents an early, explicit approach for parametric model checking of discrete-time Markov Chains (dtMCs): the probability of a path is computed symbolically by translating the dtMC into a finite automaton and obtaining a regular expression from it. Conditions for the satisfaction of a given property for a parametric dtMC, with applications to fair communication protocols, are outlined in [24]. [17,18] provide a more efficient computation of reachability properties for parametric dtMCs. The complexity of reachability properties for parametric Markov Decision Processes (MDPs) is discussed in [36]. Recent contributions in parametric model checking focus on improving generality and computational costs of the procedures [9]. An extensive illustration of verification methods for parametric Markov models is found in [22]. Applications of parameter synthesis techniques span several areas: chemical and biological networks [11,33]; optimal energy consumption [20]; renewable energy sources [28] with a parametric model of an energy network, which is then investigated under safety requirements (lack of blackouts) [30]: this is the application that drives this contribution, as the case study will outline.

This article proffers a new approach to formally verify properties on parametric, stochastic, uncountable-state systems (SDE). With focus on SDEs with specific dynamics, and affected by Uniform or Gaussian noises, we combine formal abstraction techniques with parameter synthesis problem. Given a parametric SDE and a formal specification, our procedure entails two steps: 1) a parametric formal abstraction is computed, yielding a (parametric) abstract model; 2) parameters are synthesised on the abstract model in order to satisfy the property given for the SDE. The abstraction can be iteratively refined to increase its precision. This procedure can be applied to general discrete-time, stochastic, and hybrid models. The formality of the overall algorithm is ensured by the derived abstraction error, which depends on the smoothness of the deterministic and stochastic terms of the underlying model. The remainder of this paper is organised as follows. Section 2 provides an introduction to this work. Section 3 reviews technical details of formal abstractions and introduces their parametric extensions. The core parametric abstraction procedure is presented in Sect. 3.2 and later displayed over experiments and a case study in Sect. 4, where we provide abstractions for SDE of various sorts.

2   Preliminaries

In this work we consider finite abstractions of a general-space, discrete-time SDE F $= (\mathcal{S}, T_w)$ [1]. F is defined over the pair $(\mathcal{S}, T_w)$, where $\mathcal{S}$ is a properly measurable continuous state space (e.g., $\mathbb{R}^n$), and $T_w : \mathcal{S} \to [0, 1]$ is a stochastic kernel, which assigns to each point $s \in \mathcal{S}$ a probability measure $T_w(\cdot|s)$. We can write model F in the following recursive form

$$x_{k+1} = f(x_k) + \omega_k, \tag{1}$$

where $k \in \mathbb{Z}$ is a discrete-time index, $x \in \mathbb{R}^n$ represents the variables in the state space, f is a continuous vector field $f : \mathbb{R}^n \to \mathbb{R}^n$, and ω_k denotes a stochastic term, with a distribution that is related to the kernel T_w.

We observe that if the noise term ω_k in Eq. (1) is characterised by a general distribution $\mathcal{P}(0, \sigma^2) : \mathcal{S} \to [0, 1]$, with expected value equal to zero and variance equal to σ^2, then x_{k+1} belongs to $\mathcal{P}(f(x_k), \sigma^2)$, where f is the vector field characterising the drift. For any properly measurable set $\mathcal{S}$

$$\mathbb{P}_s(\mathcal{S}) = \int_{\mathcal{S}} T_w(ds|s), \tag{2}$$

where $\mathbb{P}_s$ denotes the conditional probability $\mathbb{P}(\cdot|s)$.

An abstraction procedure accepts an SDE F $= (\mathcal{S}, T_w)$ and returns a finite-state dtMC [5], which is defined as a tuple M $= (\mathcal{Z}, T)$ where $\mathcal{Z}$ is a finite set of states, $T : \mathcal{Z} \times \mathcal{Z} \to [0, 1]$ is a discrete transition probability function that assigns, to each $z \in \mathcal{Z}$, a (discrete) probability distribution over $\mathcal{Z}$. For all states z, we require $\sum_{z' \in \mathcal{Z}} T(z, z') = 1$. The procedure [4,35] to abstract an SDE as a finite-state, discrete time Markov chain (dtMC) M $= (\mathcal{Z}, T)$ is discussed next.

2.1   Formal Abstractions of SDE: State of the Art

In the following, we briefly outline the details of the abstraction procedure, and tailor it to the computation of probabilistic safety properties that are at the core of quantitative model checking.

A quantitative safety property [10] expresses the following question: what is the probability that a process remains within a safe set $\mathcal{S} \subseteq \mathbb{R}^n$, if its initial state is within $\mathcal{S}$? Dually, we may be interested in characterising the probability of reaching an *unsafe* set $\mathcal{S}_u$ – defined as the complement of $\mathcal{S}$, i.e. $\mathcal{S}_u = \mathbb{R}^n \setminus \mathcal{S}$ – starting within $\mathcal{S}$. This can be encoded as a formula in PCTL logic, as [10],

$$\psi = \mathbb{P}_{\leq \gamma}[\lozenge^{\leq N} \mathcal{S}_u], \ N \in \mathbb{N}, \tag{3}$$

which expresses that the probability of reaching the unsafe set $\mathcal{S}_u$, within N time steps (the temporal operator $\lozenge^{\leq N}$ should be read as "eventually, within N

steps"), is smaller than a given constant $\gamma \in [0,1]$. This quantity is in general hard to express analytically over SDEs [1], which leads to the development of formal abstractions of such models.

Let us consider a finite set of abstract states $\mathcal{Z} = \{z_1, z_2, ..., z_p, z_{p+1}\}$, and a transition probability matrix over $\mathcal{Z}$, $T : \mathcal{Z} \times \mathcal{Z} \rightarrow [0,1]$. We denote $T(z, z')$ to be the probability of transitioning from state z to state z'. The finite state space $\mathcal{Z}$ is constructed by partitioning the state space $\mathcal{S}$ of the process F as $\mathcal{S} = \{S_1, S_2, ..., S_p\}$, where sets S_i are non-overlapping, and selecting arbitrary representative points $r_i \in S_i$ in each partition, thus making up the states in $\mathcal{Z}$ (point z_{p+1} refers to the entire complement $\mathcal{S}_u$). The probability of transitioning from the (abstract) state z_i to state z_j ($i = 1, \ldots, p$; $j = 1, \ldots, p + 1$), namely $T(z_i, z_j)$, is computed by marginalising the stochastic kernel T_w, conditional on r_i, over the partition S_j of $\mathcal{S}$ corresponding to the abstract state z_j. More precisely, the transition probability between two states z_i and z_j is computed as

$$T(z_i, z_j) = \mathbb{P}_{r_i}(S_j) = \int_{S_j} T_w(ds \,|\, r_i), \tag{4}$$

where the probability kernel T_w is centred in r_i, the representative point of S_i, as shown in Fig. 1. Finally, point z_{p+1} is made absorbing, namely $T(z_{p+1}, z_{p+1}) = 1$.

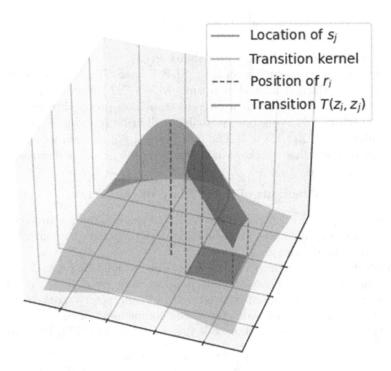

Fig. 1. Computation of the abstract transition probability.

This procedure carries an abstraction error that depends on the regularity of the kernel T_w [4]. Assuming a Lipschitz continuous kernel that can be bound by constant h_w, then the abstraction error is bounded from above as

$$\epsilon_{abs} \leq h_w \delta_s \mathscr{L}(\mathcal{S}), \tag{5}$$

where δ_s is the max among the diameters[1] of the partitions S_i and $\mathscr{L}(\mathcal{S})$ is the volume of $\mathcal{S}$. This bound can be conservative in practice: the discussion of tighter bounds is expounded in [15]. This abstraction error is to be intended as a one-step error: in other words, the probability for the system (1) of reaching, *at the next time step*, partition S_j from any point within partition S_i is confined between $\mathbb{P}_{r_i}(S_j) \pm \epsilon_{abs}$. This can be generalised to a finite-horizon, N-step property: the corresponding N-step error is upper bounded by $\epsilon_{abs} \leq N h_w \delta_s \mathscr{L}(\mathcal{S})$. This formulation allows tuning the partition size δ_s to ensure that the abstraction error is smaller than a desired, user-provided threshold ϵ^{max}, as follows:

$$\delta_s \leq \frac{\epsilon^{max}}{N h_w \mathscr{L}(\mathcal{S})}. \tag{6}$$

A smaller δ_s can thus be selected to ensure higher accuracy, but this can result in a larger (finite) state space for $\mathcal{Z}$. Qualitatively, for the model in Eq. (1) the constant h_w depends on σ^2, the variance of the noise term w_k.

Abstractions can be useful for quantitative model checking goals. Indeed, the relationship between the original SDE model and the abstract system is as follows [4]: if the abstract model satisfies a safety specification ϕ with probability δ in N steps, the probability of verifying a corresponding property for the concrete SDE lies within $\delta \pm \epsilon_{abs}$. In particular for reachability analysis, where we are interested in upper bounds on probability to reach the unsafe set (cfr. Equation (3), where we set the probability bound γ). The abstraction procedure ensures that

$$\mathsf{M} \models \phi : \mathbb{P}_{\leq \gamma - \epsilon_{abs}}[\lozenge^{\leq N} \mathcal{Z}_u] \implies \mathsf{F} \models \mathbb{P}_{\leq \gamma}[\lozenge^{\leq N} \mathcal{S}_u], \ N \in \mathbb{N}, \tag{7}$$

where $\mathcal{Z}_u$ represents the set of abstract unsafe states corresponding to the continuous unsafe region $\mathcal{S}_u$. Thus, the satisfaction of ψ for F (cf. Eq. (3)) is guaranteed by the stricter bound on M that accounts for the abstraction error ϵ_{abs}.

2.2 Parametric Models

Models are often built from data measurements that might be affected by noise or have specific parts that are not known with precision. A designer might rely on parametric models – which can be thought of as a succinct descriptions of uncountably-many possible models – and be interested in understanding whether (any or all) model parameters ensure the satisfaction of a given property under study ϕ [13] (a logical specification e.g., safety or reachability): this problem is

---

[1] Typically we consider hyper-rectangular partitions, thus the diameter is the diagonal, i.e. the longest distance between any two points within a partition.

known as *parameter synthesis*. One can be interested in finding single instantiations of satisfying parameters, or conversely the maximal region within the parameters space (known as the *feasible set* $\mathcal{T}$ of parameters) corresponding to models satisfying a property ϕ. Parameter synthesis problems usually concern finite-state models, e.g. in a probabilistic context parametric Markov chains, denoted as $\mathsf{M}(\Theta) = (\mathcal{Z}, T(\Theta))$, where $\Theta = [\theta_1, \ldots, \theta_l] \in \mathbb{R}^l$ is a vector of l continuous parameters and where $T(\Theta)$ represents a parametric transition matrix.

3   Formal Abstractions of Parametric SDE

We observe that on the one hand, research on parametric models and parameter synthesis is rich and well-established, with several available techniques (e.g. Gaussian elimination, ETR encoding [22]) and tools (e.g. PRISM [23] and Storm [14]). On the other hand, formal abstractions are used is a variety of contexts, from biology to control synthesis [12,34,35], to translate continuous models (such as SDEs) into discrete ones. This work aims at bridging the gap between these two areas: to the best of our knowledge, this is the first attempt at presenting parametric formal abstractions and verification of classes of SDEs. More precisely, we tackle the problem of formal abstractions of classes of parametric SDEs, as in Eq. (1): we shall focus on how parameters enter in the dynamics, and on specific forms of noise (Uniform, Gaussian) of wide usage.

As we have seen above, formal abstractions traditionally reduce SDEs to finite-state Markov models, performing a finite partitioning of the continuous state space of the SDE and computing probabilities between discrete states by marginalisation of the SDE transition kernel. In this work (cf. Fig. 2) we consider instead parametric SDEs, denoted as $\mathsf{F}(\Lambda)$, where Λ is a p-parametric vector $\Lambda = [\lambda_1, \ldots \lambda_p] \in \mathbb{R}^p$, $p \in \mathbb{N}$. We aim at synthesising regions (to be denoted as $\mathcal{L}$) within the parameters space Λ, such that $\mathsf{F}(\Lambda)$ satisfies a given property ψ. We shall abstract the SDE into a finite-state Markov model with parameters Θ, and automatically compute set $\mathcal{T}$, such that the corresponding abstract models satisfy ϕ, as outlined in Fig. 2. Properties ψ and ϕ for the SDE and the abstract Markov model, respectively, are related via the abstraction error ϵ_{abs}, as detailed

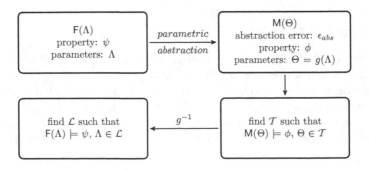

Fig. 2. Depiction of the procedure for abstraction and parameter synthesis.

in Eq. (7). Finally, we shall translate the synthesised set $\mathcal{T}$ into a region $\mathcal{L}$ for the vector Λ of the parametric SDE. Notice that, in general, $\Lambda \neq \Theta$: Λ represents the parameters vector for the original SDE, whereas Θ represents the parameters entering the abstract transition probability matrix: we expect Θ to be a function of Λ, say $\Theta = g(\Lambda)$, where $g : \mathbb{R}^p \to \mathbb{R}^l$.

3.1   Formal Abstractions of Parametric SDE

Let us now introduce a special class of parametric SDEs, as in Eq. (1), namely

$$x_{k+1} = f(x_k, \lambda_1) + \lambda_2 \cdot \omega_k, \tag{8}$$

where we have specialised how the parameters in the vector $\Lambda = [\lambda_1, \lambda_2]$ enter the dynamics. This parametric SDE considers two kinds of parametrisations:

- λ_1, a parameter within the deterministic drift, and
- λ_2, a parameter that is multiplicative on the noise term.

The distinction between these two kinds of parameters is necessary, in view of their effect on the abstraction error. However, as we shall see shortly, parametric abstractions will mostly have to deal with the second parameter λ_2 affecting the noise term. Recall that the term h_w, i.e. the Lipschitz constant of the kernel density (see Eq. (6)), depends on the variance of the distribution. The multiplication by the constant λ_2 influences the noise variance (this notably is multiplied by a factor λ_2^2), and thus ultimately the abstraction error. The actual expression of $h_w(\lambda_2)$ depends on the distribution under consideration and can be analytically obtained in a pre-processing step. The term $h_w(\lambda_2)$ hence becomes *parametric* (it is not a "constant" any more). The partition sizing procedure of Eq. (6) may be rewritten as a function of δ_s and λ_2 as

$$\delta_s \cdot h_w(\lambda_2) \leq \frac{\epsilon^{max}}{N\mathscr{L}(\mathcal{S})}. \tag{9}$$

This inequality defines a feasibility region within the (δ_s, λ_2) space, as illustrated in the following example.

Example 1. A Gaussian kernel with variance σ^2 can be upper bounded by the Lipschitz constant [4]

$$h_w = \frac{1}{\sigma\sqrt{2\pi}}. \tag{10}$$

Let us assume a formal abstraction procedure with $N = 10$ and $\mathscr{L}(S) = 1$, and for which we require an error $\epsilon^{max} = 0.1$. Condition (9) thus becomes

$$\delta_s \cdot \frac{1}{\sigma\sqrt{2\pi}} \leq \frac{\epsilon^{max}}{N\mathscr{L}(\mathcal{S})} \implies \delta_s \leq \sqrt{2\pi} \cdot 10^{-2}\sigma, \tag{11}$$

displaying a linear relationship between δ_s and σ. So, assuming that we select a partitioning value $\delta_s = 0.01$, then in order to guarantee an abstraction error below ϵ^{max}, we must have $\sigma \geq \frac{1}{\sqrt{2\pi}}$. □

We have seen that, once a value of δ_s is selected, this raises a constraint on parameter λ_2. Furthermore, recall that the formal abstraction procedure returns a parametric transition matrix, on which parameter synthesis techniques can be applied. Notice that the parameters Θ that are obtained in the abstract transition matrix are related to, yet different from, the parameters Λ of the original SDE. The parameter synthesis on the abstract model $\mathsf{M}(\Theta)$ defines a satisfiability region $\mathcal{T}$ of the parameters Θ. As we shall see, this region can then be mapped into the concrete SDE parameters Λ, defining a feasibility region $\mathcal{L}$.

Finally, we must check the condition in Eq. (9), i.e. whether the condition on the pair (δ_s, λ_2) intersects with the obtained feasibility region $\mathcal{L}$. If the intersection is empty, the abstraction must be repeated with a finer δ_s.

Example 2. Let us assume that the given SDE is a simple, parametric random walk, which is formally written as

$$x_{k+1} = \lambda_2 w_k,$$

where $w_k \in \mathcal{N}(0, 1)$ and $x_0 = 0$. Consider a safe set $\mathcal{S} = [0, 1)$, and thus $\mathscr{L}(\mathcal{S}) = 1$. Assume also that we aim at computing the safety probability at the next step ($N = 1$) with an abstraction error bounded by $\epsilon^{max} = 0.5$. Recalling the expression of h_w from Eq.(11), assume that we set $\delta_s = 0.5$. From (9), we receive

$$\lambda_2 \geq \frac{1}{\sqrt{2\pi}} \simeq 0.399. \tag{12}$$

The selected value of δ_s implies that the safe set is divided into two partitions, $\mathcal{S}_1 = [0, 0.5)$ and $\mathcal{S}_2 = [0.5, 1)$; the unsafe set is thus $\mathcal{S}_u = (-\infty, 0) \cup [1, +\infty)$. The abstract model $\mathsf{M}(\Theta)$ is formed by three states z_1, z_2, z_u, corresponding to $\mathcal{S}_1, \mathcal{S}_2, \mathcal{S}_u$, respectively. The parametric transition matrix results in

$$T(\Theta) = \begin{bmatrix} \Sigma_s & \Sigma_o & 1 - \Sigma_s - \Sigma_o \\ \Sigma_o & \Sigma_s & 1 - \Sigma_s - \Sigma_o \\ 0 & 0 & 1 \end{bmatrix},$$

where $\Sigma_s = \mathrm{erf}\left(\frac{0.25\theta}{\sqrt{2}}\right)$ and $\Sigma_o = \frac{1}{2}\left[\mathrm{erf}\left(\frac{0.75\theta}{\sqrt{2}}\right) - \mathrm{erf}\left(\frac{0.25\theta}{\sqrt{2\theta}}\right)\right]$. The parameter vector Θ is, in this example, the scalar parameter θ, which corresponds to the inverse of λ_2, i.e. $\theta = g(\lambda_2) = \lambda_2^{-1}$. The initial condition is $x_0 = 0$ hence the initial state is z_1. The probability of remaining within the safe set at the next time step is $\Sigma_s + \Sigma_o$,

$$P_{safe} = \frac{1}{2}\left[\mathrm{erf}\left(\frac{0.75\theta}{\sqrt{2}}\right) + \mathrm{erf}\left(\frac{0.25\theta}{\sqrt{2}}\right)\right].$$

For the sake of simplicity and to manipulate the value of θ easily, let us approximate the erf function with its Taylor expansion of the first order

$$P_{safe} \approx \frac{1}{2}\left[\frac{0.75\theta}{\sqrt{2}} + \frac{0.25\theta}{\sqrt{2}}\right],$$

and assume we are interested in $P_{safe} \geq 0.5$, we thus obtain

$$\theta \geq \sqrt{2} \Longrightarrow \lambda_2 \leq \frac{1}{\sqrt{2}}. \tag{13}$$

Finally, we get the range of feasible values of λ_2 by combining Eqs. (12) and (13),

$$\frac{1}{\sqrt{2\pi}} \leq \lambda_2 \leq \frac{1}{\sqrt{2}}.$$

Let us remark that, if soundness is to be claimed for the abstraction procedure, then the approximation introduced by the erf function would need to be quantified. This aspect is further discussed in the next section.   □

3.2   On the Parametrisation of Probability Distributions

The formal abstraction procedure described above translates a continuous SDE into a Markov chain $(\mathcal{Z}, T)$ via kernel marginalisation, as per Eq. (2). As the entries in $T(\Theta)$ are obtained from evaluations of the kernel $T_w(\Lambda)$, in the case of parametric SDEs they become parametric functions. The expression of the kernel T_w influences the relationship between the parameters Λ and Θ.

Ideally, we seek to *analytically* manipulate parameter values, particularly in the context of parameter synthesis. However, Example 2 highlights the main issue of parametric abstractions, namely dealing with parameters Λ that are arguments of transcendental (non-polynomial) functions. The Gaussian cumulative distribution function is an example of an analytically hard-to-handle function. In the presence of transcendental functions, we envision two paths to mitigate their untractability: either *a)* to numerically approximate the abstract transition probabilities, as done in Example 2; or *b)* to approximate the *original* distribution by means of a tractable one.

We discuss both cases, focussing on the relevant instance of SDEs with Gaussian noise: the associated distribution can be approximated with polynomial expressions [32]. These approximations are, in general, valid only over a finite domain, which is anyways a natural setting for formal abstraction procedures. More precisely, any Gaussian cumulative distribution function is a linear combination of erf functions, which can be approximated via (truncated) MacLaurin series as

$$\text{erf}(x) = \frac{2}{\sqrt{\pi}} \left(x - \frac{x^3}{3} + \frac{x^5}{10} \cdots \right), \tag{14}$$

or via rational expansions [6] as

$$\text{erf}(x) \simeq 1 - \frac{1}{(1 + a_1 x + a_2 x^2 + a_3 x^3 + a_4 x^4)^4}, \tag{15}$$

where the coefficients a_i, $i = 1, \ldots 4$ are known and given. As expected, a high-order polynomial approximation holds high accuracy, but potentially hampers the computational tractability related to parameter synthesis. The error introduced by these approximations can be quantified: as an example, the rational expansion in Eq. (15) carries a maximum error of $\xi = 5 \cdot 10^{-4}$. Recall Example 2 and assume that we use a rational expansion to approximate the associated erf function. We have computed the safety probability as the expression $\Sigma_s + \Sigma_o$, where each term carries (at most) a numerical approximation bounded by ξ, thus for a total incurred approximation error bounded within $\pm 2\xi$. As such, if we are given a safety probability threshold $P_{safe} \geq 0.5$, we must account for the newly introduced approximation, and thus aim at synthesising a parameter that satisfies $P_{safe} \geq 0.5 + 2\xi$ (the choice of the sign $\pm$ depends on that of inequality, enforcing a more conservative requirement). More generally, we should account for the approximation error arising from each term within the n-dimensional abstract transition probability matrix. At each time step, the upper bound [2] on this error is $n(n-1)\xi$. Repeating the operations over an N-step logical specification (as in Eq. (7)), we must account for a total approximation of $Nn(n-1)\xi$.

An alternative approach approximates the *original kernels* (not the abstract transition probabilities, as above) with polynomial distributions. In the specific instance of Example 2, we propose the use of Bates distributions to approximate Gaussian kernels [21]. The Bates distribution is computed as the mean of d Uniform distributions, and its probability distribution function is (piecewise) polynomial. Interestingly, for $d = 1$ we have a standard Uniform distribution, and for $d = 3$ we already have a distribution that "closely resembles" a Gaussian, as depicted in Fig. 4a. Whilst the Gaussian distribution has unbounded support, the Bates distribution is defined solely over a bounded set. We thus trade an unbounded and hard-to-handle distribution for the tractability of a (piecewise) polynomial expression over a finite support. The two distributions are rather similar, having a KL divergence [27] of $3.9 \cdot 10^{-3}$ (Bates distribution with parameter $d = 3$ vs. Gaussian), which reduces to $0.4 \cdot 10^{-3}$ for $d = 10$. Within the formal abstraction framework, we ought to compute an error bound on the marginalisation (integrals of kernels) obtained from the two distributions. Assume the procedure has selected the partitioning step δ_s. The approximation bound can be computed as the integral over a partition that maximizes the difference between the two distributions as

$$\epsilon_{distr} = \max_{S_i \in \mathcal{S}} \int_{S_i} (p_\mathcal{N}(x) - p_\mathcal{B}(x))dx, \qquad (16)$$

where $p_\mathcal{N}$ and $p_\mathcal{B}$ represent the probability distribution function of the Gaussian and Bates distributions, respectively. Notice that the integration is performed over S_i, namely over the partitions of the state space $\mathcal{S}$. The procedure should be carried out in an offline pre-processing step.

4   Experimental Results and a Case Study

In this section we outline a few experiments, including bounded-support noise (Uniform) and unbounded-support noise (Gaussian) - the latter under both

---

[2] Notice that the maximum approximation error is $n(n-1)\xi$, rather than $n^2\xi$: the last row of T (comprising the absorbing state z_{p+1}) is by default composed only of zeros and a single one on the diagonal position.

abstraction approaches discussed in Sect. 3.2. Finally, we prove the effectiveness of this technique with an industrial case study, concerning a synthesis problem for the heterogeneity ratio of a population of solar panels connected to the electricity grid.

4.1   Formal Abstraction with Parametric Uniform Noise

Let us consider a parametric SDE, as

$$x_{k+1} = \lambda_{1,a} + \lambda_{1,m} \cdot x_k + \lambda_2 \cdot w_k,$$

where $\lambda_{1,a}$ is an additive parameter, $\lambda_{1,m}$ is a multiplicative parameter, and λ_2 affects the variance of the Uniform noise $w \in \mathcal{U}(0,1)$. Consider a safe set $\mathcal{S} = [0,1)$, or dually the unsafe set $\mathcal{S}_u = (-\infty, 0) \cup [1, \infty)$, and the probabilistic reachability specification $\psi = \mathbb{P}_{\leq 0.5}[\lozenge^{\leq 1} \mathcal{S}_u]$. Recalling Eq. (9), we consider $N = 1$ and $\mathscr{L}(\mathcal{S}) = 1$, hence an upper bound for the abstraction error ϵ_{abs} is

$$\epsilon_{abs} \leq \delta_s \cdot h_w(\lambda_2) = \delta_s \cdot \frac{1}{2\sqrt{3}\lambda_2}.$$

Note that this bound is conservative, as it accounts for the probability mass over the whole partition. Let us select an upper bound $\epsilon_{abs} \leq 0.25$, thus we choose $\delta_s = 0.5$ leaving $h_w \leq 0.5$, resulting in $\lambda_2 \geq \sqrt{3}^{-1}$.

Let us now divide $\mathcal{S}$ into two partitions, $\mathcal{S}_1 = [0, 0.5)$ and $\mathcal{S}_2 = [0.5, 1)$, with boundary points $b_1 = 0$, $b_2 = 0.5$, $b_3 = 1$ and representative points $r_1 = 0.25$ and $r_2 = 0.75$. These are represented by the abstract states z_1, z_2, respectively, whereas the unsafe set is represented by z_3. The transition probability matrix T results in

$$T = \begin{bmatrix} t_{11} & t_{12} & 1 - t_{11} - t_{12} \\ t_{21} & t_{22} & 1 - t_{21} - t_{22} \\ 0 & 0 & 1 \end{bmatrix},$$

where $t_{i,j} = \frac{1}{2\sqrt{3}\lambda_2} \max\{0, y_{i,j}\}$, $y_{i,j} = \min\{b_{j+1}, \sqrt{3}\lambda_2 + \lambda_{1,a} + \lambda_{1,m}r_i\}$ $- \max\{b_j, \lambda_{1,a} + \lambda_{1,m}r_i - \sqrt{3}\lambda_2\}$.

Assume the initial state is $x_0 = 0$, which is mapped to the abstract state z_1. To account for the abstraction, we aim at verifying $\lozenge^{\leq 1} z_3$ with probability smaller than $0.5 - \epsilon_{abs} = 0.25$. We are to solve an inequality

$$t_{11} + t_{12} = \frac{1}{2\sqrt{3}\lambda_2}[\max\{0, y_{11}\} + \max\{0, y_{12}\}] \geq 0.75 \Leftrightarrow$$

$$\max\{0, y_{11}\} + \max\{0, y_{12}\} - 1.5\sqrt{3}\lambda_2 = q(\lambda_{1,a}, \lambda_{1,m}, \lambda_2) \geq 0. \qquad (17)$$

In particular, the set $q(\lambda_{1,a}, \lambda_{1,m}, \lambda_2)$ offers solutions only for values of $\lambda_2 \leq 2/3\sqrt{3}$, that is $\lambda_2 \leq 0.34$, which is disjoint from $\lambda_2 \geq 1/\sqrt{3}$, hence there is no solution for this instance of the parametric verification.

We then consider a smaller partition step $\delta_s = 0.25$, which results in a wider set of solutions $\lambda_2 \geq (2 \cdot \sqrt{3})^{-1}$. The property ϕ is now satisfiable with the upper probability bound $0.5 + \epsilon_{abs} = 0.75$, which results in the set depicted in Fig. 3a.

4.2 Formal Abstraction with Parametric Gaussian Noise, 1/2

Let us discuss an abstraction procedure of an SDE in presence of a Gaussian noise, by means of the first of the two approaches detailed in Sect. 3.2, which works on the abstraction and approximates the erf function with a polynomial expansion. Let us consider a safe set $\mathcal{S} = [0, 1)$, the unsafe set $\mathcal{S}_u = (-\infty, 0) \cup [1, \infty)$ and the reachability property $\psi = \mathbb{P}_{\leq 0.5}[\lozenge^{\leq 1} \mathcal{S}_u]$, and the SDE model

$$x_{k+1} = \lambda_{1,a} + \lambda_{1,m} x_k + \lambda_2 w_k,$$

where $\omega_k \in \mathcal{N}(0, 1)$ and the initial state is $x_0 = 0$.

The parameter λ_2 must be positive in view of its representation of stochastic noise variance, whereas $\lambda_{1,m}$ and $\lambda_{1,a}$ belong to $\mathbb{R}$. The verification of $\phi = \mathbb{P}_{\leq \gamma}[\lozenge^{\leq 1} z_{unsafe}]$ over the abstraction must account for the associated error, as $\gamma = 0.5 - \epsilon_{abs}$: for illustration purposes, let us define the bound $\epsilon_{abs} = 0.25$, so that $\gamma = 0.25$. As per Eq. (9), we choose

$$\delta_s h_w(\lambda_2) = \delta_s \frac{1}{\sqrt{2\pi}\lambda_2} \leq \epsilon_{abs}, \quad \delta_s \leq \sqrt{\epsilon_{abs}}, \quad \lambda_2 \geq \frac{1}{\sqrt{2\pi}\epsilon_{abs}},$$

defining a first feasibility region $\lambda_2 \geq (2\pi\epsilon_{abs})^{-1/2}$. We select $\delta_s = 0.5$, dividing $\mathcal{S}$ into two partitions $\mathcal{S}_1 = [0, 0.5)$, $\mathcal{S}_2 = [0.5, 1)$ represented by the abstract states z_1, z_2, respectively, whereas $\mathcal{S}_u$ is represented by state z_3. Let us define the boundary points $b_1 = 0$, $b_2 = 0.5$, $b_3 = 1$, and representative points $r_1 = 0.25$ and $r_2 = 0.75$. The transition probability matrix results in

$$T = \begin{bmatrix} e_{11} & e_{12} & e_{13} \\ e_{21} & e_{22} & e_{23} \\ 0 & 0 & 1 \end{bmatrix},$$

where the elements $e_{i,j}$ can be written as

$$e_{i,j} = \frac{1}{2}\left[\mathrm{erf}\left(\frac{b_j - (\lambda_{1,m}f(r_i) - \lambda_{1,a})}{\sqrt{2}\lambda_2}\right) - \mathrm{erf}\left(\frac{b_i - (\lambda_{1,m}f(r_i) - \lambda_{1,a})}{\sqrt{2}\lambda_2}\right)\right],$$

for $i, j = 1, 2$, whereas $e_{i3} = 1 - e_{i2} - e_{i3}$ for $i = 1, 2$.

As discussed in Sect. 3.2, we approximate the erf function with the polynomial expansion in Eq. (14): the approximation error is bounded from above by 10^{-4}, and we have 4 terms ($e_{i,j}$ for $i, j = 1, 2$) introducing such approximation. We have accounted for this error by increasing the probability bound $\gamma - \epsilon_{abs}$ by $4 \cdot 10^{-4}$. We aim at synthesising parameters that verify $\mathbb{P}_{\leq \gamma - \epsilon_{abs}}[\lozenge^{\leq 1} z_3]$: this can be written as an inequality $q(\lambda_{1,a}, \lambda_{1,m}, \lambda_2) \geq \gamma - \epsilon_{abs}$, where $q(\lambda_{1,a}, \lambda_{1,m}, \lambda_2)$ is a polynomial function (omitted for brevity). The surface $q(\lambda_{1,a}, \lambda_{1,m}, \lambda_2) = \gamma - \epsilon_{abs}$ is depicted in Fig. 3b. This region of parameter space, combined with set $\lambda_2 \geq (2\pi\epsilon_{abs})^{-1/2}$, defines the parameters where $\mathbb{P}_{\leq 0.5}[\lozenge^{\leq 1} \mathcal{S}_u]$ is satisfied.

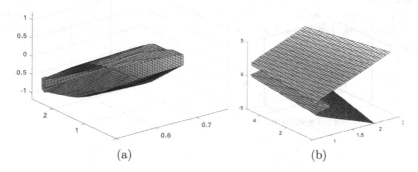

(a)   (b)

Fig. 3. Depiction of the surface $q(\lambda_{1,a}, \lambda_{1,m}, \lambda) = 0$ for the satisfiability region of the case study in Sect. 4.1 (left) and plot of the surface $q(\lambda_{1,a}, \lambda_{1,m}, \lambda_2) = \gamma - \epsilon_{abs}$ for the Gaussian case study (right.)

4.3 Formal Abstraction with Parametric Gaussian Noise, 2/2

Let us now work with the second of the two approaches detailed in Sect. 3.2, which works on the concrete SDE and replaces the Gaussian kernel with a Bates one. We shall compare the results considering a similar problem setting, namely a safety property characterised by safe and unsafe sets. We use the same partitioning function as above, so that $\mathcal{S}_1 = [0, 0.5)$, $\mathcal{S}_2 = [0.5, 1)$ with representative points $r_1 = 0.25$ and $r_2 = 0.75$. The Bates distribution is formed by the mean of d Uniform distributions with support $[a, b]$. Its variance can be written as

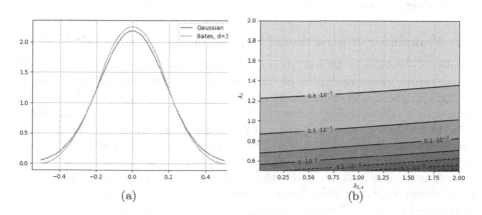

(a)   (b)

Fig. 4. A Bates distribution ($d = 3$) compared against a Gaussian one (left); difference between the solution $q(\lambda_{1,a}, \lambda_{1,m}, \lambda_2)$ obtained with the Bates approximation and that with approximation of the erf function (cf. Sec 4.2) (right).

$$\lambda_2^2 = \frac{(b-a)^2}{12d},$$

and imposing $a = -b$ (symmetry around zero) we get that the distribution support is defined as $b - a = \sqrt{12d}\lambda_2$. Recalling that $a = -b$, we get $b = \sqrt{3d}\lambda_2$. For simplicity, we set $d = 3$ as per Fig. 4a. The Bates kernel density can be written as

$$t_{Bates}(d, x) = \frac{d}{2(d-1)!} \sum_{l=0}^{d} (-1)^l \binom{d}{l} (dx - l)^{d-1} \text{sgn}(dx - l). \tag{18}$$

Each entry of the transition matrix T is computed as

$$T_{i,j} = \int_{S_j} t_{Bates}\left(d, \frac{x - a - \lambda_{1,a} - \lambda_{1,m} r_i}{b - a}\right), \tag{19}$$

where we substitute $a = -\sqrt{3d}\lambda_2$ and $b - a = \sqrt{12d}\lambda_2$, as discussed above. Notice that each entry is a polynomial of order three, hence the parameters satisfying the property ϕ (cf. case study in 4.2) can be found solving a cubic equation of three variables. In order to show the efficacy of this approach, we compute the difference between the surface $q(\lambda_{1,a}, \lambda_{1,m}, \lambda_2)$ found using the erf approximation (see previous case study in Sect. 4.2) and with the Bates distribution used here. Figure 4b shows the absolute difference between the values of $q(\cdot)$, with of $\lambda_{1,a}$ ranging within $[0, 2]$, λ_2 ranging within $[0.5, 2]$ and fixing the value $\lambda_{1,m} = 1$ for visualisation purposes. We notice that the value of $\lambda_{1,a}$ does not influence significantly the results, as this represents simply a shift in the distributions: the difference is likely caused by numerical approximations. The approximation reliability of the approach is instead sensitive to the value of λ_2, i.e. the variance of the Bates distribution, which is proportional to its support, hence defining the feasibility region for the distribution.

4.4   Parametric Abstraction of Populations of PhotoVoltaic Systems

Finally, we outline a formal abstraction procedure for a parametric model of a heterogeneous population of PhotoVoltaic (PV) systems, as presented in [28, 29, 31]. The model encompasses a population of heterogeneous PV systems connected to the electricity network. A single PV device may be considered a hybrid system: it (re-)connects to and disconnects from the network according to the value of the electric frequency. Further, the reconnection is a delayed procedure: in order to reconnect safely to the network, a device ought to wait for a predefined time interval. A device thus can be in three possible states: ON when connected, OFF when disconnected and W when "waiting" to reconnect, as outlined in Fig. 5. Transition among these states as defined as $a(k)$, representing the probability of disconnecting from an active state, $b(k)$ representing the probability of reconnecting from an inactive state, and $\varepsilon(k)$ denoting the probability that the reconnection delays has expired. Notice that the transitions depend on the current value of the electric frequency, hence time-varying.

The reconnection and disconnection thresholds vary over a large population of devices in view of different regulations (European countries may impose narrower or wider thresholds according to the renewable penetration), different age

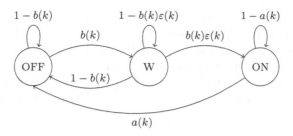

Fig. 5. Schematic representation of the heterogeneous population of PV systems.

and manufacturer. The works in [28, 29, 31] then consider probabilistic thresholds to model a heterogeneous population of devices. With respect to the model in [28, 29, 31], we leverage a few assumptions: we will consider Uniform reconnection and disconnection thresholds, Uniform frequency noise and we will ease the electricity grid dynamics. We aim at synthesising a value of the variance of the disconnection threshold distribution that guarantees safe network operations. Let us define $a(k)$, the cumulative distribution function of the disconnection thresholds, which may be written as

$$
a(k) = \begin{cases} 0 & \text{if } f(k) < -\sqrt{3}\lambda_2 + \lambda_1, \\ \dfrac{f(k) - \lambda_1}{2\sqrt{3}\lambda_2} + \dfrac{1}{2} & \text{if } |f(k) - \lambda_1| \leq \sqrt{3}\lambda_2, \\ 1 & \text{otherwise,} \end{cases}
\tag{20}
$$

where λ_1 represents the average value and $2\sqrt{3}\lambda_2$ is the distribution domain written in terms of the distribution variance λ_2. Similarly, we may write $b(k)$ the cumulative distribution function of the reconnection thresholds.

The population model immersed in the electric network can be written as

$$
\begin{cases} \Delta f(k+1) = \alpha \Delta f(k) + \beta \Delta P_{PV}(k) + \omega_f(k), \\ x(k+1) = (1 - a(k))x(k) + b(k)\varepsilon(k)y(k), \\ y(k+1) = b(k)(1 - x(k) - \varepsilon(k)y(k)), \\ P_{PV}(k) = \bar{P}Nx(k) + \omega_P(k), \end{cases}
\tag{21}
$$

where x and y represent the probability of being in states ON and W, respectively. The frequency evolves according to a first-order difference equation, with coefficients α, β. We consider ω_f and ω_P belonging to a Uniform distribution. Notice that these stochastic signals are not parametric, and the only parameters are within $a(k)$ and $b(k)$.

Let us define the state variable $s = [\Delta f, \Delta P_{PV}, y]$, where we can omit x as it is the "deterministic version" of ΔP_{PV}. Let us define the safe state space $\mathcal{S}$ as the set-product of three sets, $\mathbb{F} = [-0.8, 0.8]$, $\mathbb{P} = [0, \bar{P}N]$, $\mathbb{X} = [0, 1]$ and such that the three-dimensional safe set $\mathcal{S} = \mathbb{F} \times \mathbb{P} \times \mathbb{X}$. Simultaneously we define the unsafe set $\mathcal{S}_u$ as the complement of $\mathcal{S}$. We produce a partitioning grid with $\delta_s = 0.01$ that ensures an abstraction error $\epsilon_{abs} = 0.1$.

For the first test, we set the average value of the disconnection distribution equal to $\lambda_1 = -0.2$. We aim at computing the variance of the Uniform noise λ_2^2 that guarantees that the probability of entering the unsafe set is smaller than 0.1 after 2 time steps. Our procedure returns the analytical solution $\lambda_2 \leq 0.080$, which is then corroborated by the numerical evaluation depicted in Fig. 6a. We read this result as a requirement for a low degree of population heterogeneity.

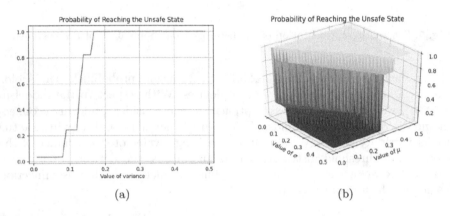

(a)   (b)

Fig. 6. Probability of reaching the unsafe state varying solely the variance (left) or the mean and variance (right) of the distribution.

Similarly, we repeat the test considering λ_1, the average value of the disconnection threshold distribution, as a parameter. The procedure returned a rather complex inequality expression, which provided the solution

$$\lambda_2 \leq 0.81\lambda_1 - 0.08, \tag{22}$$

which is numerically confirmed by the depiction of Fig. 6b. We can practically interpret Eq. (22) as follows. Heterogeneity (λ_2) and disconnection average (λ_1) should increase (or decrease) in parallel. Namely, the overall system dynamics can withstand high heterogeneity when the disconnection average is far enough from the nominal operating frequency f_0.

5   Conclusions and Future Work

In this work we have presented a method to perform parameter synthesis over parametric SDEs using formal abstraction techniques. Formal abstractions are employed to transform the continuous-space SDE into a discrete-space parametric Markov chain, on the parameters of which synthesis is performed via formal verification techniques. Such new parametric abstractions carry an error that certifies the verification technique, and which is used to obtain sets of parameters for the concrete SDE satisfying the given specification. Several experiments show possible applications of this methodology.

Future work will further push the computational scalability of this procedure and implement it in a software tool, possibly extending FAUST^2 [35] or StocHy [12]. The use of alternative abstraction techniques [25] can help investigating infinite-horizon properties, thus extending the results in this work.

References

1. Abate, A., Prandini, M., Lygeros, J., Sastry, S.: Probabilistic reachability and safety for controlled discrete time stochastic hybrid systems. Automatica **44**(11), 2724–2734 (2008)
2. Abate, A., et al.: Arch-comp19 category report: stochastic modelling. In: 6th International Workshop on Applied Verification of Continuous and Hybrid Systems, vol. 61, pp. 62–102 (2019)
3. Abate, A., et al.: Arch-comp20 category report: stochastic models. In: 7th International Workshop on Applied Verification of Continuous and Hybrid Systems (ARCH20), vol. 74, pp. 76–106 (2020)
4. Abate, A., Katoen, J.P., Lygeros, J., Prandini, M.: Approximate model checking of stochastic hybrid systems. Eur. J. Control **16**(6), 624–641 (2010)
5. Abate, A., Soudjani, S.E.Z.: Quantitative approximation of the probability distribution of a Markov process by formal abstractions. Log. Methods Comput. Sci. **11** (2015)
6. Abramowitz, M., Stegun, I.A.: Handbook of Mathematical Functions with Formulas, Graphs, and Mathematical Tables, vol. 55. US Government printing office (1948)
7. Alur, R.: Timed automata. In: Halbwachs, N., Peled, D. (eds.) CAV 1999. LNCS, vol. 1633, pp. 8–22. Springer, Heidelberg (1999). https://doi.org/10.1007/3-540-48683-6_3
8. Alur, R., Courcoubetis, C., Henzinger, T.A., Ho, P.-H.: Hybrid automata: an algorithmic approach to the specification and verification of hybrid systems. In: Grossman, R.L., Nerode, A., Ravn, A.P., Rischel, H. (eds.) HS 1991-1992. LNCS, vol. 736, pp. 209–229. Springer, Heidelberg (1993). https://doi.org/10.1007/3-540-57318-6_30
9. Baier, C., Hensel, C., Hutschenreiter, L., Junges, S., Katoen, J.P., Klein, J.: Parametric Markov chains: PCTL complexity and fraction-free Gaussian elimination. Inf. Comput. **272**, 104504 (2020)
10. Baier, C., Katoen, J.P.: Principles of Model Checking. MIT press, Cambridge (2008)
11. Cardelli, L., et al.: Syntax-guided optimal synthesis for chemical reaction networks. In: Majumdar, R., Kunčak, V. (eds.) CAV 2017. LNCS, vol. 10427, pp. 375–395. Springer, Cham (2017). https://doi.org/10.1007/978-3-319-63390-9_20
12. Cauchi, N., Abate, A.: StocHy: automated verification and synthesis of stochastic processes. In: Vojnar, T., Zhang, L. (eds.) TACAS 2019. LNCS, vol. 11428, pp. 247–264. Springer, Cham (2019). https://doi.org/10.1007/978-3-030-17465-1_14
13. Daws, C.: Symbolic and parametric model checking of discrete-time Markov chains. In: Liu, Z., Araki, K. (eds.) ICTAC 2004. LNCS, vol. 3407, pp. 280–294. Springer, Heidelberg (2005). https://doi.org/10.1007/978-3-540-31862-0_21
14. Dehnert, C., Junges, S., Katoen, J.-P., Volk, M.: A storm is coming: a modern probabilistic model checker. In: Majumdar R., Kunčak V. (eds) Computer Aided Verification. CAV 2017. LNCS, vol 10427, pp. 592–600. Springer, Cham (2017). https://doi.org/10.1007/978-3-319-63390-9_31

15. Esmaeil Zadeh Soudjani, S., Abate, A.: Adaptive and sequential gridding procedures for the abstraction and verification of stochastic processes. SIAM J. Appl. Dyn. Syst. **12**(2), 921–956 (2013)
16. Hahn, E.M., et al.: The 2019 comparison of tools for the analysis of quantitative formal models. In: Beyer, D., Huisman, M., Kordon, F., Steffen, B. (eds.) TACAS 2019. LNCS, vol. 11429, pp. 69–92. Springer, Cham (2019). https://doi.org/10. 1007/978-3-030-17502-3_5
17. Hahn, E.M., Hermanns, H., Zhang, L.: Probabilistic reachability for parametric Markov models. Int. J. Softw. Tools Technol. Trans. **13**(1), 3–19 (2011)
18. Han, T., Katoen, J.P., Mereacre, A.: Approximate parameter synthesis for probabilistic time-bounded reachability. In: 2008 Real-Time Systems Symposium, pp. 173–182. IEEE (2008)
19. Hartmanns, A., Hermanns, H.: The modest toolset: an integrated environment for quantitative modelling and verification. In: Ábrahám, E., Havelund, K. (eds.) TACAS 2014. LNCS, vol. 8413, pp. 593–598. Springer, Heidelberg (2014). https:// doi.org/10.1007/978-3-642-54862-8_51
20. Herrmann, L., Baier, C., Fetzer, C., Klüppelholz, S., Napierkowski, M.: Formal parameter synthesis for energy-utility-optimal fault tolerance. In: Bakhshi, R., Ballarini, P., Barbot, B., Castel-Taleb, H., Remke, A. (eds.) EPEW 2018. LNCS, vol. 11178, pp. 78–93. Springer, Cham (2018). https://doi.org/10.1007/978-3-030-02227-3_6
21. Johnson, N.L., Kotz, S., Balakrishnan, N.: Continuous Univariate Distributions, volume 2, vol. 289. Wiley, New York (1995)
22. Junges, S., et al.: Parameter Synthesis for Markov Models (2019)
23. Kwiatkowska, M., Norman, G., Parker, D.: PRISM 4.0: verification of probabilistic real-time systems. In: Gopalakrishnan, G., Qadeer, S. (eds.) CAV 2011. LNCS, vol. 6806, pp. 585–591. Springer, Heidelberg (2011). https://doi.org/10.1007/978-3-642-22110-1_47
24. Lanotte, R., Maggiolo-Schettini, A., Troina, A.: Parametric probabilistic transition systems for system design and analysis. Formal Aspects Comput. **19**(1), 93–109 (2007)
25. Laurenti, L., Lahijanian, M., Abate, A., Cardelli, L., Kwiatkowska, M.: Formal and efficient control synthesis for continuous-time stochastic processes. IEEE Trans. Autom. Control **66**(1), 17–32 (2021)
26. Lavaei, A., Khaled, M., Soudjani, S., Zamani, M.: AMYTISS: parallelized automated controller synthesis for large-scale stochastic systems. In: Lahiri, S.K., Wang, C. (eds.) CAV 2020. LNCS, vol. 12225, pp. 461–474. Springer, Cham (2020). https://doi.org/10.1007/978-3-030-53291-8_24
27. MacKay, D.J., Mac Kay, D.J.: Information Theory, Inference and Learning algorithms. Cambridge University Press, New York (2003)
28. Peruffo, A., Guiu, E., Panciatici, P., Abate, A.: Aggregated Markov models of a heterogeneous population of photovoltaic panels. In: International Conference on Quantitative Evaluation of Systems, pp. 72–87 (2017)
29. Peruffo, A., Guiu, E., Panciatici, P., Abate, A.: Synchronous frequency grid dynamics in the presence of a large-scale population of photovoltaic panels. In: Power Systems Computation Conference (PSCC). IEEE (2018)
30. Peruffo, A., Guiu, E., Panciatici, P., Abate, A.: Model-based formal reliability analysis of grid dynamics with solar energy sources. In: 15th European Workshop on Advanced Control and Diagnosis. Springer (2019)

31. Peruffo, A., Guiu, E., Panciatici, P., Abate, A.: Aggregation and control of a heterogeneous population of solar panels over the grid frequency. IEEE Trans. Control Syst. Technol. **29**(4), 1420–1436 (2021)

32. Richards, W.A., Antoine, R., Sahai, A., Acharya, M.R.: An efficient polynomial approximation to the normal distribution function and its inverse function. J. Math. Res. **2**(4), 47 (2010)

33. Rizk, A., Batt, G., Fages, F., Soliman, S.: On a continuous degree of satisfaction of temporal logic formulae with applications to systems biology. In: Heiner, M., Uhrmacher, A.M. (eds.) CMSB 2008. LNCS (LNAI), vol. 5307, pp. 251–268. Springer, Heidelberg (2008). https://doi.org/10.1007/978-3-540-88562-7_19

34. Soudjani, S.E.Z., Abate, A.: Aggregation and control of populations of thermostatically controlled loads by formal abstractions. IEEE Trans. Control Syst. Technol. **23**(3), 975–990 (2015)

35. Soudjani, S.E.Z., Gevaerts, C., Abate, A.: FAUST 2: Formal abstractions of uncountable-STate STochastic Processes. In: Baier C., Tinelli C. (eds) Tools and Algorithms for the Construction and Analysis of Systems. TACAS 2015. LNCS, vol 9035, pp. 272–286. Springer, Berlin, Heidelberg. https://doi.org/10.1007/978-3-662-46681-0_23

36. Winkler, T., Junges, S., Pérez, G.A., Katoen, J.P.: On the complexity of reachability in parametric Markov Decision Processes. arXiv preprint arXiv:1904.01503 (2019)

Author Index

Printed in the United States
by Baker & Taylor Publisher Services